AF291315

SALVATOR ROSA

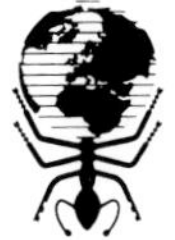

Books in the RENAISSANCE LIVES series explore and illustrate the life histories and achievements of significant artists, rulers, intellectuals and scientists in the early modern world. They delve into literature, philosophy, the history of art, science and natural history and cover narratives of exploration, statecraft and technology.

Series Editor: François Quiviger

Already published

Artemisia Gentileschi and Feminism in Early Modern Europe *Mary D. Garrard*

Blaise Pascal: Miracles and Reason *Mary Ann Caws*

Botticelli: Artist and Designer *Ana Debenedetti*

Caravaggio and the Creation of Modernity *Troy Thomas*

Donatello and the Dawn of Renaissance Art *A. Victor Coonin*

Erasmus of Rotterdam: The Spirit of a Scholar *William Barker*

Giorgione's Ambiguity *Tom Nichols*

Hans Holbein: The Artist in a Changing World *Jeanne Nuechterlein*

Hieronymus Bosch: Visions and Nightmares *Nils Büttner*

Isaac Newton and Natural Philosophy *Niccolò Guicciardini*

John Donne: In the Shadow of Religion *Andrew Hadfield*

John Evelyn: A Life of Domesticity *John Dixon Hunt*

Leonardo da Vinci: Self, Art and Nature *François Quiviger*

Leon Battista Alberti: The Chameleon's Eye *Caspar Pearson*

Michelangelo and the Viewer in His Time *Bernadine Barnes*

Paracelsus: An Alchemical Life *Bruce T. Moran*

Petrarch: Everywhere a Wanderer *Christopher S. Celenza*

Piero della Francesca and the Invention of the Artist *Machtelt Brüggen Israëls*

Pieter Bruegel and the Idea of Human Nature *Elizabeth Alice Honig*

Raphael and the Antique *Claudia La Malfa*

Rembrandt's Holland *Larry Silver*

Rubens's Spirit: From Ingenuity to Genius *Alexander Marr*

Salvator Rosa: Paint and Performance *Helen Langdon*

Titian's Touch: Art, Magic and Philosophy *Maria H. Loh*

Tycho Brahe and the Measure of the Heavens *John Robert Christianson*

SALVATOR ROSA

Paint and Performance

HELEN LANGDON

REAKTION BOOKS

Published by Reaktion Books Ltd
Unit 32, Waterside
44–48 Wharf Road
London N1 7UX, UK
www.reaktionbooks.co.uk

First published 2022

Copyright © Helen Langdon 2022

Printed and bound in India by Replika Press Pvt. Ltd

A catalogue record for this book is available from the British Library

ISBN 978 1 78914 573 1

COVER: Salvator Rosa, *Self-portrait*, c. 1647, oil on canvas. The Metropolitan Museum of Art, New York (bequest of Mary L. Harrison, 1921).

CONTENTS

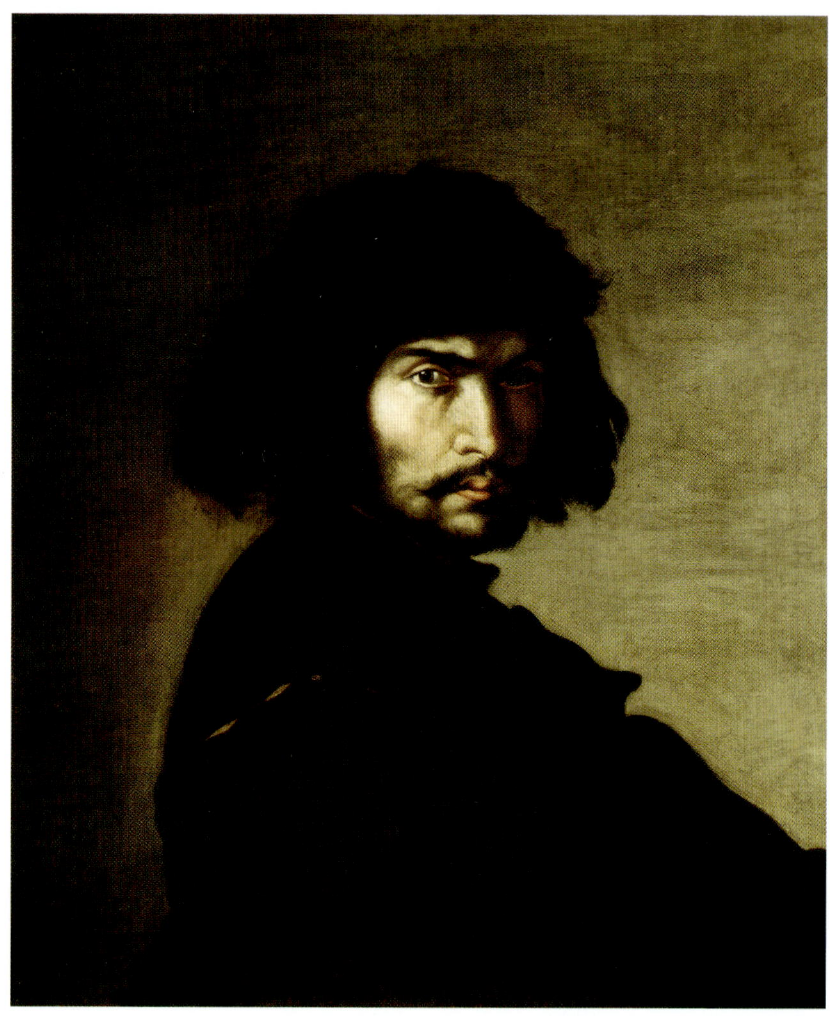

Introduction

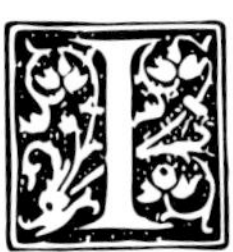

t was impossible, wrote Filippo Baldinucci, Salvator Rosa's biographer, to describe to one who did not know the artist his spirited conversation, and the vivacity and sweetness of his thought.[1] A Neapolitan, with arresting dark eyes and thick black hair that fell in waves across his shoulders, his curious and sprightly presence captivated those around him.[2] Often described as 'spiritoso', 'stravagente' or 'bizzarro', he was one of the most charismatic and engaging personalities of seventeenth-century Italy, well known as both artist and phenomenon, and celebrated as a multitalented virtuoso, actor, musician, prolific correspondent, poet and painter. Vain, often boastful and tirelessly self-assertive, Rosa was above all ambitious, possessed by an overriding love and thirst for glory, and an inordinate desire to claim a place as 'the first man of the century'.[3]

In this book I trace the strategies of self-fashioning that the artist developed to claim the cultural pre-eminence he so desired, as he moved from Naples to Medici Florence and on to the grandest stage of Rome. Initially he painted genre scenes, landscapes and battle pictures, but his ambition grew, and he strove to cast off his lowly origins in the back streets of Naples, where dealers affectionately nicknamed

1 Salvator Rosa, *Self-portrait*, 1649–50, oil on canvas.

him Salvatoriello, to be feted in Rome as a philosopher-painter of serious and esoteric themes. A series of self-portraits painted in Florence formed a dazzling publicity campaign, foregrounding his many roles, and at the same time displaying his skill. He presented himself as a court painter seeking immortal fame through art; as an actor in the role of Pascariello, subversive, provocative, a dark Neapolitan prancing across the Medici stage; and as a philosopher-scholar, enjoying an ideal of solitude and retreat. In the early 1640s he launched his career as a satirical poet, and, in the tradition of the Roman poet Juvenal, created a harsh and angry persona. He saw himself as heir to the great Stoics and Cynics of antiquity, the moral mentor of his age, virulently denouncing the corruption of modern times. In aspiring to excel in both poetry and painting, Rosa followed a Florentine ideal of artist-writers, promulgated by Vasari and most splendidly represented by Michelangelo. In Florence, too, Rosa saw the power of a circle of learned men to spread his fame. He enjoyed the life of the cultural academies, with their playful names and love of wit and jokes, where literature, art, poetry and theatre were discussed. These academies created large cultural networks, indispensable to an artist seeking to increase his social mobility. Rosa shone in these circles, and in the more informal *conversazione*, with their lively artistic debates that were held sometimes in bookshops and in artists' studios. Skill in *conversazione* was increasingly a social marker in this time, and an area in which Rosa excelled. Many *letterati* wrote poems and eulogistic letters in his praise, and these circulated widely.

For a brief period in the 1640s Rosa was court painter to the Medici. Success at court was central to an artist's career and it was with some courage that Rosa soon aggressively rejected it, claiming instead a new kind of professional freedom. He was to turn down prestigious invitations from four heads of state – King Louis XIV of France, Queen Christina of Sweden, Archduke Ferdinand Karl of Austria and Emperor Ferdinand III – commenting to his closest friend and chief correspondent Giovanni Battista Ricciardi, 'I value, and will always value, a single moment of complete freedom more than centuries, even if golden, spent working in other people's command.'[4] Rosa wished to live where he liked, surrounded by his friends, and to paint what he liked, and when he liked. This did not mean that he was free of the demands of patrons and clients, and he remained at their mercy. Wishing to cast off the traditional channels of advancement, he had to find new means, and, more enthusiastically than any artist before him, Rosa saw the possibilities of the public exhibitions in Rome to make his name. Here he could present startlingly original works and attract new buyers. He constantly asserted his right to choose his subjects and refused to agree on a price beforehand, once remarking rudely to a prospective client, 'go to a barrel-maker or a builder, as they work to order.'[5]

Nonetheless, Rosa's subjects were sometimes chosen for him, and many of his paintings entered the great aristocratic collections of Rome. Yet he aspired to be acclaimed, as his contemporary Nicolas Poussin was, as a philosopher-painter, and to engage a new public of learned men, poets, scientists, bankers and many close friends, who replaced the conventional patronage networks and enjoyed his rare subjects. It is important to stress that in no way did Rosa create a private or consistent body of work, even less an art of dissent. He often poses in the then fashionable role of Stoic but he does not ponder any abstract philosophical doctrines, instead plucking motifs from them when it suits his aims. His satires, a series of lengthy literary self-portraits, present Rosa the Stoic, but in a manner rooted in the conventions of classical satire. Often his choice of subject seems casual, as when he asks Ricciardi for 'something new, without too many figures, and if there's also some figure in the air over a cloud or something else it won't be a problem'. He stressed the value of novelty above all, 'since Rome has learned that I'm most fantastical in my inventions and I must live up to that as much as possible'.[6] Clearly he chased novelty, but his subjects would not have caught on without his intense awareness of the strains of thought and feeling that dominated the intellectual life of his learned friends. He chose themes that were central to seventeenth-century debates, such as whether the intellectual or moral man could live at court, the virtues of the simple life and the corrupting power of wealth. Seventeenth-century gallery-goers enjoyed paintings that provoked discussion, and some of Rosa's choices of ambiguous and mysterious subjects would have pleased them.

In his later years Rosa became ever more obsessed with the baroque cult of *novità*, seeking rare subjects that would astonish his public. Again his themes – of magic and divination, of the earliest days of philosophy and learning – were central to contemporary culture, especially that of the scientific world of the Jesuits, and Rosa claimed there his place, as an intellectual or scientific persona. He was a showman, with an eye for a striking image, whose pictures reflected the wonders or *meraviglie* that were enthralling such eccentric natural philosophers as Athanasius Kircher, and he engaged with contemporary debates on the emerging aesthetic of the sublime. The originality of his art was complemented by his creation of a bizarre and often outrageous persona, one that was provocative and arrogant, a dark outsider whose hatred of mankind was modelled on that of the great misanthrope Timon of Athens. He had a gift for preserving his outsider image while putting himself at the centre of intellectual worlds.

Rosa's appetite for fame resounds through all his letters, and his creation of an alternative world of patronage was remarkably effective, but for a man of the seventeenth century there was no true greatness without social recognition. Rosa, rebel and outsider, was, paradoxically, entirely at one with this. His boastful letters are rich in descriptions of the visits of cardinals, ambassadors and men of letters to his studio, visits that increased his glory and spread his fame through Rome. He had, since his earliest years, been most successful as a landscape painter. This success caused him misery, for his deepest desire was to be accepted as a great figure painter of historical subjects and sacred histories, and, above all, for his pictures to adorn the great churches of Rome. In this ambition he was aligned with the critical canons of his time that acknowledged figure painting as the artist's highest achievement. Rosa wished to become part of the canon, to take his place beside the grandest of Old Masters, as can be seen from his etching *The Genius of Salvator Rosa* in which he personifies Painting through a well-known figure from Raphael's *Transfiguration.*

In this book I have presented the conflicts and paradoxes of Rosa's career, and woven through the narrative of his art and life his strategies of self-promotion. I have chosen a series of remarkable works that represent his ambitions and have suggested the strains of thought and feeling to which he was so shrewdly responding. The book is ordered chronologically, showing how his ambitions were formed by and evolved in relation to the painters and writers around him, and how versatile his response was to new places and ideas. The landscapes, on which his fame in England has so long depended, here play a minor role, but perhaps Rosa himself would be pleased at this strong emphasis on his subject paintings. The artist's letters, recently made available in English by Alexandra Hoare, are a remarkable resource. Nothing remotely like them is available for any other artist and they are invaluable to an understanding of the art world in seventeenth-century Italy. Through them I have tried to keep something of the texture of everyday life, as Rosa recounts his triumphs and his despair, his often black melancholy and his subversive humour.

ONE

Salvatoriello Goes to Rome

'Salvator Rosa', wrote Giovanni Battista Passeri, his friend and biographer, 'was born in the city of Naples, the garden of the world.'[1] An ancient Greek city, Naples had long been renowned as an earthly paradise, its natural beauties enhanced by the scattered ruins of classical antiquity. In the seventeenth century this Arcadian setting framed a newly magnificent cosmopolitan city, the second largest in Europe. It was the Spanish capital of the Kingdom of the Two Sicilies, reigned over by an absent monarch, Philip IV, and governed by a succession of Spanish viceroys, the splendour of whose court was renowned. The city boasted a rich literary, artistic and scientific life. Caravaggio had introduced a dramatic naturalism and chiaroscuro that had transformed its painting, while the most celebrated Italian poet of the age, Giambattista Marino, had in 1623 returned in triumph from Paris to his native Naples, bringing with him a passion for all that was new and wondrous, and a fascination with an aesthetic of horror. Naples stood in the forefront of the new empirical science then challenging deeply rooted Aristotelian traditions. The natural philosopher, dramatist and author of *Magia naturalis* (1558) Giambattista della Porta was a resident of Naples and admired throughout Europe. The apothecary

Ferrante Imperato's Dell' Historia Naturale museum, with its display of wonders and curiosities, was a famed attraction in the city. Dialect poets, above all Giulio Cesare Cortese and Giambattista Basile, in an astonishing and unusual corpus of dialect literature, were creating a new sense of identity for the city, and giving, for the first time, a voice to the vivid street types – maids, servants, fishermen, bandits – of the boisterous Neapolitan world. But beneath all this magnificence and vitality lurked another, darker reality. Vesuvius loomed over the magical seas and skies, symbolically evoking the city's long association with natural disaster and rebellion, and with social tensions and banditry. In 1631 the volcano, which had been silent for five centuries, burst into terrifying life, a prelude to an overwhelmingly harsh decade. In these years the demands of the viceroys for men, money and arms to serve the political interests of Spain caused grave economic crises and extreme oppression. Naples became the stage for a tumultuous civic life: sumptuous court spectacles contrasted with uprising and revolts, scenes of extreme cruelty were common and the chains of men pressed into service created intense anger. The city's stark differences, the parallel worlds of the idyllic and the dark and brutal, are woven together throughout Rosa's art.

Rosa was born in Arenella, a small village set high above the bay of Naples, on 21 July 1615.[2] His father was Vito Antonio de Rosa, a land surveyor and master builder, and his mother Giulia Greco, daughter of Vito Greco, whose family included several artists and a lute maker. Her father and her brother, Domenico Antonio Greco, were both undistinguished painters, who probably made cheap devotional images. Soon after Rosa's birth the household moved to Naples, where, by 1619, Vito Antonio had built a home for them near the convent of Gesù e Maria. However, a ruinously expensive illness and his death in 1621 left the family in desperate poverty. Rosa's mother remarried in 1625 and in 1632 Rosa's grandfather, Vito Greco, was named legal guardian of her three children, Giuseppe, Salvator and Giovanna.

The Rosa brothers were fortunate in being placed in a school for poor children run by the Piarist order and received an education unexpectedly rich with promise. The Piarist schools had been established in Rome by the priest St Giuseppe Calasanzio, the founder of this religious teaching order, and a man who was passionately concerned to bring free education to impoverished children. He opened schools in the most deprived areas of Naples, driving out the cardplayers and vagabonds and replacing, he boasted, six hundred prostitutes with six hundred schoolboys.

Rosa (now aged eleven) and his brother, Giuseppe, attended a school near their house and somehow, in spite of the harsh and sometimes chaotic classrooms (in one school two low rooms contained one hundred boys), from very early on they stood out as exceptional students. They caught the attention of Calasanzio himself, and he was to continue to take an interest in their careers. Calasanzio was a true Catholic Reformation saint, harshly ascetic, and a rigid disciplinarian, but he was a courageous supporter of the ideal of free education for all classes and, perhaps most surprisingly, the Piarists were to be unusually open to the new science and sympathetic to Galileo. Rosa attended classes in grammar, where he would have studied Cicero and Virgil's *Aeneid*, and then advanced to rhetoric and logic, based on the works of Seneca and Martial, and so acquired the rudiments of a classical education that was to serve him well in later years. The brothers entered the novitiate as trainee priests – Giuseppe in 1629, when he took the name of Domenico di San Tommaso Aquino, and Salvator in 1630, with the name of Salvator di San Pietro. The following year, however, Rosa abandoned the novitiate and went to live with his mother's family in their workshop on the via Toledo near the Piazza della Carità.[3] He was already attracted to painting, and when his sister, Giovanna, married the young artist Francesco Fracanzano in 1632, Rosa, a witness at the wedding, signed himself as a painter with a studio in the neighbourhood of the church of Spirito Santo.[4] Rosa had also been studying painting with his uncle, Domenico Antonio Greco; now his brother-in-law, Fracanzano encouraged him to copy his paintings in oil.

Rosa's situation in these early years was entirely typical for a young Neapolitan artist. Artistic communities were close-knit, their families interlinked and painters, sculptors, carvers and gilders lived near one another. The Piazza della Carità, and the adjoining neighbourhood of Spirito Santo, teemed with artists. And yet, from this first moment, Rosa seemed to be touched by something exceptional. His early biographers, perhaps encouraged by Rosa himself, weave around him all the biographical topoi long associated with the discovery of artistic talent. Rosa, who was quick to reveal his many gifts and spirited charm, was beset by not only servile poverty but obstacles of every kind. Impatient with books, he firmly halted his school studies at grammar and rhetoric and declared that he wished to be an artist. His family objected.

They acknowledged his unusual gifts, but encouraged him to study architecture, music and poetry instead, and dreamed that he might become 'the miracle of his times in the world of letters', or perhaps a lawyer, with the power to restore the family fortunes. But Rosa began to draw, so exuberantly that there was no wall in his home, or anywhere else, that he did not cover with charcoal drawings, 'creating little figures and small landscapes'. He was even reprimanded for covering the walls of a cloister.[5]

Rosa's first paintings were small sketches of the coastline around Naples. The art historian Bernado De Dominici creates a charming picture of these very early years, recalling how, when Rosa was still almost a boy, he and a sixteen-year-old Marzio Masturzo (today known only as a minor battle painter) enjoyed taking a boat out to 'draw views of the beautiful coast of Posillipo and towards Pozzuoli, and other similar spectacles produced by nature'.[6] Rosa, unusually, made landscape sketches in oil on paper and then graduated to small canvases. These were novel works, whose freshness, spontaneity and graceful figures 'delighted all who saw them', and Rosa was quick to work out a highly successful commercial strategy.[7] He sold his works cheaply to the second-hand dealers whose shops were clustered around the via Toledo and, to get the best publicity possible, concentrated on those in the street's busiest piazzas. Rosa's efforts were crowned with unexpected success, for his small landscapes, which were exhibited anonymously, caught the eye of the celebrated painter Giovanni Lanfranco, who was in Naples in 1634 to work on the frescoes in the church of Gesù Nuovo. Lanfranco so liked these works that he paid a dealer over the asking price, and others he bought and gave to friends as gifts. One day, as the artist passed the shop of the dealer Pietro di Martino in his carriage, he saw hanging outside a Rosa, *Landscape with Hagar and the Angel*, which he bought immediately and took back with him to Rome. Rosa's fame spread. The dealers were so impressed by the great Lanfranco's esteem that they asked the young artist for more work. Rosa, 'who never lacked shrewdness', swiftly raised his prices.[8] Rosa's precocious urgency, and the chance discovery of his youthful talent by a well-known artist, are common motifs in artistic biography. Rosa already had a strong sense of self, and the combination of a quick commercial awareness and an ability to attract the glamour of artistic myth remain characteristic of the artist. It is striking that he retained the name 'Salvator' when he became a novice. Rosa's biographer Filippo Baldinucci stresses that he 'was himself both pupil and master' – and would go on to foster the image of Rosa as the independent and original artist.[9]

The chronology of how Rosa spent the years circa 1635–8 is unclear, and the early sources are conflicting. It seems likely that at the start of the 1630s, by now in his early twenties, Rosa worked first in the studio of José de Ribera and then that of Aniello Falcone.[10] In 1635 he went to Rome and over the next two years shuttled back and forth between there and Naples. He probably returned to Naples in 1637, and spent a second period in Falcone's studio in 1638. In the autumn of 1638 he left for Viterbo in the entourage of Cardinal Brancaccio, and in 1639 settled in Rome.

Rosa's spirit and wit, and his many talents, enchanted his contemporaries, and encouraged his rise in these Neapolitan studios. Francesco Fracanzano, Rosa's brother-in-law, probably introduced him to Ribera, and the young artist, 'with his playing of the lute and singing, obtained the favour not only of Ribera but of all his sons as well'.[11] Ribera was to be overwhelmingly important for Rosa. From him comes the younger artist's fascination with horror, his expressive power and the brutal naturalism of his large-scale figure paintings. Rosa's early closeness to the Spanish artist was long to cast its lustre around him, and, above all, he appropriated two of Ribera's most celebrated subjects to establish his own reputation in Rome and in Florence. First came the horrific suffering of the *furias*, depicted in vast canvases that show mighty figures in complex poses, subjects which, after a period of silence in the late sixteenth century, had been reborn in the 1620s and '30s. Ribera painted a superlative and original series on the theme, the learning and ambition of which challenged the famous prototypes by Titian and Rubens.[12] The subject offered artists the opportunity to display their skill in portraying extreme emotion and complicated postures, and Rosa would long remember Ribera's *Tityus* (illus. 2), where he foregrounded the figure of the Greek giant, thrusting the screaming face, open palms and angular limbs towards the spectator, so heightening the overwhelming and disturbing horror of the thread of intestine being pulled out from his stomach by an eagle. Next come the half-length philosophers and hermit saints, the two most popular genres issuing from Ribera's studio; his assistants were commissioned to paint veritable squadrons of these types. The ancient philosophers, heirs to a genre established in the Renaissance for the decoration of libraries, are now ugly and tattered, in torn clothes tied up haphazardly by bits of string or bizarrely patched together. Ribera's

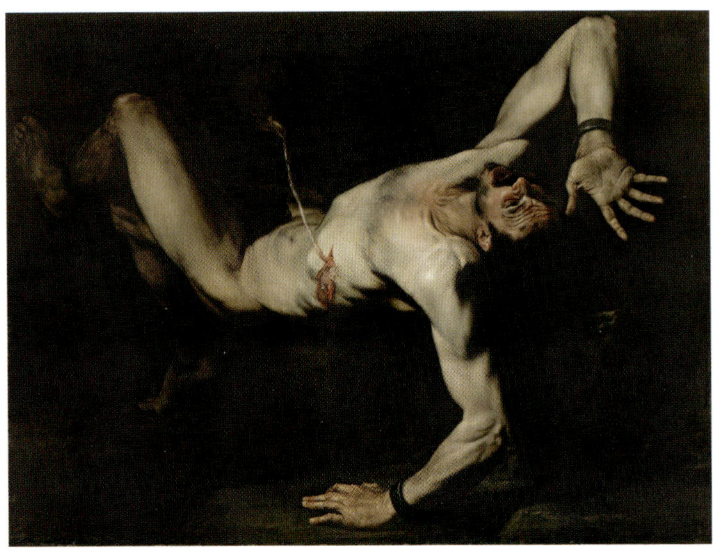

Democritus (1630; illus. 3) and *Diogenes* (1637) have an astonishing vitality, suggesting the dark world of the marginal and dispossessed in the alleys of Naples, or perhaps the beggar heroes of the picaresque novel. Yet these are learned works, intended to delight the erudite, and often based on the immensely popular *Lives and Opinions of the Eminent Philosophers* by the biographer Diogenes Laërtius (3rd century AD), or the satires of the Greek poet Lucian (2nd century), both rich in amusing descriptions of the eccentric behaviour of the ancients. Giovanni Battista della Porta's *Della fisionomia dell'uomo* (The Physiognomy of Man; 1586) includes descriptions of ancient philosophers, sometimes based on literary sources, sometimes on ancient sculptures. Della Porta's brother, Vincenzo, had a celebrated 'museo', and Giovanni describes his bust of Plato as having a head 'a little too great' (a sign of a sublime intellect). Artists enjoyed the opportunity to bring to new life such expressive

2 José de Ribera, *Tityus*, 1632, oil on canvas.

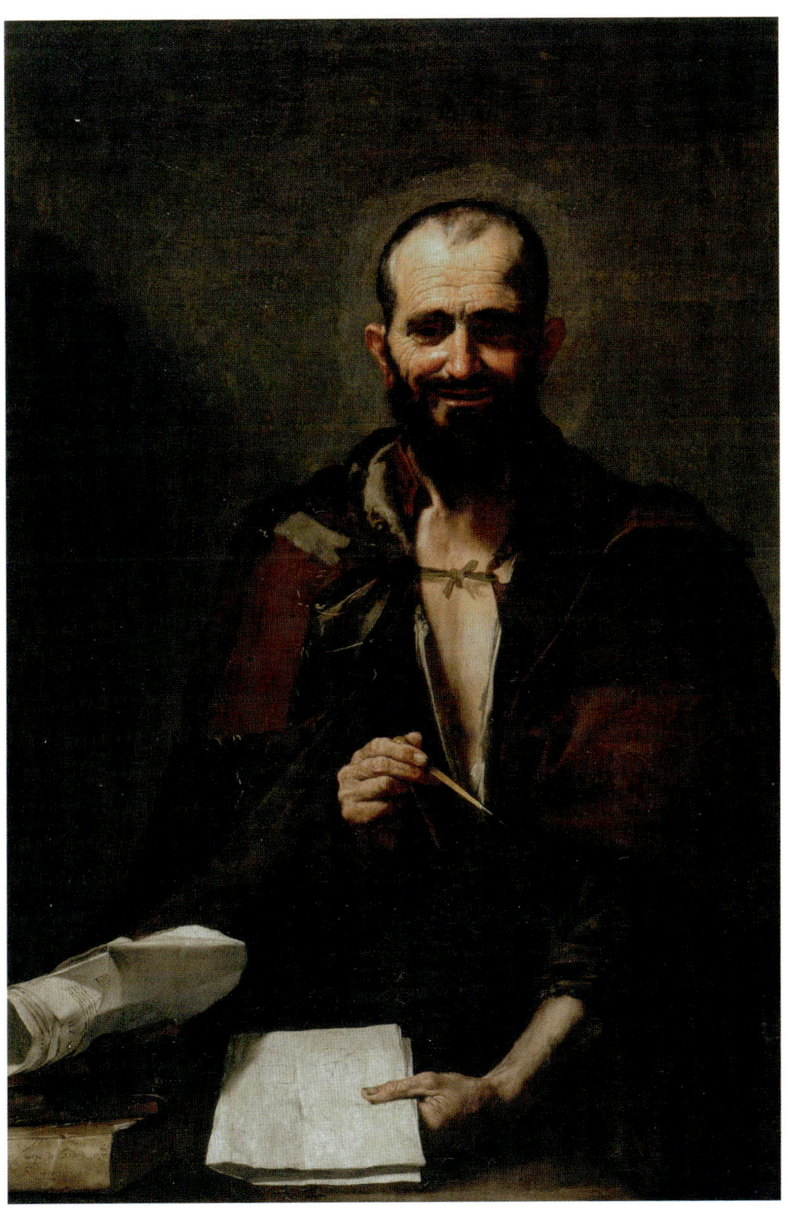

3 José de Ribera, *Democritus*, 1630, oil on canvas.

heads, and in the seventeenth century the philosophers live on, hovering between comedy and nobility.[13] They were to become a major theme in Rosa's art.

Aniello Falcone's studio produced small cabinet pictures – battle paintings, still-lifes, landscapes and genre paintings – for collectors, and here Rosa worked with many talented artists, among them Andrea de Lione and Domenico Gargiulo (known as Micco Spadaro). These artists were together creating a new kind of vividly naturalistic art. They drew from nature incessantly, making red chalk academic studies of life models and sketching genre figures such as peasants and fishermen going about their everyday activities along the seashore. Falcone, Gargiulo and Rosa together made sketching trips into the countryside, capturing the play of light on water and rocks, and shadowy caverns and grottoes. Falcone himself,

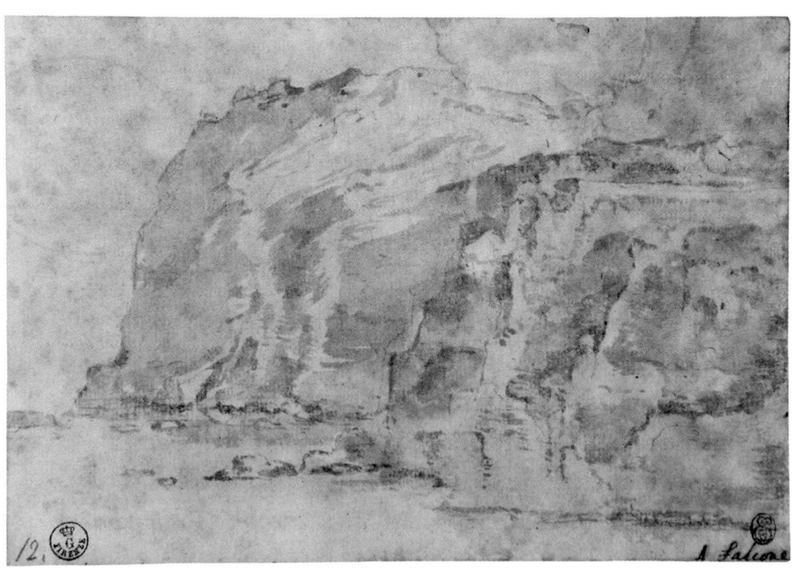

4 Aniello Falcone, *Landscape Study of a Rocky Cliff*, n.d., pencil and red wash on paper.

elegantly dressed and with a sword and dagger, was quarrel-some and quick to draw. He was 'brave and daring', prized for his 'bizarre genius' and able to delight his patrons with his 'humorous and bizarre way of speaking'.[14] The artist was perhaps a role model to the young Rosa, and seems to have recognized in his pupil a kindred spirit, for he loved him more than any of his other students, prizing his spontaneous wit and high spirit. Rosa's first signed and dated picture is a *Battle Scene* from 1637, a 'battle scene without a hero', which is very close to those of his teacher. Falcone, comments De Dominici, was not tempted by jealousy to impede his pupil's path to glory, setting an example 'certainly most rare'.[15]

In these early years Rosa became well known for his novel views of the Neapolitan coastline. A taste for small poetic land-scapes, especially those by Filippo Napoletano and Goffredo Wals, already flourished in the city, but Rosa developed a fresh and spontaneous naturalism and, with Micco Spadaro, he created the genre of the rocky southern bay. Naples had long been seen as the epitome of beauty. It lured the early Grand Tourist, and Fynes Moryson in 1611 had exclaimed, 'Here the beautie of all the world is gathered as it were into a bundle.'[16] Prints and contemporary guidebooks spread an Arcadian image of the city throughout Europe. Giovanni Battista del Tufo's *Il Ritratto o modello delle grandezze, delizie e meraviglie della nobilissima città di Napoli* (A Portrait or Model of the Grandeurs, Delights and Marvels of the Most Noble City of Naples; 1588) celebrated its unique 'delights, pleasures, sea, sky and setting', and cata-logued its customs and daily life in a series of small folkloristic vignettes. In the sixteenth century the poet Jacopo Sannazaro had published his piscatorial eclogues, a collection of poems

that substituted fishermen for the traditional pastoral scenes
of Arcadia, and this new genre was revived in Giulio Cesare
Capaccio's collection of eclogues *Mergellina* (1598). Here the
poet wanders with the fishermen along the celebrated sites
of the Gulf of Pozzuoli, the rocky and cavernous shores of
'immortal' Posillipo, the Torre del Greco, the volcanic islet of
Nisida, ringed by orange trees, and the shady cliffs of Sorrento.
Capaccio created a mythic landscape, of antiquities and memories, recalling an ancient way of life. His coast is a *kunstkammer*,
an abundance of wonders and curiosities, overflowing with
rare fish and treasures, fragments of ancient stuccoes and frescoes, corals and pearls. All this he contrasts with the harsh life
of the fishermen of the present, and the miseries of his times.
His eclogues were hugely popular, and were sung on the

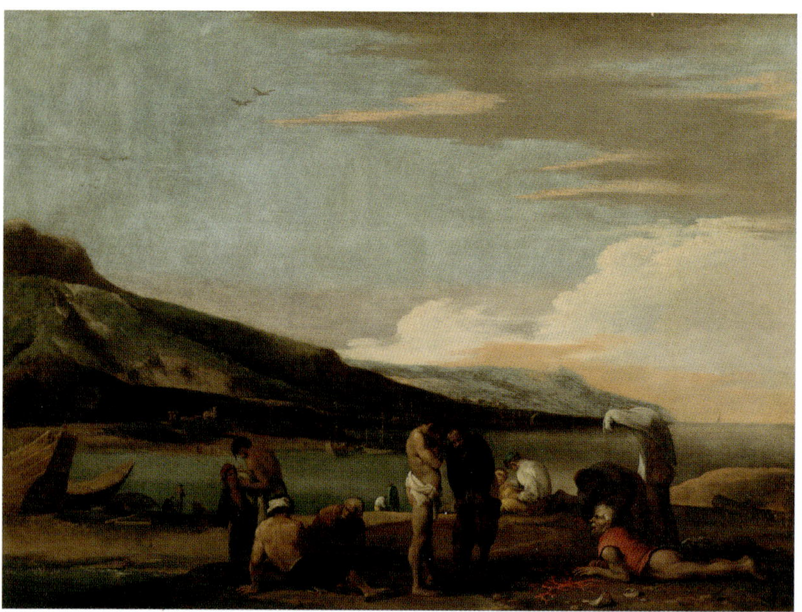

5 Salvator Rosa, *The Coral Fishermen*, c. 1637, oil on canvas.

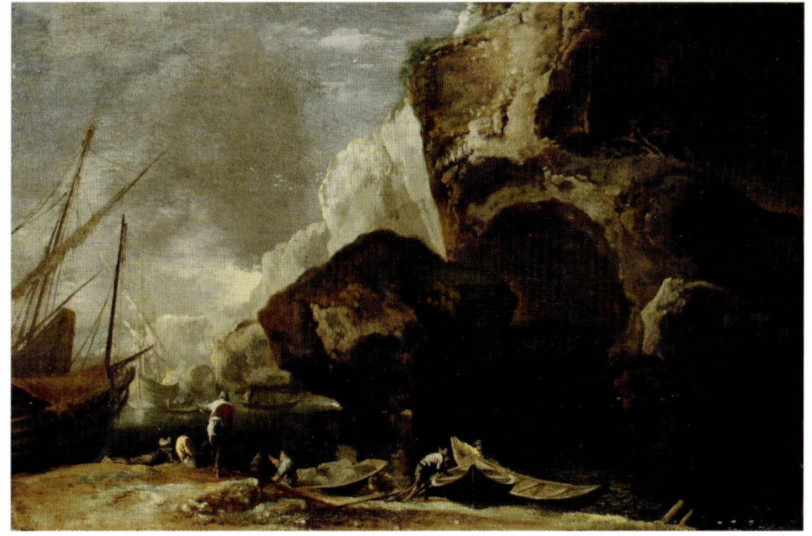

quayside. At the same time dialect poets gave lively voice to
the Neapolitan fishermen, who became emblematic of the
city. The shores of Naples became a theatre, and the spectacle
of seaside life enchanted travellers and aristocrats. Marino,
whose *Marittimi* – themselves a homage to Sannazaro – were
particularly well known in Naples, described the beauties of
Posillipo: 'this seaside setting is a most glorious theatre, where
every evening the nobility of Naples come by gondola to enjoy
the air of Paradise.'[17]

Among Rosa's early coastal scenes is the startlingly naturalistic *The Coral Fishermen* (illus. 5) of around 1637. The
landscape is swiftly brushed in, in planes of light and dark,
sharp and clear beneath the warm glow of the setting sun.
Shells and branches of coral hint at the mythic richness of
the Neapolitan shore, but Rosa subverts this Arcadian tradition, linking an ancient past to the 'the misery of our times'.

6 Salvator Rosa, *Marine Landscape with Fishermen*, c. 1636, oil on canvas.

Boldly at the centre, dividing the composition, stands the almost naked, aggressively naturalistic, fisherman, the fruit of Rosa's studies from the life model. Around him cluster groups of strongly characterized Neapolitan types, white-haired, weathered and ungainly, having endured a harsh way of life. In the following years Rosa developed a new, more lyrical type of coastal scene, with smaller figures; he began to use the device of a framing curtain of rocks, enhancing the effect of theatre, and creating a stage for the varied activities of the fishermen. The prominently signed *Marine Landscape with Fishermen* (illus. 6) from around 1636 is an early example that suggests the poetry of dark caves and grottoes, their deep shadows set against the unusual silvery tonality of the cliffs. The great boulder, perilously unstable, is daringly central. It divides the picture in two, and rocks and cliffs add a thrill of fear and mystery to the fragile world of the everyday.

It may be this type of painting that Rosa took with him on his first visits to Rome. Passeri tells us that Rosa, impatient to win a reputation, did not hesitate to work for Roman dealers, and sold small paintings with spirited little figures and a lively touch, but of lowly subjects.[18] His paintings delighted Romans with the novelty of their Neapolitan themes, and perhaps Neapolitan collectors enjoyed the evocation of the places they knew so well – the castle at Nisida, the Torre di San Vincenzo, the Gulf of Pozzuoli and the strongly characterized Neapolitan types.[19]

In the early 1630s, in Naples and Rome, Rosa had formed a trio of remarkable friends – Girolamo Mercuri, Cardinal Francesco Maria Brancaccio and Niccolò Simonelli – who were to stir his ambition and to create a network that remained astonishingly constant throughout his life. He perhaps met Mercuri, an exuberant Neapolitan, in the studio of Falcone, where Mercuri studied drawing as an amateur. Mercuri was *maestro di casa* to Brancaccio, and he encouraged Rosa's visit to Rome in 1635, when he was welcomed to the Roman household of Cardinal Brancaccio.[20] There Rosa was introduced to Simonelli, then *guardaroba* (Master of the Wardrobe) in the same household and later to become the most celebrated *maestro di casa* of the seventeenth century. Melancholy and avaricious, Simonelli was very different in character from Mercuri, but his gifts as a connoisseur and his knowledge of the ancient world reigned supreme, and he was exceptionally skilled in promoting young artists. Brancaccio, the key figure in the launching of Rosa's career, was made a cardinal in 1633, and moved in the most advanced cultural circles in both Naples and Rome. He was 'greatly devoted to pleasure, hence he often appears in dances and comedies';[21] his very distinguished library suggests deep learning and a desire to remain abreast of all the developments in literature and music, and in the new science. When Brancaccio left Naples in 1638 to take up his episcopal see in Viterbo, he took Rosa with him.

In these years, as Rosa moved back and forth between the art worlds of Naples and Rome so too did he deepen his literary culture in both cities, and he became increasingly aware of the power of the *letterati* to spread his fame. Brancaccio, above all, was the link, and it was he who opened up to the young artist the world of the literary academies that were to become so immensely important to his self-promotion. As a young boy, De Dominici tells us, Rosa was introduced, probably by his grandfather, to the household of Don Angelo Pepe, 'a dilettante of painting', with the precise aim of winning 'the affection of people'.[22] There was no tradition of artist-writers in Naples as there was in Florence, but Don Angelo Pepe, a shadowy figure, seems to have pioneered a discourse between the art and literary worlds. Massimo Stanzione, who dominated painting in Naples, had a library and after dinner read poetry and history. He became a writer on art after enjoying symposiums and *conversazioni* at the house of Don Angelo Pepe, who also welcomed to his house, as honoured friends, painters such as the renowned Viviano Codazzi and the much-loved Domenico Gargiulo.[23] De Dominici also describes with charm the artist Battistello Caracciolo's love of reading and writing poetry, and the pleasure he took in sociable evenings at the house of the learned poet and writer Giovanni Battista Manso. These figures may well have served as exemplars to Rosa, whose charisma attracted the *letterati* and all around him, and who was to become skilled in conversing with the rich and powerful.

In 1611 Brancaccio, then only nineteen, was a founder member of the Accademia degli Oziosi, which became one of the most celebrated literary academies in Italy. He was also a member of the Roman Umoristi, and the two academies shared several projects.[24] It is not clear whether Rosa ever attended a meeting of the Oziosi, and the visual arts were not at the forefront of their concerns. This was an official academy, controlled by the Spanish, which forbade the discussion of religion or politics, and much energy was spent on trivial topics and improvised comedies. However, the brothers Cesare and Francesco Fracanzano, both painters, were closely connected to the Oziosi, and were admired by academy member Giambattista Basile, whom perhaps Rosa met. Occasionally there is a hint of possible interest in painting, as when the Genoese poet and collector Gian Vincenzo Imperiale listened to a dialogue at the Oziosi on which was superior, the laughter of Democritus or the tears of Heraclitus (a popular topic and one reflected in the subjects of Ribera's beggar-philosophers).[25] And yet somehow, in the shadows, around its edges, a strong anti-court invective was finding a voice, a voice that was to leave a deep mark on Rosa. Torquato Accetto's prose work of 1641, *Della dissimulazione onesta* – a guide to the preservation of self, truth and liberty amid the perilous lies and hypocrisies of the court – took shape at this date. Basile, too, in his celebrated collection of fairy stories *Tale of Tales* (1634), conveys a harsh sense of the degradation of the intellectual and of the uncertain life of the courtier. His tales initially included subversive eclogues – spirited satirical poems about Neapolitan society, where only the unworthy were honoured – a theme to which Rosa returned obsessively throughout his life. In Rome Rosa may have attended meetings of the Umoristi where, in 1636, Antonio Abati read his *News from Parnassus*, a laboured attack on contemporary literary culture. Abati was to become a satirical poet celebrated throughout Europe, prized both by princes and the literary world. Rosa may first have met him in Rome, and Abati played a major role in promoting Rosa's career as both painter and poet. Later, in Viterbo, Abati and Rosa were to enjoy a warm friendship. They spent entire days together, exploring their shared passion for poetry. Later the two were to become bitterly estranged, and their friendship poisoned by rivalry and envy. But at this date, as the art historian Lione Pascoli poetically puts it, 'the Muses of Abati, with whom he had formed a strong friendship, woke his own Muses to song.'[26]

These early years in Rome were vitally important to Rosa, and it was here that he acquired the learning so essential to his later ambitions as a philosopher-painter. Back in Naples, in 1637, Niccolò Simonelli commissioned from him a large painting of *Tityus*, and by 1638 Rosa had sent this work to Rome.[27] He was dissatisfied with his status in Naples, and felt the growing threat from Micco Spadaro's success as a landscape artist. His 'inbred conceit' and his 'desire to win the name of a great painter' made him long for the grander stage of Rome.[28] To keep his memory there alive Rosa planned an astonishing publicity campaign. His first step, orchestrated by Simonelli, was to display, in the art exhibition held yearly at the Pantheon, a large painting of Tityus. This yearly exhibition, which took place on 19 March, was arranged by the Congregazione dei Virtuosi and in the 1630s was becoming well organized and a highpoint of the artistic year. The paintings were hung, crowded together with tapestries, under the portico of the Pantheon and, to seize the attention of the exhibition-goer, they needed to be large and dramatic. Rosa showed one work, one intended to astonish, deploying for the first time a strategy to which he would return. This strategy was itself indebted to Ribera, for a well-known anecdote relates that Ribera had won his position at the vice regal court by exhibiting a *Martyrdom of St Bartholomew* (1634) close to the Palazzo Reale, and his intense depiction of horrific cruelty caused a sensation in Naples. This occasion was probably the yearly exhibition of the Festa dei Quattro Altari, an exhibition similar to that held in Rome at the Pantheon.[29]

The subject, too, is taken from Ribera. The giant Tityus suffered the perpetual punishment of being chained to a boulder in Tartarus while an eagle eternally devoured his liver.[30] Ribera, foreswearing the heroism of the illustrious precedents of Michelangelo and Titian, had painted him with brutal realism, feeding into a quintessentially Neapolitan aesthetic of violence and horror. To Giambattista Marino, Tityus was an epitome of terror, who, 'freed from his binding prison and risen to his feet, if the ravenous and cruel bird that devours his fecund entrails should ever allow him to breathe and rise from the nine fields where he lies spread out' would summon up images of evil and horror.[31] The young Neapolitan now boldly claimed his place in Rome with this gory subject, one long established as an artistic opportunity

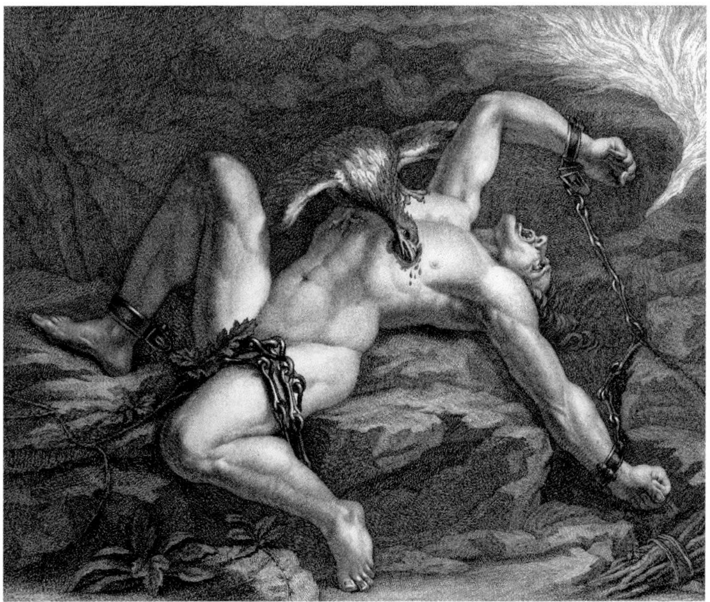

7 Ferdinando Gregori, *Tityus*, 1786, engraving after Salvator Rosa's *Tityus* (*c.* 1638, now lost).

for vying with an illustrious tradition.[32] The painting that Rosa sent is now lost, known to us only through an engraving by Ferdinando Gregori (illus. 7). Rosa followed the horizontal format pioneered in Naples but, for a Roman setting, he toned down Ribera's violence, and strove instead to showcase a monumental, Michelangelesque treatment of anatomy.

Rosa's debut was orchestrated by Niccolò Simonelli, and both artist and connoisseur were concerned to suggest Rosa's erudition. Simonelli, and perhaps Rosa, may have known that the ancient painters Euanthes and Parrhasios had displayed versions of a related subject, Prometheus, in temples of Zeus and Minerva.[33] Simonelli wrote a poem to accompany the painting, naming his friend 'the Demosthenes of painting', and the support of one so eminent in the Roman art world ensured the painting's success.[34] Demosthenes, a celebrated classical rhetorician and orator, was a title carefully chosen, and it suggested a fiery artist, with the power to express passionate emotion. This is the first moment in which Rosa is linked to the aesthetic of the classical sublime, for, as Longinus, author of the first-century AD treatise *On the Sublime*, tells us, Demosthenes 'may be likened to a thunderbolt or flash of lightning, as it were burning up or ravaging all that is before him'.[35]

The young Neapolitan arrived with éclat on the Roman scene. His painting triumphed; it won 'universal fame and a thunderous applause'. The Neapolitan 'Salvatoriello' had come of age, and was now more respectfully known as Salvator Rosa.[36] This episode, so early in his career, encapsulates Rosa's later strategies of bold display and the recognition of a man of letters. His was also a bravely independent move, for major artists were too cautious to risk using the exhibitions as a tool for self-promotion.

Poised on the threshold of a re-entry to Rome, Rosa spent a few months with Brancaccio in Viterbo, underemployed and carrying out odd jobs created for him by the cardinal. Here, he won his first commission for an altarpiece, *The Incredulity of St Thomas* (illus. 8), in which he included his first self-portrait, thereby carrying a proud statement of his worth and origins. This painting, for the high altar of the Chiesa dell'Orazione e Morte in Viterbo, is a clumsy derivation from Caravaggio's *Doubting Thomas* of 1601–2. Yet Rosa conveys immense pride in his achievement, including, on the right, a self-portrait, elegant and assured, engaging the spectator, while his companion looks at him reverently. Chiming with this portrait, on the ground before him, is his prominent signature on a *cartellino* – an illusionistic piece of paper with a curling corner – inscribed 'Salvator Rosa *neapolitanus fecit*'. Portrait and paper together exhibit and designate the artist. The signature on the *cartellino* is a form more common in the early Renaissance, but several Spanish artists had favoured its use, insistently inscribing their presence in their art. Rosa here follows Ribera, who had painted a *cartellino* being devoured by a snake in his *Drunken Silenus* of 1626, signing himself 'Josephus de Ribera, *Hispanus, Valentin/ et adcademicus Romanus faciebat/ partenope*'. Like Ribera, Rosa uses Latin, and stresses his nationality. He showcases, for his Neapolitan patron but in a painting destined for Viterbo, the illusionistic skill of a Neapolitan artist. He was later to return to Ribera's snake-born *cartellino*.

In 1639 Rosa finally settled in Rome, never to return to Naples. Rome of the late 1630s was the centre of the European

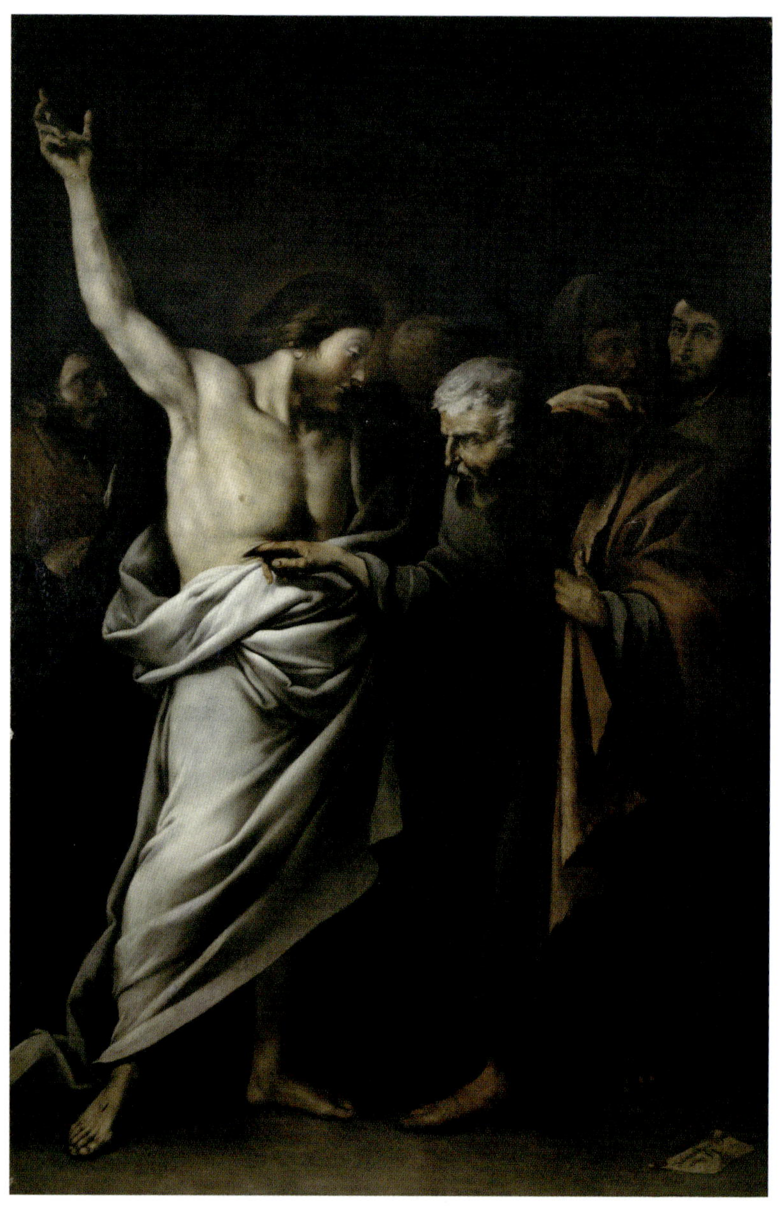

8 Salvator Rosa, *The Incredulity of St Thomas*, c. 1639, oil on canvas.

art world, enjoying the new artistic splendour created by a triumphant Catholic church and enhanced by magnificent palazzi, with ever richer collections of art, amassed by the Popes, the cardinals and the aristocrats. The Neapolitan sculptor Gian Lorenzo Bernini reigned supreme over the public art world, and Pietro da Cortona was completing his vast fresco, *An Allegory of Divine Providence*, in the grand *salone* of the Palazzo Barberini. At the Accademia di San Luca a vigorous theoretical debate raged between supporters of Cortona's abundant and epic style and classicist artists who believed that art should follow the Aristotelian rules of tragedy, with their emphasis on unity and concentration. Nicolas Poussin's *The Israelites Gathering Manna in the Desert* (1639) became a key work of Aristotelian classicism, unfolding a sequence of events before the viewer and displaying a range of emotions and reactions. Around these elite art worlds flocked the crowds of mainly northern artists, known as the *bamboccianti*. Named after the Dutch painter Pieter van Laer – nicknamed '*Il bamboccio*' (or clumsy puppet) on account of his ungainly physical appearance – they painted another Rome, a place of vice and misery, inhabited by the marginal and dispossessed, beggars, bandits, street sellers, brawling in taverns or eking out harsh lives among the lime-kilns and ruins of the city. Pieter van Laer was known for his highwayman scenes, and his popular *Large Lime-kiln* (illus. 9), now known through an engraving from the mid-1630s, had started a trend. There was a growing demand for landscape, and the painters Herman van Swanevelt and Claude Lorrain stood at the threshold of distinguished careers.

For a young and almost unknown Neapolitan artist, a debut in this rich art world, despite the success of the *Tityus*,

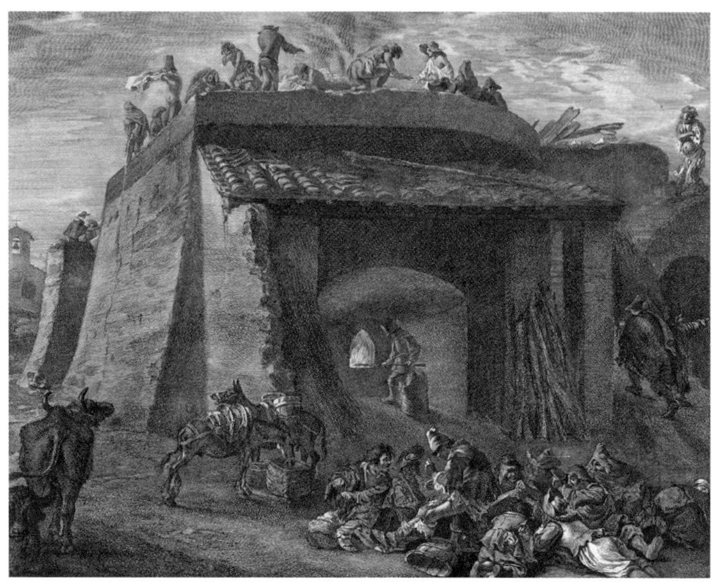

was immensely difficult. Rosa's restless ambition became immediately apparent, and this year in Rome forecasts his later colourful and sometimes provocatively challenging strategies of self-promotion. He sought fame but he also sought independence, and at this moment his desire to be free from the fetters of the court first manifests itself. On his return to Rome from Viterbo he left the household of Brancaccio and took a house on the via del Babuino.[37] This was in the colourful centre of artistic Rome where the north European artists lived, among them Claude and Swanevelt. Many artists, forbidden by the Accademia di San Luca to own a shop, sold their works from their homes, and hung them throughout the rooms. Rosa advertised the range of his art with four overdoors, two landscapes – one with an arsenal and a view of a port – a battle scene and a genre scene of a lime-kiln showing

9 Cornelis Visscher, after Pieter van Laer, *The Large Lime-kiln* (detail), 1638–58, etching and engraving.

many spirited figures. With this choice Rosa, the creator of the
Tityus, sets himself squarely among the *bamboccianti*, and he
competed with their novel topics. Two subjects stand out:
the bandit scene, which offered the thrill of the topical, of
traveller's tales and picaresque novels; and the lime-kiln, an
ambiguous symbol of both destruction and rebirth – both
specialities of van Laer. Rosa's *Attack by Bandits* (illus. 10), from
around 1639, is very close to the Dutch artist. In Naples Rosa
had painted small scenes of armoured bandits, or soldiers,
mingling with beggars and travellers, and evoking the poverty
of the countryside, of misery and dejection. This Roman scene
is quite different. It is, for Rosa, unusually highly finished, and
the travellers, so unprepared, so defenceless, are painfully realistic, but touched by a comic theatricality. Bandits were a very

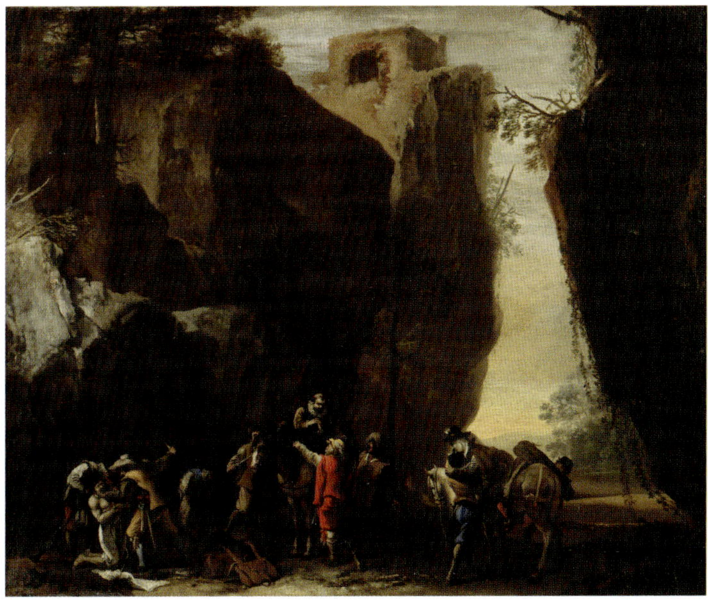

10 Salvator Rosa, *Attack by Bandits*, c. 1639, oil on canvas.

real threat, and this painting may well have reminded the viewer of the contemporary kidnapping of Jean Orefice, a French nobleman, by the notorious outlaw Giulio Pezzola. Rosa's ambitious *Beggar's Encampment* (illus. 11) is probably close in date, and its ebullience seems an attempt to rival the lime-kiln paintings of van Laer and fellow Dutch painter Jan Both.[38] The figures, unusually small, eke out a squalid existence in the ruins of ancient Rome, a dark underworld of sordid misery set among the traces of a heroic past. An astonishing catalogue of beggars seems pressed low into the earth, like the cats that now lurk among the ruins of the Mausoleum of Augustus, while above the stone pines and the soft light of the sky open into the world of nature. Bones and skeletons suggest the harsh passing of time, and the flimsy tent, glimpsed beyond the ruins, evokes the transience of this pitifully marginal population. Rosa's *bambocciate* were popular, but his desire to

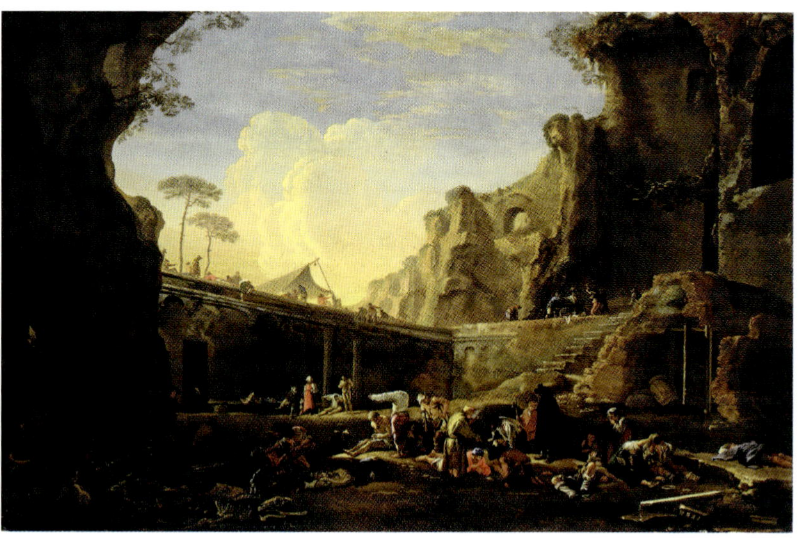

11 Salvator Rosa, *Beggar's Encampment*, 1640s, oil on canvas.

compete with the Dutch painters was to be a short-lived episode, and one which he was bitterly to regret. But the paintings were sought after; Baldinucci, who gives the later history of the four overdoors, suggests that they became the valued possessions of distinguished collectors. The painting of the lime-kiln was in the collection of Carlo de Rossi, a lifelong admirer of Rosa.[39]

At his house Rosa enjoyed the company of his many friends, and of his 'troups of partisans'. Impatient for success, dissatisfied with his lack of acclaim, with their support he now plunged into the world of theatre – a shortcut to fame.[40] The Roman academies, including the small Intrigati, Infiammati and Desiosi, and the grander and more distinguished Umoristi, were enthralled by dilettante theatre. They enjoyed *commedie ridicolose*, which, written by amateur authors, adapted the masks of the professional *commedia dell'arte*. The painter Giuseppe Cesari had staged such works with actors and artists, and the same men now gathered around Rosa.[41] Dominant was the celebrated painter-playwright-actor Giovanni Briccio and together he and Rosa created an extraordinary vehicle of self-display for the young artist. The now elderly Briccio, who was self-taught and sometimes mocked for his lowly origins, was spirited and amusing. His breadth of interests and his gifts as artist and writer dazzled the world: he was for Rosa the perfect partner. In Briccio's many surviving comedies the world of the *commedia ridicolosa*, gypsies and magicians, braggart soldiers and comic Neapolitans, beggars, the lame and the halt, the world of Rosa's *Beggar's Encampment*, spring to life. Pascariello, a well-known Neapolitan mask who was witty, lively and colourful in his language, was a favourite. And it was as 'Pascariello Formica' that Rosa made his debut on the Roman stage, a character that he would undoubtedly have found personally attractive.

Rosa first appeared in this role at the Roman carnival of 1639. Rosa and his masked friends, in the streets thronged with carnival revellers, pretended to be charlatans, pausing in squares and at street corners, handing out fake prescriptions. Rome's streets and squares were themselves a kind of theatre, with a lively array of pedlars, jesters, buffoons and vendors of every kind. Among them the real charlatan was a kind of hero, who cannot be imagined without his handbill or flyer, and often he blurred with the performers of professional troupes. Rosa's handbills, fake prescriptions invented by Briccio, had a long history. Their language was notoriously creative, and often they were weapons of political or religious polemic. They may well have been Rosa's first foray into the art of satire. The performances probably took place on wagons that were drawn by oxen, with collapsible stages, and presented a kind of theatre within a theatre, where art and reality mingled. Rosa's performance was immensely successful. 'The chief of everything, and well speaking', his charisma attracted half of Rome.[42] Rosa had an unusual gift for moving easily between high and low cultures, from the sublimity of his *Tityus*, to the colourful world of popular culture, and the theatre of the piazza. It is possible that, at the end of his performance, he drew off his mask to reveal himself as the famed painter of the *Tityus*.

Rosa's next step was more perilous: he dared to attack the theatre of the great Bernini. Bernini, now forty, and universally recognized as a man of genius and a consummate court artist with a vast and adulatory following, was also a brilliant actor, skilled in exactly those Neapolitan roles in which Rosa himself excelled. He 'wonderfully performed all parts, the serious and the ridiculous, and did so in all languages'.[43] His performances included startlingly harsh and biting attacks on a corrupt society, but his prestige ensured that he could speak with unusual freedom.[44] Above all Bernini was celebrated for his extraordinary theatrical machinery and wondrous illusionistic effects, most famed among them his presentation of the flooding of the Tiber and of a Roman street, replete with carriages, horses and people on foot. To Rosa Bernini was both model and challenge. He emulated his *napolitanità*, his harsh satire and wit, and followed him into the Roman world of actors, artists and playwrights. In the summer of 1639, missing the glamour of the starring role he had won in the carnival, he performed two comedies in the gardens of the Villa Mignanelli, and directed by the celebrated preacher and connoisseur of paintings Niccolò Musso, whose name lent lustre to the proceedings. His first performance caused a stir, and the second attracted a distinguished audience, among them Bernini himself and two well-known painters, Giovanni Francesco Romanelli and Guido Ubaldo Abbatini. Passeri, who was sitting in the same row as these artists, gives an amusing account. Rosa, as Formica, opened the evening with an inflammatory attack on Bernini's comedies: 'I do not want us to act comedies like certain people who spread dirt about here and there, because in due course, you can see that the dirt spreads faster than the poet's ink. And I do not want us to bring on stage couriers, brandy sellers, goatherds, and rubbish of that sort which is the folly of an ass.'[45] Earlier that summer Bernini, with his stage director Ottaviano Castelli, had put on a commedia with just such effects. Passeri quickly sneaked a glance at Bernini, who feigned dignified indifference. Castelli, however, shook his head crossly and uttered bitter sighs. Passeri himself comments that Bernini's work had flouted the Aristotelian rules of unity for dramatic structure, which forbade the addition of such extraneous characters. His observations are suggestive of the debates at the Accademia di San Luca at the time over the use of peripheral figures in a composition and it is clear that Rosa was aware of the theoretical questions absorbing intellectual Roman artists. Later Castelli attempted an ill-judged and feeble act of revenge. He made a vicious attack on Rosa, but one which, vulgar and vituperative, seemed to encompass the whole profession of painting, and both Passeri and Bernini angrily left his audience. Rosa, with unusual prudence, withdrew from the contest, and concentrated on promoting his paintings. The episode, whose importance is stressed by Passeri, demonstrates Rosa's vaulting ambition and fearless but rash self-assertion.[46] Young and unknown, he used the popular theatre to attack courtly culture and the highest echelons of the elite world; but he does this in the name of erudition, underpinning his charge with the support of Aristotle, spiritedly mixing and crossing genres.

Rosa's bid for fame was perilous but successful. His circles widened and he began to catch the attention of collectors from outside Rome. In 1639–40 he won a prestigious commission from Francesco I d'Este, Duke of Modena, who was an enthusiastic collector of northern landscape paintings. The duke's ambassador in Rome, Francesco Mantovani, looked to Rosa's theatrical friend Niccolò Musso for advice on painting and, through him, the young artist won the commission for three landscapes destined for the Palazzo Ducale at Sassuolo. The duke had recently been to Madrid, where he had seen the vast cycle of hermit landscapes that Philip IV of Spain had commissioned for the Buen Retiro Palace in Madrid. From Rome the poet Fulvio Testa encouraged the duke to emulate, at the Ducal Palace at Sassuolo, the decorative landscape cycle of the Palazzo Pallavicini Rospigliosi in Rome, where Cardinal Bentivoglio then lived. Here Filippo Napoletano had created country landscapes and marine scenes with grottoes and rock arches, which were much admired.[47] Rosa sent three landscapes to Sassuolo: *View of a Bay* (illus. 12), *Erminia Carving Tancred's Name on a Tree* (illus. 13) and *Landscape with Lake and Herds* (illus. 14). He sets himself in the vanguard of Roman landscape, responsive above all to the abundant naturalistic detail and effects of light of Claude and Swanevelt. He pairs

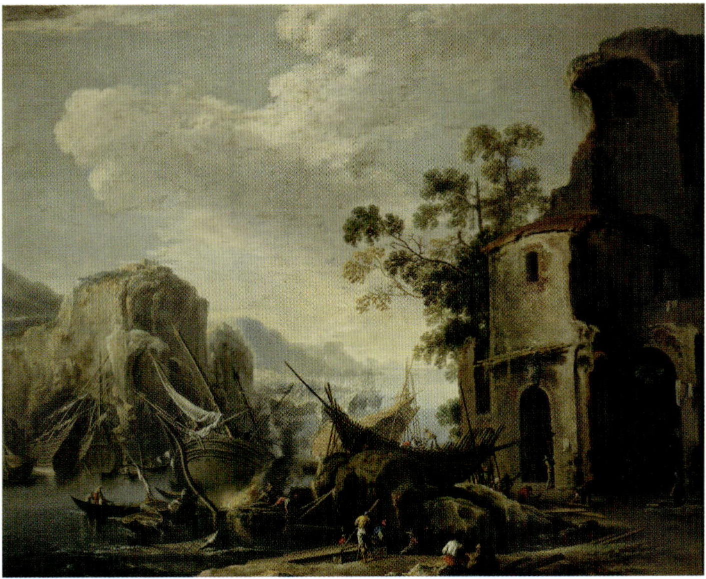

12 Salvator Rosa, *View of a Bay*, c. 1640, oil on canvas.

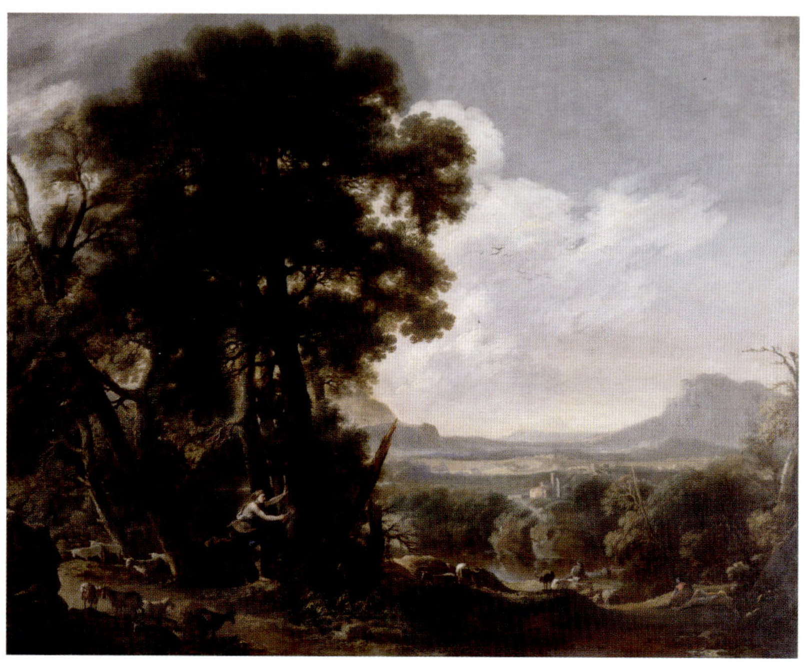

a landscape and a seascape, as Claude had done, but these are chiefly pastoral scenes, of a kind long recommended by Renaissance writers for the decoration of country villas. Shepherds rest and dream in the lovely place of Virgilian pastoral, light shimmers on lakes and rivers and creates deep shadows among darkly massed tree trunks, and soft atmospheric distances enchant the imagination. These Claudean distances, the '*sfumato nell'aria*', so new in landscape painting, particularly pleased the duke.[48] Claude was to remain a dominant influence on Rosa until at least the mid-1640s.[49]

Between 1639 and 1641, while Rosa was creating the landscapes for a courtly setting, Antonio Abati wrote an extended ekphrasis, or description, of his paintings – a very deliberate

13 Salvator Rosa, *Erminia Carving Tancred's Name on a Tree, c.* 1640, oil on canvas.

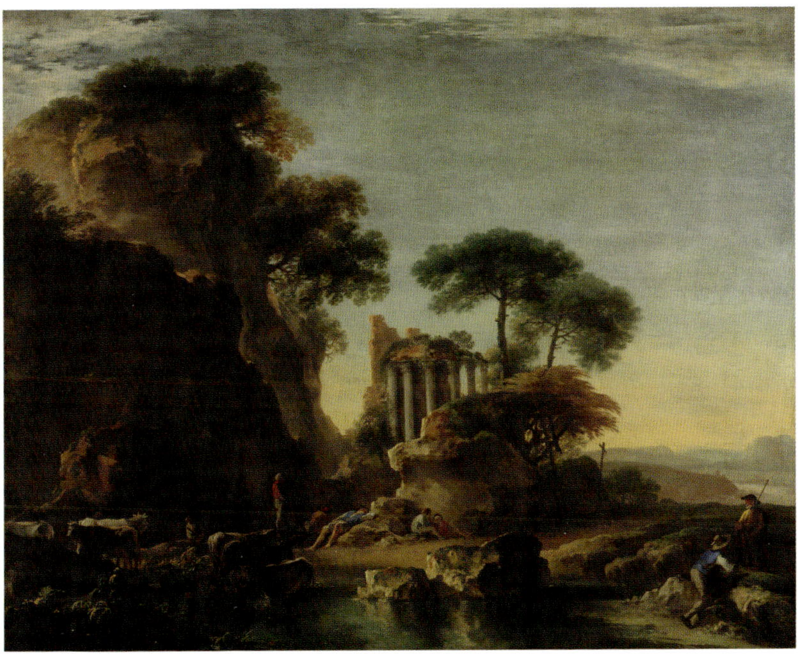

attempt to promote his friend as an elevated and noble genius and, for the first time, as a satirist.[50] The letter is addressed to Conte Diego Gera, the '*gran letterato*' (great man of letters) and member of various literary academies and perhaps the writer of comedies. It was written in response to Gera's wish for a long letter full of news about the art world in Rome, and most importantly of the rising young star, Salvator Rosa. Its subtext is a plea from Abati to Gera to put in a good word for him at the Medici court, for he and the noble art of poetry itself are so little prized in Rome. The poet opens with an exalted praise of landscape painting, defending it against the narrow aims of the figure painter. Man, writes Abati, created in God's image, and so separate from the rest of creation, can himself conjure

14 Salvator Rosa, *Landscape with Lake and Herds*, c. 1640, oil on canvas.

up seas and lands and skies; himself a *meraviglia*, or wonder, he can re-create an astonishing world. He was perhaps aware of Leonardo's defence of the artist as a lord capable of creating 'whatever exists in the universe, in essence, in appearance, in the imagination'.[51] He is also perhaps uneasily aware that Rosa, the painter of lime-kilns and other low subjects, does not excel as a figure painter, a role fundamental to the artist who wished to succeed in the highest genres of painting, where *historia*, *disegno* and *idea* reigned supreme. There followed a lengthy encomium of his landscapes. Rosa, whose touch was so light and fresh, and who painted so fast, excelled in effects of the rising and setting sun, of clouds that seemed to threaten storms, of rocky promontories reflected in the sea. He created, writes Abati, a sense of journeying through terrains that enchant with their variety and their mixture of pleasure and fear. Abati marvels at the figures, so varied and spirited – the goats clambering on the hillsides, reaching up to nibble the tops of bushes, the shepherds leaning on their crooks and, perhaps above all, the vivid life of the seashore, where fishermen mend nets and light little fires, and swimmers hug themselves to keep warm. After this brilliant evocation of Rosa's early landscapes, which Abati clearly knew and loved, he moves on to a description of one painting, the now untraced *Pittura Solitaria*, or 'Solitary Painting', which the Medici agent Fabrizio Piermattei had invited him to see in his house in Rome. Here, in a desolate rocky landscape, surrounded by barren trees, Rosa showed Painting in the attitude of Melancholy. She is personified as a most beautiful woman in a sky-blue robe, her brush and palette cast off on the ground. Painting has fled the city; she declares her independence, for 'Virtue is its own theatre and tribunal.' She need no longer flatter the rich and powerful but here, in a desolate wilderness, can choose her own subjects, perhaps scenes from Ovid's *Metamorphoses*. She can, most of all, praise the virtues of a simple and frugal life, and here Abati introduces a series of those literary topoi that are to be so fundamental to Rosa's paintings and satires – setting the corrupt luxury of life at court against the purity of the life of the country, where the wild rose, the sparkling water of the brook and the simple fare delight more than all the gilded finery of courtly life.

Painting and letter are a turning point. Rosa strove to cast off his reputation as an artist associated with the *bamboccianti*, the northern followers of Pieter van Laer – a mission that was increasingly to obsess him – and many literary men were to aid him, by constructing with him a new persona as philosopher-painter and satirist. At the same date there is a hint that Rosa was also trying to enlist the aid of Nicolas Poussin. An intriguing note, written on the back of a drawing, suggests that Rosa sent, through an intermediary, a drawing to Poussin.[52] This drawing, *Study of Three Heads and a Caricature*, is of expressive heads, and perhaps Poussin's *Israelites Gathering Manna*, a master-class in expression and gesture, encouraged Rosa to send it. Raphael had sent such a gift to Albrecht Dürer to display his drawing ability, and Rosa follows this tradition, as he was frequently to do later in his career.[53]

His painting criticized the court but, at this date, Rosa was striving to move from the world of dealers to a courtlier ambience. He had delivered paintings to Francesco I d'Este; and he had perhaps already accepted an invitation from Giovan Carlo de' Medici in Florence, or was about to do so.

The troubles caused by his attack on Bernini may have made life difficult for him and his way was perhaps smoothed by the presence of his brother in Florence, who was well placed to introduce him to the city's scientific circles. Certainly Calasanzio continued to take an interest in him and, in June 1640, wrote to Rosa's mother saying that he would ask her son to write to her. Rosa, he notes, is doing well in Rome, and is being looked after by Brancaccio and praised by many others for his great gifts as a painter.[54] It seems likely that Fabrizio Piermattei had sent *Pittura Solitaria* to Florence, where it hung in Giovan Carlo's casino on the via della Scala, the decorative scheme of which centred on the idea of retreat from the court.

TWO

Courtier and Painter-poet

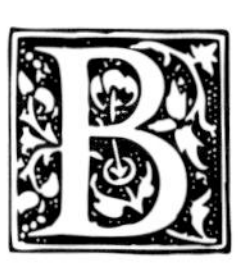y the autumn of 1640 Rosa had settled in Florence under the protection of Prince Giovan Carlo de' Medici.[1] The 1640s ushered in a period of brilliant patronage of the arts and sciences in Medici Florence. The Grand Duke Ferdinand II, and his three brothers, Giovan Carlo, lover of luxury and spectacle, the military Prince Mattias, and Cardinal Leopoldo, supporter of the new science, each had apartments in the Palazzo Pitti. In the Palazzo's Planetary Rooms the frescoes of Pietro da Cortona introduced to Florence the splendour of the Roman Baroque and eulogized the virtues of the ideal ruler, triumphant in both war and peace. In the summer apartments the decorative cycles of the Florentine painters Giovanni da San Giovanni and Francesco Furini struck a different note, uniting deep learning with wit and irreverence (illus. 15). Here the ancient philosophers, amusing parodies of the stately figures in Raphael's famed *School of Athens*, celebrate the golden age of Medici patronage. This juxtaposition of the solemn and the grandiose with the burlesque and the eccentric runs through the city's culture and was at the heart of the many cultural and small theatrical academies that were frequented by Medici princes and patricians and which were central to Rosa's constant

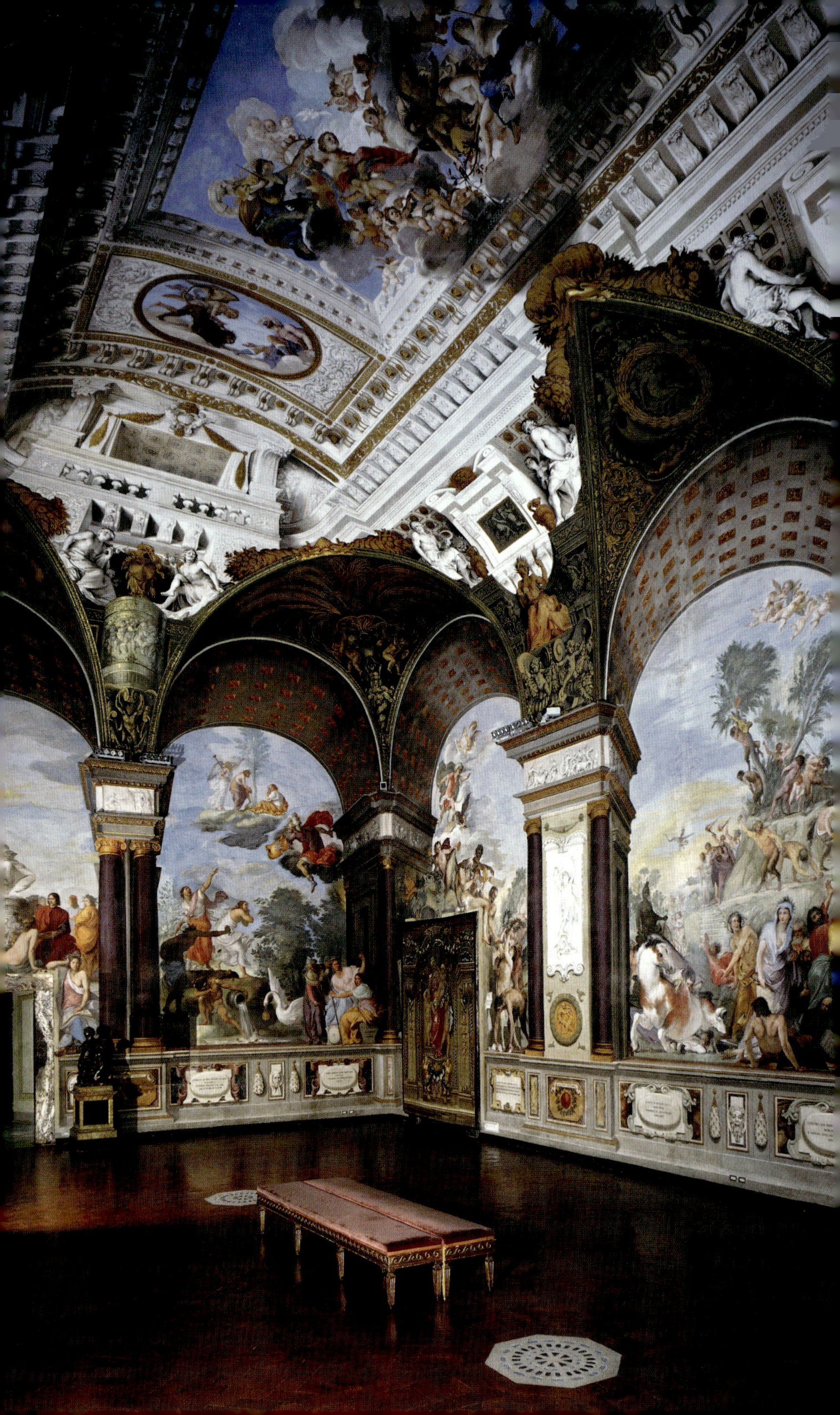

search for social acclamation. Florence, far more than Rome, encouraged an uninterrupted tradition of painter-poets, and here Rosa was to follow in the steps of Giovanni da San Giovanni, Francesco Furini and Baccio del Bianco, all of whom delighted in burlesque poetry and the mock heroic and parodic.

Each of the Medici brothers bought paintings from Rosa but Giovan Carlo de' Medici was his main patron. His terms were favourable: he lived in his own house, with a regular salary, and received payment for each of his paintings and permission to work for other patrons. Outside the court he soon met the three people who were to be of immense importance to him. He became acquainted with Ugo Maffei, a descendent of the ancient Volterra family, while he was in Rome, and through him he met his brother, the merchant Giulio Maffe, who became a close friend. Around 1640 he also got to know Giovanni Battista Ricciardi, a distinguished Pisan academic. Ricciardi was a writer of comedies and burlesque poetry. He was also a scholar and moral philosopher, an admirer of Lucian, Petronius and Juvenal, and Rosa often turned to him for advice on literary matters. Rosa's most interesting letters are written to Ricciardi – they are emotionally urgent, wavering between high-flown professions of Ciceronian friendship, which is based on the ideal of the friend as a second self, a kindred spirit in virtue and interests, and endless boasting, querulous complaints, demands and melancholic lamentation, and sometimes touching descriptions of domestic life. Those to Giulio are in a lower key; he and Ricciardi often stayed in the Maffei family's country houses near Volterra, and Rosa writes charmingly of the many pleasures of country

15 Sala degli Argenti, Palazzo Pitti, Florence, with frescos by Francesco Furini, Cecco Bravo and Giovanni da San Giovanni, 1635.

life. In 1640 Rosa met Lucrezia Paolina, who became his model and companion. She was a married woman but, when Rosa left Florence to stay with the Maffei, Lucrezia went with him, as company and solace.[2] Their first son, Rosalvo, was born in August 1641, probably at Volterra. These nine years in Florence, perhaps the happiest of Rosa's life, were transformative. Rosa, up until that point a painter of genre and landscape, become a renowned painter-poet, whose philosophical works were celebrated throughout Europe and described, in the most poetic language, by many distinguished men of letters. This was a decade rich in self-invention, and a dazzling series of self-portraits – as court painter, actor, poet, philosopher and hermit – run through these years, displaying his many-sided and restless ambitions.

Rosa undoubtedly intended to shine at court. He painted fast, he was witty and learned, a gifted musician with a good contralto voice, and brilliant conversationalist. His theatrical gifts endeared him to Giovan Carlo, and he was valued as an intellectual, able to interpret complex iconographic programmes in praise of the Medici. Rosa seemed to be endowed with all the gifts of the court painter, and was the perfect heir to the quirky French printmaker Jacques Callot and to Filippo Napoletano, who had introduced a modern and naturalistic art to Florence.

Giovan Carlo's own career had started a little shakily, but in 1638 the Medici prince had been invested with the prestigious title of *Generalissimo* of the Spanish seas. In 1642 he led an expedition from Livorno against a rebellious Catalonia and, in January 1641, he sent his painter, Salvator Rosa, to Livorno to paint the Medici galleys in preparation there for the voyage. Rosa was offered accommodation by Leopoldo de' Medici, but preferred to choose his own lodgings and enjoy the company of his friends, as he had done in his Roman house. Though he had done very little, Leopoldo commented uneasily to his brother, Rosa was anxious to return swiftly to Florence for Easter.[3]

In the sixteenth century Livorno had expanded and was now the premier port of call in the Mediterranean for ships travelling to the Levant, and renowned for its fortifications and lighthouse. The city, and its colourfully diverse population, had attracted many artists, among them Callot, Stefano della Bella and Baccio di Bianco, all of whom had made prints of the Medicean galleys and of lively incidents at the waterside. Rosa's two vast paintings, his *Marine with Lighthouse and Ships* and *Harbour Scene at Sunset*, brought an entirely new scale to this tradition. In the first (illus. 16), the two masted galleys, some of which flaunt the banners of the Order of St Stephen, fan

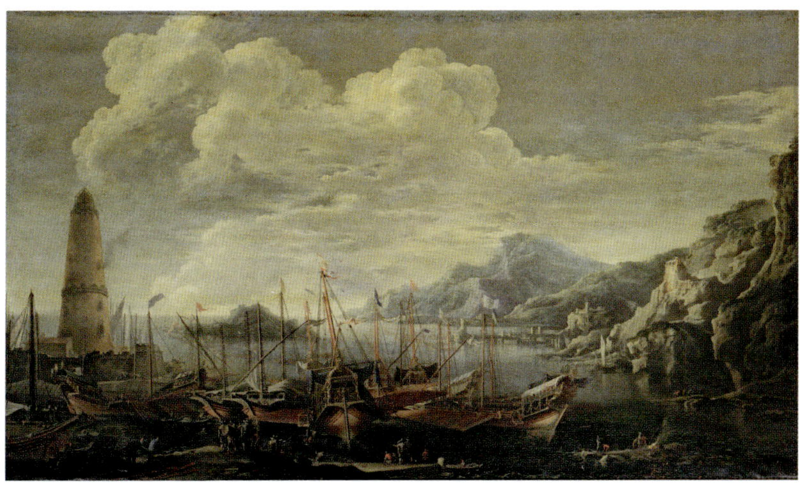

16 Salvator Rosa, *Marine with Lighthouse and Ships*, c. 1642, oil on canvas.

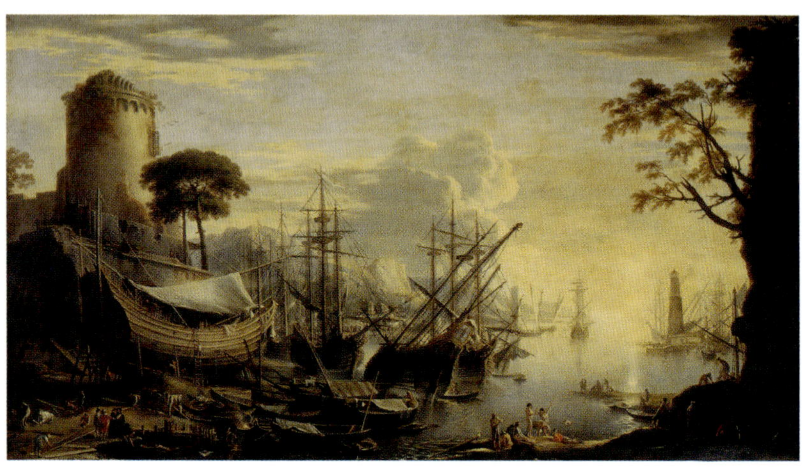

out across a foreground filled with small everyday scenes. The
Medici arms are carved into the poppa of the galley at the
very centre, and close to the viewer, immediately attracting
the eye. The painting is highly detailed, a little drily painted
and, aiming to please the specialist viewer, shows a wealth of
informative small incidents connected with manning the fleet.
There is a sharp jump from foreground to distance, where the
soft light and drenched atmosphere recall the Neapolitan
landscape. The *Harbour Scene at Sunset* (illus. 17) is very different. Its subject is a working shipyard where, in the light of the
setting sun, three masted men-of-war vessels are being refit-
ted and recaulked. It is predominantly a tribute to Claude,
whose *Seaport with Villa Medici* had been bought in 1637 by the
young Leopoldo de' Medici. Rosa's painting, both in its classical structure, and in the shimmering track of light across the
water, is indebted to this work. In the evening sun, their day's
work done, a group of workmen strip off to enjoy a late swim.
They shiver in the cold, or float, feigning dead; a clothed

17 Salvator Rosa, *Harbour Scene at Sunset*, 1641–2, oil on canvas.

figure peers comically at the naked and ungainly bottom before him. The figures look back to Rosa's Neapolitan works, and have much of the humour of *The Coral Fishermen*; they seem to poke fun at the charming lovers and musicians who fill the foreground of Claude's painting. This small group, so vivid and lively, inject a burlesque note into the grandeur of the seascape, delighting Rosa's Florentine viewers. Such vast harbour scenes had never before been seen in Florence. Rosa himself promoted this scale, an indication of his great ambitions. Giovan Carlo was nervous that the pictures would be too big for the room but was reassured by his *maestro di casa*, Filippo Niccolini, that the painter would 'submit to his taste'.[4]

Giovan Carlo's naval expedition proved disastrous on every level. He was chastened but rose again to be made a cardinal in 1644. In 1645 he travelled to Rome for his investiture, taking with him his painter, Salvator Rosa. In Florence the cardinal now dedicated himself to artistic projects, both at the Palazzo Pitti and at the Casino of the Orti Oricellari on the via della Scala, which his brother had presented to him in 1640. At the casino Giovan Carlo created an enchanted world – including a garden embellished with grottoes, joke fountains, mock ruins and artificial mountains – that delighted all the senses. Within was the *salone*, where the cardinal and his painter, Salvator Rosa, together created a celebration of his power. For the ceiling Pietro da Cortona painted an *Allegory of Peace*, and the Roman painter's presence may itself have fed the growing ambition of Rosa. Here hung his marine paintings, *Marine with Lighthouse and Ships* and the *Harbour Scene at Sunset*, and to complement them Rosa painted two further works, *Alexander and Diogenes* (illus. 18) and *Cincinnatus Called from the Plough* (illus. 19), noble scenes from Greek and Roman history, and only a little smaller than the harbour pictures. These paintings no longer suggest the world of affairs but a different model for the ideal life of the prince, now enjoying the pleasures of his city villa and his role as patron of the arts. The amusing and provocative Diogenes, who lived in a celebrated tub beneath the porticoes of the Athenian temples, was one of the most popular philosophers in the seventeenth century. Rosa showed a famous moment from his life. Alexander visited Diogenes in Corinth, and asked the philosopher if he could do anything for him. Diogenes rudely replied, 'Stand out of my light.' Rosa's painting is closest in spirit to the account given by Plutarch in the *Moralia*, in which the two figures seem

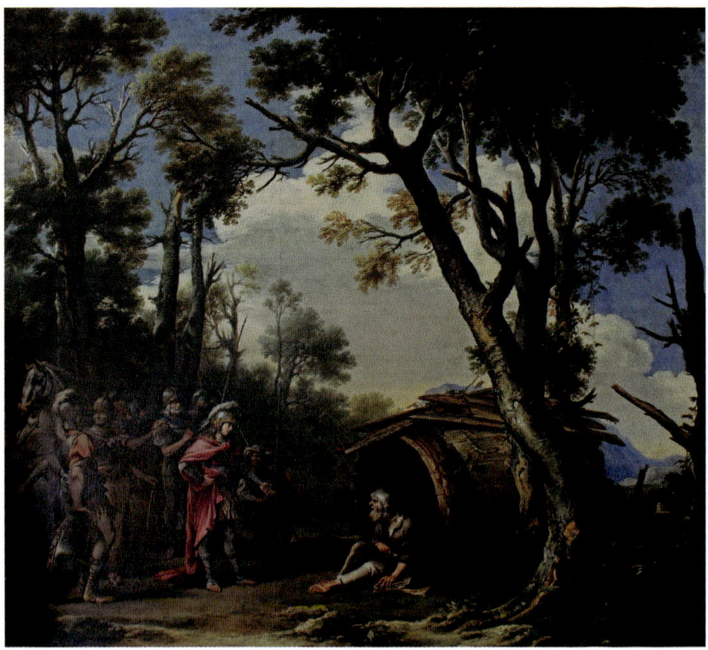

18 Salvator Rosa, *Alexander and Diogenes*, c. 1643, oil on canvas.

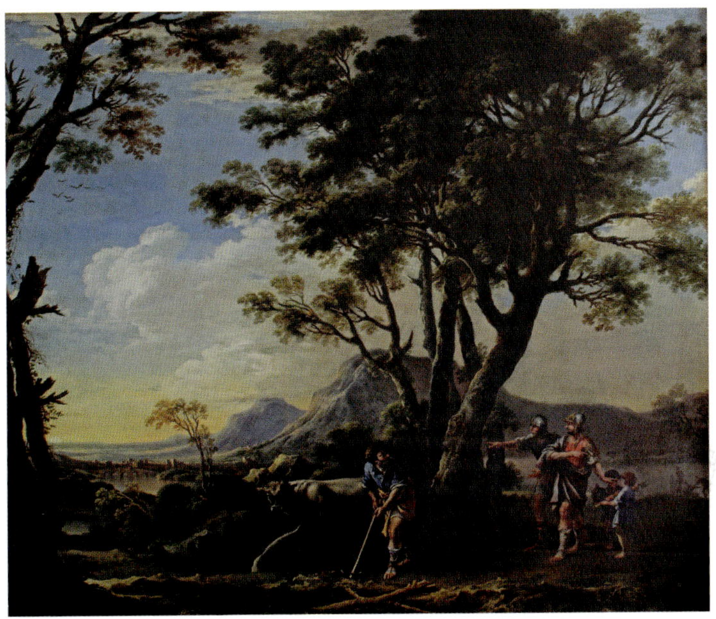

equal. Plutarch describes Alexander as being surrounded by a glamorous entourage of companions who laugh and jest at the philosopher's daring. But Alexander himself is impressed, and later he stresses how 'awed and astounded' he was with the life and worth of Diogenes, and how he resolved to spread his name throughout the world.[5] King and philosopher appear as complementary sources of power and the story had earlier been used by members of the Medici family seeking to celebrate their roles as patrons of learning and wise men. It occurs in the summer apartments at the Palazzo Pitti and in the Palazzo Vecchio where Alexander and Diogenes, representing philosophy, accompany figures of Geometry and Poetry.

Cincinnatus Called from the Plough (illus. 19) shows a different kind of virtue. Cincinnatus, who had retired from his service

19 Salvator Rosa, *Cincinnatus Called from the Plough*, c. 1643, oil on canvas.

to the Roman Empire to enjoy the simple pleasures of the countryside, was called back when brutal war threatened, and made a dictator. He was well known for both answering this call to duty and happily returning to his farm after sixteen days of total power. He became a model of civic virtue, of humility and selflessness and of the virtuous life of the countryside. Rosa shows him, as Livy had described him, working on the land, in rough clothes and covered in dust and sweat. There he was found by representatives of the state, elegantly bearing the insignia of office, who ask him to put on his toga so that they may tell him the mandates of the senate.[6]

It is not known who wrote the programme for this room but it is possible that it may have been Rosa himself. It is likely that the works were painted after the visit to Rome in 1645, for both landscape and figure style suggest an awareness of Roman painting, of Claude's landscapes of the 1640s and the figure style of Poussin and Domenichino.[7] Elsewhere in the casino, in the small upper rooms by the terrace, hung a wealth of more informal works by Rosa. These were small oblong landscapes, landscapes in gouache and paintings of maps and cities, the whole creating a magical space, which evoked, within the cardinal's garden, the charms of solitude and of the arts.

In 1642, while Giovan Carlo was away, Rosa received a commission from Ferdinando II, Grand Duke of Tuscany, for the *Battle between Turks and Christians* (illus. 20), to celebrate the birth of a male Medici heir, the future Cosimo III. The priest Reginaldo Sgambati wrote 'An address to Rosa, the famous artist, on the birth of the Grand Prince of Tuscany', which prophesied the future valour of the infant prince:

Take up your brushes, Rosa, prophesy
In paint the mighty infant's destiny . . .
Depict a thousand Arab ships in flight,
A thousand savage walls collapse in flames,
The blood of infidels spread like a flood
Across their impious seas and godless lands.[8]

Medici triumphs on sea and land, against Turks and Moors, had long been celebrated in the fresco cycles that decorated the family's Tuscan villas and palaces, while Mattias de' Medici's victorious campaigns in the Thirty Years War in northern Europe had displayed afresh the military might of the House of Medici. As Rosa painted, the Wars of Castro were unfolding and, in 1643, the Grand Duke was to enjoy a celebrated victory against the papal forces in Umbria.[9] Military prints and

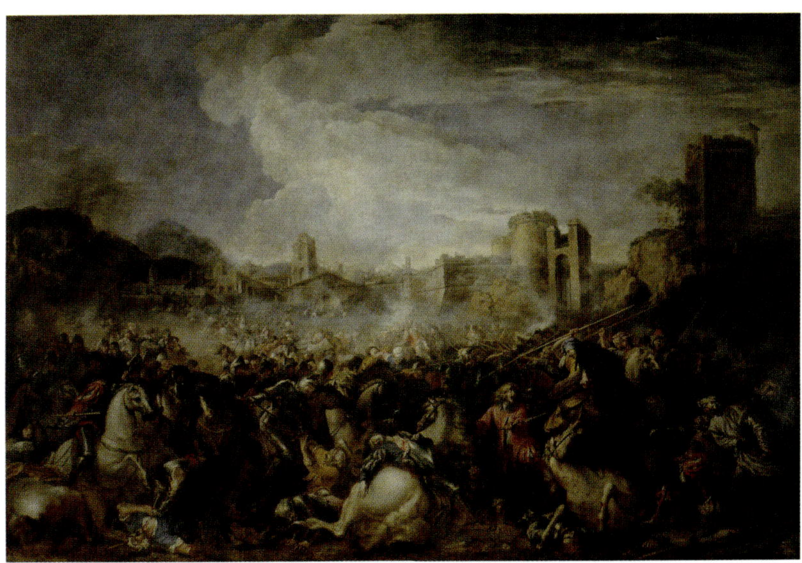

20 Salvator Rosa, *Battle between Turks and Christians*, 1642, oil on canvas.

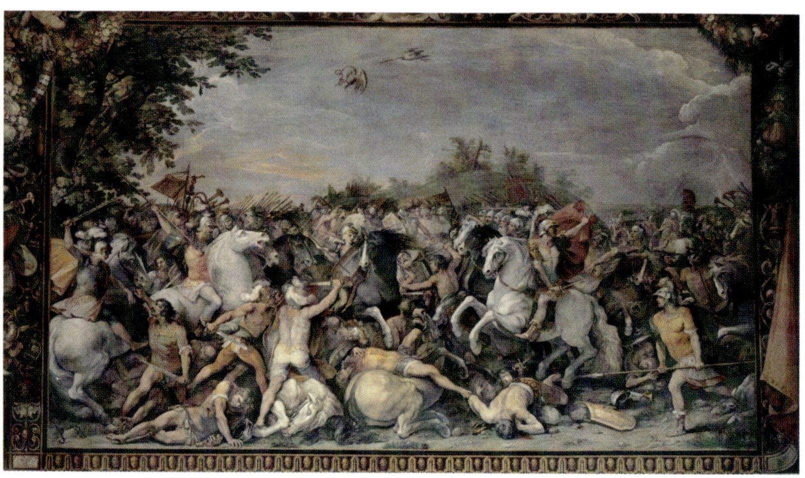

drawings of contemporary battles were popular in Florence and collectors enjoyed discussing their wealth of documentary detail.

Rosa's battle, in sharp contrast, is imaginary and anonymous, blending contemporary dress and antique armour and suggesting past, present and future, in homage to the infant prince. His composition pays tribute to Giuseppe Cesari's fresco, the *Battle of Tullius Hostilius* (illus. 21) in the Roman Palazzo dei Conservatori. Both artists build up their compositions around symmetrical groups, with a strong emphasis on the centre, where soldiers lie dead on fallen horses. In the clear bright light of his fresco Cesari idealizes battle, aesthetically weaving together a variety of movements and figures and displaying his skill in complex poses often underpinned by evocations of celebrated antique sculptures. His is an abstract concept of battle, and the ecclesiastical writer Giovanni Michele Silos later commented that so attractive were Cesari's

21 Cavaliere d'Arpino (Giuseppe Cesari) and workshop, *Battle of Tullius Hostilius Againsthe Inhabitants of Veii and Fidenae*, 1598–1601, fresco.

warriors that Mars himself did not attain ferocity.[10] Rosa remade Cesari's picture, creating a savage Neapolitan horror that was new in battle painting. It is likely that he knew the Notebooks of Leonardo da Vinci, where Leonardo had described war as 'most bestial madness', and his urgent instructions to the painter seem to be rooted in appalled observation:

> Make the conquered and beaten pale, with brows raised and knit, and the skin above their brows furrowed with pain . . . Show someone using one hand as a shield for his terrified eyes with the palm towards the enemy; while the other rests on the ground to support his half raised body. Represent others shouting with their mouths wide open, and running away.[11]

Rosa's painting is full of such detail, of sound and fury, of terror and pain. The fallen Christian soldier, spotlit against the white horse, no longer has the elegance of Cesari's central figure but, a martyr to the ferocity of the Turks, his naked chest streaming with blood, he reaches out, with tragic pathos, to the spectator. His pathos is juxtaposed with the sickening violence, more extreme than in earlier art, of the fallen warrior on the left, whose arm is bloodily severed at the elbow and whose bare hand clasps the dagger of his enemy.[12] In the distance, in the shadow of the walls of a city that evokes Florence, the horsemen merge with clouds of dust, a motif again made famous by the notebooks, where Leonardo describes the dust-laden air, the combatants scarcely visible in the turmoil and soldiers slipping and falling in the mud-stained mire.[13] It is tempting to see Rosa's picture as a condemnation of the destruction of war and the enormity of suffering, a strong theme both in his own poetry and in contemporary Florentine writing. But the painting was done for the Medici, and the bestial horrors of war convey their grim heroism.

Cesari, who enjoyed arms and armour and loved to ride proudly through Rome on horseback, his sword at his side, included a self-portrait at the left of his symmetrical frieze of heroic warriors. He perhaps inspired Rosa to add, at the left of his painting, a bystander self-portrait. Both artists may have been aware of Plutarch's description of the Greek sculptor Phidias' self-portrait, 'a bald old man lifting up a stone with both hands,' which Phidias included in a relief of the battle of the Amazons decorating the shield of his celebrated Athena.[14] Cesari, his face individual and contemporary and his shield displaying his arms, draws the eye into the ranks of Roman warriors. Rosa, in sharp contrast, hollows out a still space, a little apart from the great brutality of the battle. Here he stands, aloof and elegant, both intensely aware of the spectator and consciously posed at the opening of a brilliant career, the Phidias of a new age. He bears a shield with the head of Medusa, traditionally associated with the goddess Athena, and used in battle for protection and for defeating the enemies of reason and knowledge. The shield is inscribed 'Sarò', meaning 'I shall be', and in this way the painter declared – with a typically Florentine love of wordplay and anagram – the eternity of his art. The shield's gleaming surface will reflect his fame to later ages.[15] The painting dramatizes Rosa's success at the Medici court. It became celebrated and Rosa received for it a high payment of 300 scudi. He was later to express his dislike of battle painting, but it was a genre already viewed in classical times as the highest artistic challenge. Here he displayed his skill in the depiction of expression and complex movement as well as his powers of invention, qualities that enabled him to entirely remake the genre.

Rosa aimed to excel at court but was bitterly disappointed by his reception. The artist was always generous, his liberality a conscious expression of the greatness of his gifts and intellect, and he lavished money on sumptuous banquets for the courtiers. They were happy to enjoy his hospitality but, glimpsing him from their carriages the next day, ruthlessly cut him dead, though he had imagined that he would be admitted to their *conversazione*. This, he reported resentfully, taught him to steer clear of the great of this world. Rosa, aware of his lowly origins, began to hate the court, where adulation and dissimulation reigned supreme. He began to write verse in the early 1640s, and a bitter wail of rejection runs through these early poems. His *Lament* (early 1640s) veers between rueful humour and bleak anger: 'Remember, Fortune, that I am of this world, and that I too am of flesh; For me alone, the sky is deaf, the sun is dark, and dry the earth.' If he goes to the palace, he complains, the satraps of the court gossip maliciously about him; he has no villa, nor yet a room. But his spirit revives as he remembers his great calling: he can imagine no greater destiny than that of painter, who can scatter galleys across the seas and create worlds for others, though he has not a handful of earth.[16] He unites fury at rejection with an exultant sense of the landscape artist's power of creation.

Rosa's friend, the satirist Antonio Abati, was later to write, 'Knowing how to kill the famous vices of the century with the blows of satire is today the most efficacious way of winning commendation and the eternity of letters.'[17] In these years, Rosa too saw the power of satire to win fame on a wider stage and he wrote his first three satires, *Music*, *Poetry* and *War*, in Florence. At the Roman Accademia degli Umoristi, and stimulated by Abati, a lively interest in satire had flourished. Rosa looked to Abati but also built on a distinguished Florentine tradition, of such poets as Michelangelo Buonarroti the Younger and Jacopo Soldani. The Roman monologue satire had been reborn in the sixteenth century, and in the seventeenth the model was the Roman satirist Juvenal, whose harsh voice was replacing that of the more amusing Horace. Juvenal declared that he was inspired by righteous fury to inveigh against the chaotic degeneracy of contemporary Rome – his heart burned dry with rage (*Satire* 1, l. 45) and it was hard not to write satire. Rosa's anger echoes Juvenal's: he cannot remain silent and moral passion spurs him on (*Poetry*, l. 81). Whatever their ostensible theme, Rosa's satires are linked by his passionate hatred of the court, where the noble perish, while the unworthy are honoured and his own merits languish unrecognized. His use of a variety of forms – monologue, dialogue, fables and proverbs – derives from classical satire, as does his mix of language – of the learned and the mundane, the high-flown and the parodic, the noble and the obscene. He chose a Dantesque terza rima, commonly used for didactic poetry, and aspired with increasing passion to be recognized as the self-elected moral mentor of his age, 'spotless in his way of life'.[18] Through his varied material Rosa wove highly selected personal details that vaunted his courage, his freedom and the modesty of his needs, and presented him as being one who longed for 'no bed more precious than a bower of traveller's joy, among the meadows and the canopy of the woods' (*Music*, ll. 358–60). He constantly berated the evils of the court and the crowd of degenerates who frequented that infernal site – the adulator, the madman, the spy, the gentlemen of the bedchamber, the cheat (*Music*, ll. 342–3) – and set the luxury and corruption of his day against the heroism of ancient times and the simple lives of the Cynic and Stoic philosophers. This strategy was a convention of classical satire, as was Rosa's satiric persona, and his claiming of the Stoic virtues of frugality and simplicity. There is a very tight connection between the themes of his satires and the scenes from the lives of the ancient philosophers that entered his art at the same time. Rosa was not only a Juvenalian poet, but a Juvenalian painter.

At the end of his life Rosa planned to publish the satires, but they were initially a kind of drama, a performance presented to his friends and to a select circle of intellectuals: his persona of anger and indignation was inherent to his cherished ideal of freedom. His poetry amused and delighted. Rosa, who as Pascariello had cut a dashing figure in the squares of Rome, now dazzled his friends and the Florentine literary academies with his performances of the satires. His verses, like those of Juvenal, were a kind of drama. As early as 1641 he wrote to Giulio Maffei that he had read his satire in Siena and half the city had flocked to hear him.[19] Passeri later described his performances, his 'wonderful tone of voice' and the 'vivacity of gestures that he painted with language'.[20] In Florence and Rome, Filippo Baldinucci tells us, the leading intellects of the day marvelled at 'the vividness, the witticisms, the sharpest sayings'. They enjoyed the brio of the dark Neapolitan, so vital in expression and gesture, and commanding of attention through imposing silences. The artist became a kind of wit personified and Baldinucci wrote of his satirical persona, concluding that his verses were 'a true and most like self-portrait'. A little later Baldinucci added a more critical description, of Rosa's fury when his audience did not laugh enough. This can happen, writes Baldinucci severely, even to a cultured man, so obsessed was he with glory, and so inordinately vain.[21]

Rosa now dominated the literary world, and was celebrated for his double laurels. He attracted the finest intellects in Florence. Men clustered around him, competing for his attention; cardinals and princes came to watch him work, and to listen to his pronouncements. Rosa used this power to attract, and his house at the Croce del Trebbio became a stage, where he himself shone as impresario and star. He mixed not with painters but with men of letters, whose *bella conversazione* soon blossomed into an academy, the Accademia dei Percossi. Its members were immensely distinguished, some of them known throughout Europe, and several also frequented the famed Accademia della Crusca. They included eminent disciples of Galileo, such as the mathematician Evangelista Torricelli and the young scientist Francesco Redi, while from the world of affairs and high church came Paolo Vendramin, the Venetian representative in Florence, and the Sienese theologian Volunnio Bandinelli, later a cardinal, and known for his stern moral virtues. Classical scholars, among them Carlo Dati, the perfect man of letters, and Valerio Chimentelli, professor of moral philosophy and Greek at the University of Pisa, nourished Rosa's erudition and knowledge of ancient literature and language. Among the poets were

Francesco Rovai, a learned poet and amateur painter, and Pietro Salvetti, creator of both sparkling witticisms and bitter satire. These were multitalented men, who, in true Florentine vein, enjoyed both philosophy and high culture, and practical jokes and wordplay, keeping alive the legacy of the sixteenth-century burlesque poet Francesco Berni. At the academy all was humorous and festive, and it had a convivial and facetious atmosphere. Rosa was to mock Carlo Dati for his pomposity but Dati immortalized Rosa as prankster in his *Lepidezze di spiriti bizzarri* (Witticisms of Bizarre Spirits), a title which itself pinpoints the atmosphere of Florentine cultural life. Dati tells how Rosa, 'painter, and excellent Neapolitan poet' irritated by the haughty arrogance of a Spanish visitor to Rome, took him through the back door of a trattoria which opened into the Piazza Navona, nonchalantly commenting that this was the inn's *cortile* (courtyard).[22] Wit and jest were important components of the self-fashioning of artist and writer.

At the centre of the Percossi's activity was the symposium, the recreation of an ancient Greek tradition established by Plato and Xenophon, where the members gathered to eat, drink and talk, and to enjoy recitations of poetry and dramatic performances. Ideally the symposium created peace of the spirit and joy, and celebrated friendship, and Rosa's academy was 'the house of joy and the marketplace of happiness'.[23] In winter the rooms of his house were well furnished and per-fumed, while in the hot summer months an enchanting interior garden, where the visitor seemed to enter an illusionistic forest, offered shade and repose.[24] To the Florentine visitor this would have suggested Plato's well-known academy, which met in a grove near the ancient city of Athens, and had inspired the fifteenth-century Florentine Platonic academy.

The food was presented with a scenographic flair. All the courses – pastries, roast meat, mincemeats, soup and even the salad – were, with a dazzling display of ingenuity, made from the same ingredient, and yet they wittily suggested a wealth and variety of flavours.[25] Such displays delighted Florentines, and earlier the artist Andrea del Sarto had created for the 'Company of the Cauldron', a dining club of twelve artists, an octagonal temple from different foods, with music sheets of lasagne marked with pepper grain notes.[26] Many burlesque poems were addressed to such subjects as fennel and ricotta, and the Percossi decreed that Rosa's creations should be so celebrated; the Bolognese trader Francesco Maria Agli delivered a memorable mock encomium on mincemeats, a fitting subject for one who was elderly and toothless.

There followed a wide variety of dinner entertainments, ostentatiously displaying, in satires and poetry, the intellectual status of host and guests. Two discourses, Evangelista Torricelli's *Encomium to the Golden Age* and Valerio Chimentelli's *Report on Peace*, were addressed to Rosa's paintings, the *Departure of Astrea* (illus. 22) and *Peace Burning the Arms of War* (c. 1640–45), and were especially praised by Baldinucci. The *Encomium to the Golden Age* is an anthology of ancient texts on the golden age, dominated by Seneca's *Epistle XC* and interwoven with quotations from Virgil. Torricelli praised the innocent simplicity of pastoral life, far from the corrupt luxury of the court; here, as Virgil had written, 'Departing Justice left among these her latest earthly footprints. So wrote the most sublime of all poets, and so it was painted by the liveliest of brushes, that of Salvator Rosa.'[27] Chimentelli's *Report on Peace* is lost, but it was almost certainly addressed to *Peace Burning the Arms of War*. The two paintings are described as pendants by Baldinucci and they were very probably a Medici commission, painted, as was the *Battle between Turks and Christians*, to celebrate the birth of Cosimo III.[28] They go together, the first lamenting the end of the Golden Age, the second the rebirth of an era of peace.[29] Rosa's tone is humorous and Justice leaves a quirky group of peasants, including a bare-bottomed baby, pushed to the forefront, far removed from the tone of Virgilian pastoral. The connection with the Medici is significant. The Percossi here celebrated Rosa as court painter, skilfully articulating the Medicean myth of the Golden Age, which had long been part of Florentine Renaissance poetry. Their academy was not a place of dissent or subversion. Its members were courtiers, heavily dependent on Medici patronage; but at their

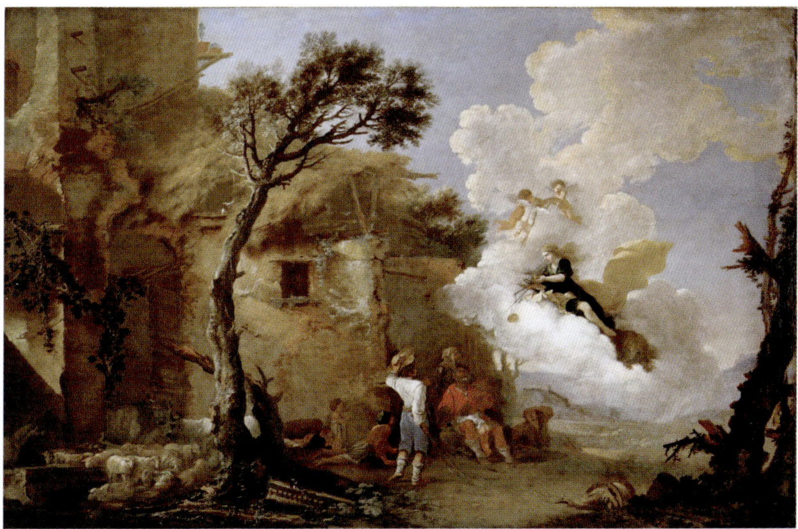

22 Salvator Rosa, *The Departure of Astrea, c.* 1640–45, oil on canvas.

academy they enjoyed close friendships and a high-spirited freedom.

Giovan Carlo de' Medici was particularly important as a theatrical patron, and under his protection a branch of the Percossi, the Accademia degli Improvvisi, put on improvised theatrical performances at the Casino di San Marco. Baldinucci describes with delight his memories of these 'most beautiful and bizarre improvised comedies', which showed 'noble and serious subjects, with the addition of comic roles'.[30] He could not speak, he exclaimed, too highly of Rosa's side-splitting performance as Pascariello. At their first performance in 1645, many women, rarely before invited to such occasions, joined the enthusiasts.[31] Rosa's centrality is celebrated in a poem by Francesco Rovai, who praises the fiery spirits of the actors, 'more ardent than the August sun'; Rosa, their mentor, inspires and moves them. He is castigator of vice, the enemy of sloth and lasciviousness, but he is also an artist so gifted that he surpasses nature herself, creating afresh all that is lovely in the earth.[32]

To his fame as poet and painter, crowned by double laurels, Rosa added another persona: Pascariello, a character from the Neapolitan *commedia dell'arte*. Rosa, as we have seen, had introduced him in Rome, and then brought him to Tuscany, where he added the mask of Coviello to his performances. Pascariello is a zanni, or servant, astute, spirited and ingenious. He is close to the *commedia dell'arte* character of the vainglorious Spanish captain, immensely popular in Naples, and well understood in other parts of Italy. He is akin, too, to the beloved Neapolitan mask of Pulcinella, who often gave voice to the hungry and oppressed of Naples. The dialect poet Sgruttendio describes

Pascariello strutting about with his sword by his side.[33] Rosa made full use of his exotic *napoletanità* on the Florentine stage; Pascariello is indeed a stereotype of the Neapolitan, whose ridiculous expressions and gestures delighted the city. His self-portrait (illus. 23) in this role is a dazzlingly complex blend of parody and wit. It is fittingly Spanish in style, and the pose, with jutting elbow and thrusting sword, suggests both the swaggering stance of the halberdier immortalized in Renaisance prints of soldiers, and a more courtly type of portraiture. The sheer size of the painting evokes his ambition and self-love; we look up to his affectedly stern and proud expression, his beard and moustache faintly absurd, as he turns a sharp eye on the world, about to denounce or mock, in an ironic vein, the degradation that he condemned in the satires. And yet all elegance is undercut by the strange gloves, so shredded and tattered. The gloves, associated with nobility and masculinity, seem a parody of such an elegant Venetian portrait as Titian's *Man with a Glove* (c. 1520). Rosa never painted a portrait celebrating rank and status, and his Pascariello seems an ironic comment on a courtly artist's self-portrait such as that of Rubens, who paints himself worldly and assured, richly dressed and ostentatiously gloved, and bearing a sword. It is possible, too, that Rosa here recalled the celebrated bandit Micco Passaro, the subject of the Neapolitan dialect poet Cortese's mock heroic *Micco Passaro 'nnamorato* (1619). The actor Bartolomeo Zito has left us a description of this historic figure, who paraded through Naples, 'armed always with sword and buckler, who at all times wore gloves, tattered and filthy'.[34] Rosa was perhaps drawn to Pascariello as a Neapolitan, and as a free and independent character with whom he could identify.

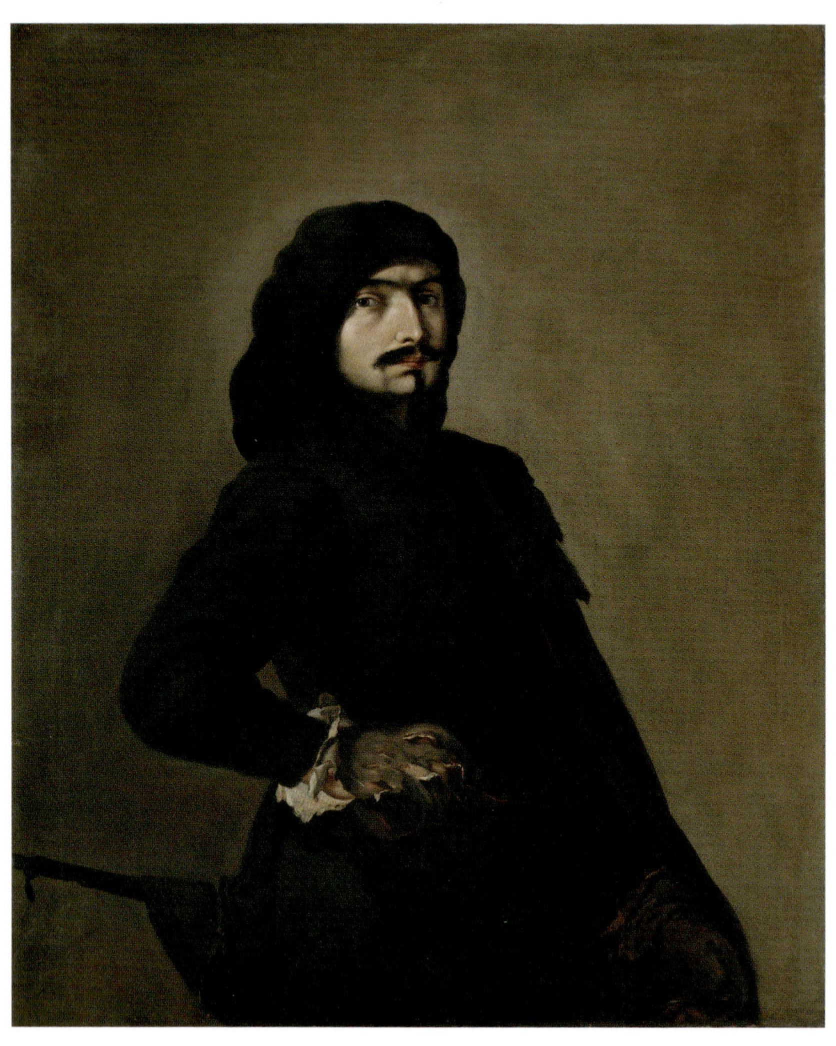

23 Salvator Rosa, *Self-portrait as Pascariello, c.* 1645–9, oil on canvas.

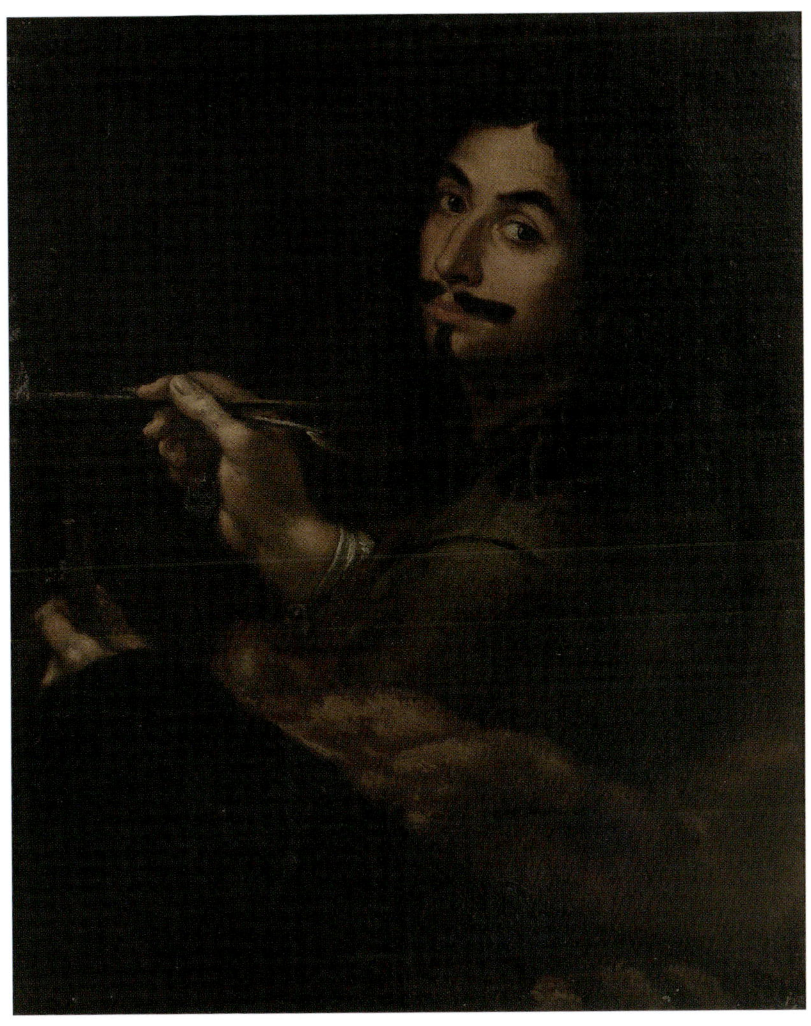

24 Salvator Rosa, *Self-portrait as Painter-poet*, c. 1642, oil on canvas.

In the same years Rosa, often with other members of the Percossi, enjoyed another kind of freedom, far removed from the intrigues of the court, in the most remote parts of Tuscany, near Volterra. Most frequently he and Ricciardi went to the villas owned by the Maffei family, at Barbaiano and Monterufoli. Here they enjoyed an enchanting way of life, reading good books and, as at the Percossi, enjoying high-spirited dinner parties and philosophical discussions with literary friends. His *Self-portrait as Painter-poet* (illus. 24), a gift to the Maffei family, recalls these creative days, when Rosa both wrote and painted; fur-wrapped, jovial, he turns from his easel to invite the viewer to the social pleasures of Monterufoli, and brush and pen suggest his double laurels. Rosa drew constantly and it was here, in this wild countryside, among the strange rock formations and densely wooded hills, that he created a new aesthetic of wild beauty, or *orrida bellezza*. A touching letter from Giovanni Battista Ricciardi to their friend Ascanio della Penna, the Medici courtier, dilettante artist and collector, describes the intensely sociable, Petrarchan solitude which the two enjoyed. Far from the vices of the city, Ricciardi writes, together they read philosophy 'among the water and shadow of the crags', sometimes satirizing the world from the mountain tops.[35] The letter was accompanied by Rosa's drawing of himself as a hermit, with a pile of books, while another young man writes on the rock, '*Hic aevi mihi prima dies*' (The first day of my life; illus. 25). The drawing suggests a comparison with Poussin's *Et in Arcadia Ego* of 1637–8, where shepherds trace out the Latin letters on a tomb.[36] Rosa's is a new landscape of philosophical retreat, a wilderness of solitude and inspiration, far removed from the sunlit valleys of Poussin's *Arcadia.*

The painter-poet Lorenzo Lippi, probably a member of the Percossi, was Rosa's closest friend in Florence. Lippi, a generous man with a fiery spirit, cut a dashing and witty figure in the literary academies, and he too moved easily between theatre, painting and poetry. His *Self-portrait* shows him looking out jestingly at the spectator, conveying an ironic intelligence that recalls Rosa's Pascariello and was a typical ingredient of artistic self-fashioning.[37] Lippi was at the court in Innsbruck, Austria, from 1647–9, a place where he wrote most of his mock heroic poem *Il Malmantile racquistato*, the story of the usurper Bertinella's attempt, aided by the witch Martinazza, to retain the ill-gotten castle of Malmantile. This poem delighted his Florentine friends and, on his return to the city from Innsbruck, Rosa encouraged him to finish it. The poem was a parody of Tasso's *Gerusalemme Liberata* (Jerusalem Delivered) and, Baldinucci informs us, where Tasso had chosen a noble subject and noble language, Lippi chose to tell folk and fairy tales, adorned with Florentine proverbs, riddles and dialect. Baldinucci describes the pleasure his friends took in suggesting new episodes.[38] Rosa introduced Lippi to Giambattista Basile's *The Story of Stories*, and Baldinucci himself 'for a most cheerful pastime and amusement' added new ideas to the Dantesque *Descent into Hell*, a stock component of epic poetry. Martinazza, a clumsily unsuccessful witch, enters dramatically in a chariot pulled by demons. She smears herself with unguent, summoning up devils with strange incantations, and jumps into a magic circle, muttering mysteriously among her jars and scraps of paper. Several stanzas describe the grisly contents of her spells, a set piece of both poetry and painting.[39] Her descent to the Underworld, an iconic feature of epic poetry, marks the

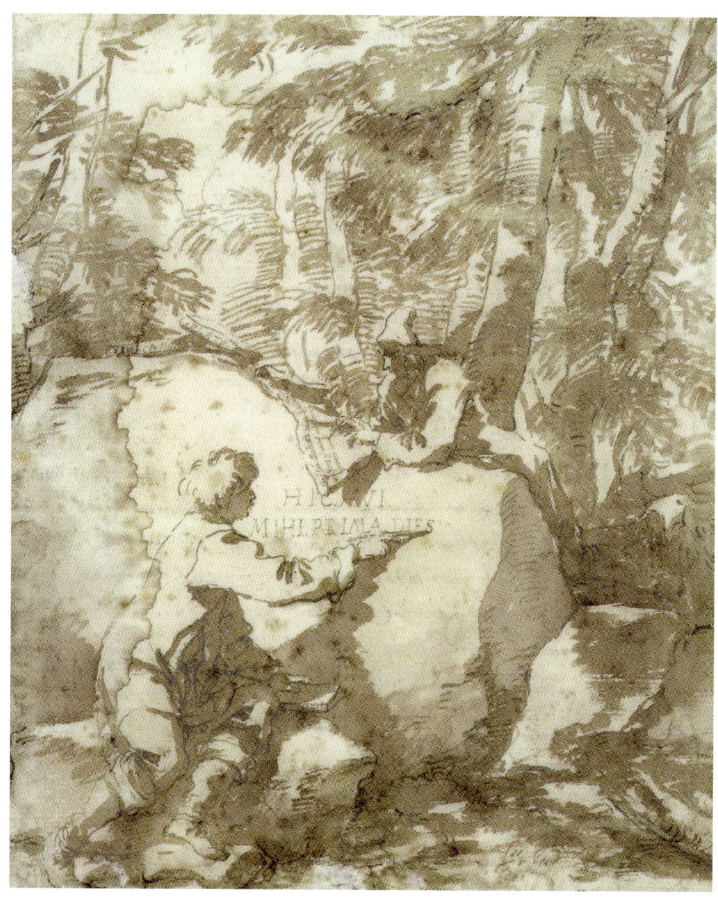

climax.⁴⁰ Here Lippi, mocking the perfumed garden of Tasso's enchantress, Armida, created a garden from Hell, planted with instruments of torture and the hangman's gibbet. Skeletons hang from trees, and against the walls are spread out monsters and hunchbacks in place of fruit trees. Lippi delighted in displaying his ingenuity; his satirical witchcraft scenes entertained and astonished.

25 Salvator Rosa, *Rosa in the Countryside*, 1640s, drawing.

At about the same time Rosa began to paint scenes of witchcraft. These scenes were rooted in the complex system of witchcraft beliefs that had spread throughout Europe from the sixteenth century, codified in the writings of erudite demonologists, above all in Martin del Rio's popular *Disquisitionum magicarum, libri sex* (1599). At their centre was the concept of the sabbath, a vast meeting of witches where the Devil was worshipped. Constantly recurring motifs were the creation of love spells, the sacrifice of babies and necromancy. The description of witches in Latin literature, even when clearly satirical, carried weight in the seventeenth century, and Rosa knew these works well. Horace, in *Epode v*, describes a bevy of old hags, and their horrific murder of a young boy, whose dried liver and marrow they need for a love potion. The poem is a horror-farce, predominantly humorous; Horace mocks the witches, who are disgusting and ridiculous. These witches set the general tone of the witches of early modernity. Lucan's necromantic Erictho in the *Pharsalia* (mid-1st century AD) was an equally powerful prototype. Erictho was the most foul of all the Thessalian witches and her dark rituals astonished with their gruesome details. Lucan creates theatrical settings, among abandoned tombs and in the darkness of night, for scenes of necromancy, piled high with horror. Erictho, her face gaunt and loathsome with decay, seizes from funeral pyres the smoking ashes of the young and blazing bones; she 'breaks with her teeth the fatal noose and mangles the carcase that hangs on the gallows'.[41] Rosa was also steeped in the chivalric epic and the traditions of the literary witch, of the poet Ludovico Ariosto's beautiful Alcina in the *Orlando Furioso* and Tasso's magician Ismen, who, in the *Gerusalemme Liberata*, practised necromancy among the ghosts and goblins of the gloomy forest of Saron. More recently Giambattista Marino had presented a gallery of witches in his epic poem *Adonis.* Marino attempted to surpass the horrors of the entire tradition of literary witches, from Lucan to Tasso, and the hyperbole of his descriptions, his aim to intrigue with his *novità*, and to play on the contrast between beauty and horror, has something in common with the extravagance of Rosa's witch scenes. But witchcraft was also very much part of contemporary reality. In 1647 an old woman, Caterina, had been accused of witchcraft at Camugliano, near Florence, and the centre of a fief belonging to the Niccolini family, who owned an important series of Rosa's witchcraft scenes. Caterina's court depositions present her astonishing imaginative life and vividly suggest how the different worlds of witchcraft, the scholarly, the theatrical and the contemporary fed into one another. In Tuscany, particularly in the rural areas where Rosa sometimes stayed, accusations of sorcery and of casting spells were frequent and often priests and friars were charged with taking part in the rituals of black magic. The wild countryside around Volterra, rich in strange rock formations and caves, conjured up demonic apparitions, and the Masso di Mandringa, a massive rock near Volterra, was thought to be the site of a witches' sabbath.[42] Rosa himself may well have witnessed exorcisms. But Rome attempted to control the zeal of the witch hunters and from the 1640s it was possible to indulge in satire and ridicule.[43] Rosa's visual sources are clear. He painted not the beautiful enchantresses of the Italian tradition but the aged and ugly hags of the north, most importantly the grotesque and fevered figures who fill the eery night-time scenes of Hans Baldung Grien's chiaroscuro woodcuts.

The oval *Scene of Witchcraft* (illus. 27) perhaps introduced his series of witchcraft scenes. Here, against a dusky sky lit by the flaming bones, a group of antic figures, repulsive yet humorous, are absorbed by their bizarre rituals. A robed magician, awkward and clumsy, peers through the pelvis of a skeletal bird; beyond, airborne witches fly to the hangman's gibbet. The support is slate, and Rosa uses the greyness of the stone to enhance the hallucinatory quality. The painting seems itself a magical object and the slate has overtones of the stones used by witches and magicians. It was probably set off by a rich gold frame. In this work Rosa contrasted horror and beauty, creating, from repulsive material, a perfectly crafted object that would have delighted collectors in Florence, where paintings on stone were a fashion. Aristotle, in the *Poetics*, had written of the pleasure to be found in the accurate representation of 'the forms of the most despised animals and corpses', and Rosa would have been aware of this aesthetic.[44] Unusually the artist makes a direct reference to the church. A priest and Franciscan friar conduct a black mass, while in the distance the motif of the hanged man on the gibbet seems a parody of the *Descent from the Cross*. Rosa may well have remembered the notorious trial in Rome in 1635, when a group of priests were accused of using black magic in an attempt to murder the pope.[45] The caricatured priest and friar are stolid, naturalistic figures, yet painted with delicate detail, and they seem to conjure up around them the horrors of a ghostly world. An elaborate still-life of the tools of magic fills the foreground, and this motif became a set piece in witchcraft scenes. Such grisly catalogues had since classical times attracted poets: Marino, in *Adonis*, presented an encyclopaedia of black magic, a hyperbolic

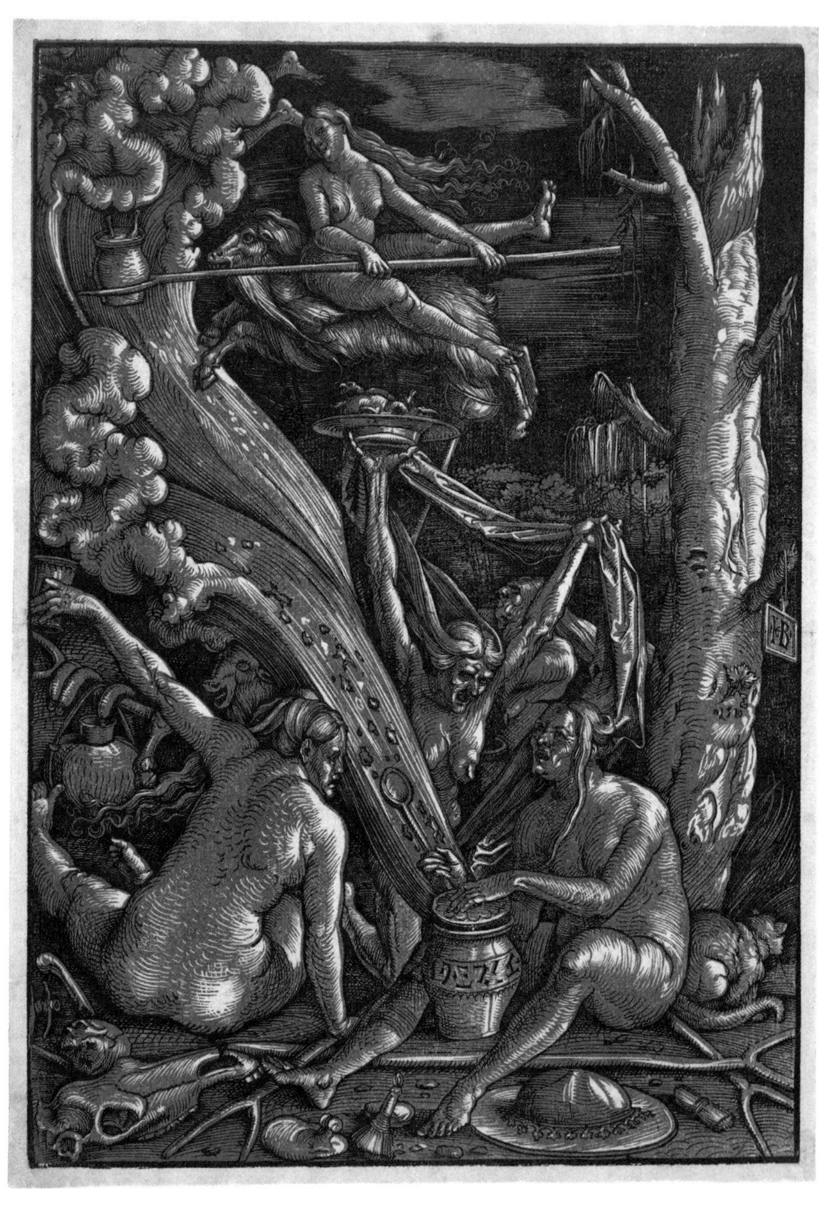

26 Hans Baldung Grien, *The Witches* (*Departure for the Sabbath*), 1510, woodcut print.

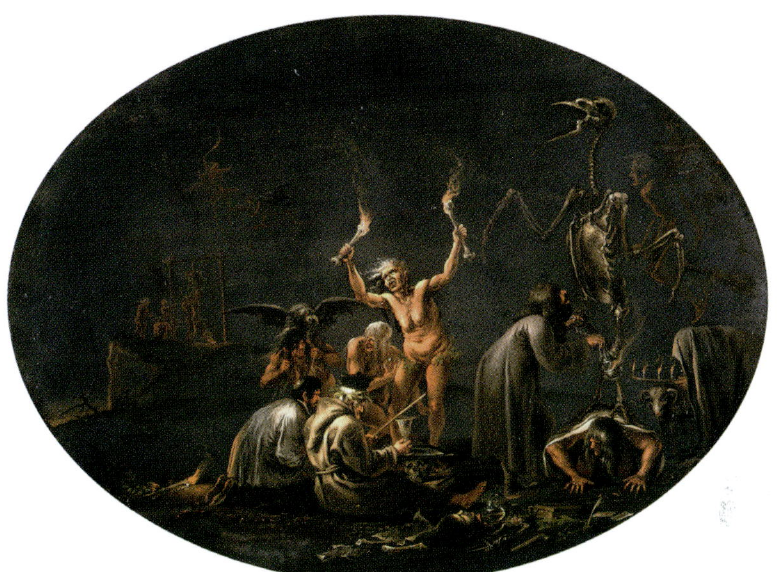

collection of the repulsive ingredients of spells. Rosa competed
with him, his *tour de force* the horrific decapitated head at the
centre; like Marino, Rosa intended to intrigue and to shock
with his *novità*.[46] His flying witches call to mind the flight of
Marino's enchantress Falsirena, who journeys through clouds
and whirlwinds to glean body parts from a desolate battlefield
(canto XIII).

In 1666 Rosa was to look back with pride on the later *Scene
of Witchcraft* (illus. 28) painted twenty years earlier, predicting
that its price would soar after his death, for 'everyone is most
intrigued by it'.[47] This painting tells no narrative; it spreads
out before the viewer, as though on a theatrical stage, a compendium of the activities of witches. Rosa weaves together a
variety of sources, both visual and literary, ancient and modern, from folklore and high culture. He remakes, with vivid

27 Salvator Rosa, *Scene of Witchcraft*, c. 1644, oil on slate.

topicality, the most well-known of earlier prints of witchcraft, from both Italian and northern traditions.

The painting falls into three groups, their relationships fluid. At the centre Rosa calls forth Hans Baldung Grien's iconic print *The Departure for the Sabbath*, evoking its night-time setting and dead tree, and the hideous hag stirring a potion in a vessel. Northern prints were popular in Florence and the visual similarities are striking. The younger witch, blonde, with ribboned hair, with wax figurine and mirror, suggests the popular love spells described by Theocritus and Virgil, and she seems to seek help from the circle of hideous old hags who cluster around. The love spells of classical poetry were often recreated by modern poets; Marino had described the wax model of a reluctant lover, pierced through the heart by a sharp splinter of myrtle and melted on the fire, so that the fire of love would destroy his spirit (canto XIII:17). But, beyond this foreground group, Rosa moves into the horrors of the modern world. The tragic corpse of the hanged man,

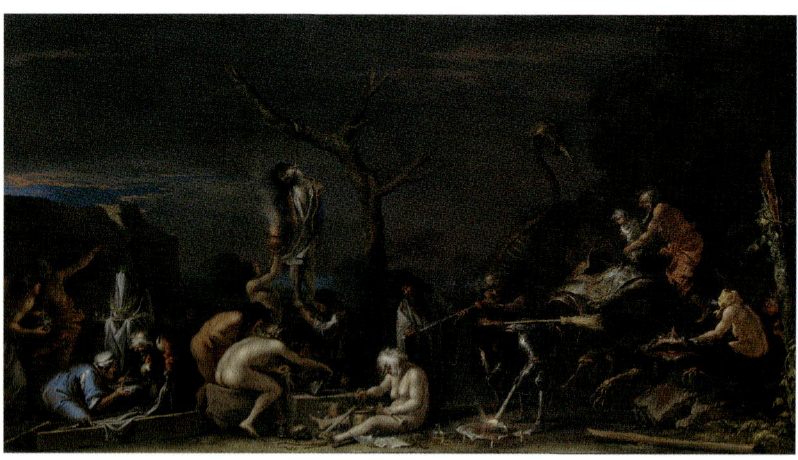

28 Salvator Rosa, *Scene of Witchcraft*, c. 1646, oil on canvas.

a prelude to Goya's sinister art, looks back to the violence of José de Ribera's Naples and perhaps to Jacques Callot's print *The Hanging*, from the series 'Miseries and Misfortunes of War'. Around the corpse cluster a naked Nordic witch, fumigating the head, paired by a realistic old hag from the Neapolitan streets, who cuts the toenails. The ransacking of graves and places of execution, a recurring motif since Lucan's *Pharsalia*, is repeated in the group to the left, where witches practise divination using the skeletal hands of an exhumed corpse. These witches, strikingly prosaic and contemporary, are the witches of the demonologists, and may have been inspired by the woodcut illustrations in Stefano Guazzo's *Compendium maleficarum* (1608), a witch-hunter's manual that describes how, 'in our day', witches steal bodies from graveyards and use the rope, the chains, the stake and the iron tools deployed at executions.[48] A learned viewer would have recognized that, underpinning this contemporary scene, was a famous Renaissance print, Agostino Veneziano's *Skeletons* (1518).

To the right of the central group cluster a trio of male witches. The white-robed magician holds out a sword bearing a pierced heart to his companion, who wields a broom. Before them a knight in armour bends over a magic circle, and his torch lights a hare: all motifs associated with love and superstition. The mixture of male and female is unusual in witchcraft paintings, and perhaps Rosa's setting of a knight in armour among aged crones hints at a parody of the witchcraft scenes in chivalric literature. This group leads to the monstrous cavalcade that closes the painting on the right. A booted witch, astride a skeleton, is poised to plunge a baby into a cauldron, recalling the hideous attempted sacrifice of a child in Horace's

Epode V. The cavalcade was an instantly recognizable reworking of another celebrated Renaissance print, *Lo Stregozzo*, by Agostino Veneziano. Such fantastic combinatory monsters had been admired in Florence since the young Michelangelo had copied Martin Schongauer's *Temptation of St Anthony*. Rosa flamboyantly remakes the monsters of the print, showing three hybrid creatures, one with perhaps the gills and scales of a fish, another with a droopy mask-like face, suggesting the Mannerist decorative motifs of the stage designer Bernardo Buontalenti, and the third a Nordic devil. All these he sets against the threatening skeletal bird adapted from Filippo Napoletano's series of etchings *Incisioni di diversi scheletri di animali* (1620–21), adding a touch of the new science to these fantasies.

The painting's mood is ambiguous. Rosa delights in a display of exuberant inventiveness but it has also a stillness and melancholy that deepens its meaning. The sun is rising, and the figures will, like a nightmare, vanish at break of day. The initiates arriving on the left suggest a transitory moment, a sudden vision or hallucination that opens up before them. The figures seem oddly inward-turned and self-absorbed, wrapped in delusion. Perhaps, at some level, they are symbols of vanitas and human folly. Rosa knew Basile's *The Story of Stories*, and his painting echoes the pessimism and satire with which Basile, in his eclogue *La Coppella*, describes the astrologer and the alchemist: 'He finds that he is blind for he has stood/ The pillars of his hopes all greased and smoked/ On vases made of glass, he's poised his thoughts/ and all his plans on spirals made of smoke'.[49]

Rosa fascinated a small group of friends and learned collectors with the range and variety of his knowledge, and with an astounding display of inventiveness; his works invited interpretation on many levels. To his contemporaries it seemed that his art itself had a magical power and Paolo Vendramin likened him to the mythological Greek enchantress Medea, playing on her power both to create and to destroy.[50] Carlo de Rossi, who owned the *Scene of Witchcraft* (illus. 28), enjoyed the painting's power to astonish, and perhaps its hint of something dangerous and forbidden, and presented it as the grand finale in a tour of his gallery in Rome, covering it with a taffeta curtain before unveiling it to an audience. These pictures have the atmosphere of the seventeenth-century cabinet of curiosities, where odd and intriguing works of art were displayed with the marvels and freaks of nature, playing on the contrast between the horror of the subject-matter and the beauty of execution. Above all they invited speculation and *conversazione*, of the kind that Lippi had so enjoyed when writing the *Malmantile*, and collectors would have taken pleasure in teasing out the web of allusions and quotations that Rosa brilliantly weaves together. Some works were unusual in form, being oval or round, and executed on unusual surfaces, several on slate.[51] His friends and patrons were interested in the scholarly discussions of the demonologists. Ricciardi, in 1652, in response to the request of an unidentified friend, sent him a list of authors on divination, dominated by Martin del Rio, and mentioning 'many, many others who have variously discussed the subject with originality'.[52] The recipient of this letter also knew Rosa, and he may have been Filippo Niccolini, who owned *Four Witchcraft Tondi*, and had in his library several of the esoteric texts mentioned by Ricciardi.[53]

During this time Rosa brought to Florence another novel theme, the representation of ancient philosophers, a subject associated with his role as satirist and with the lively debates at the Percossi. Neapolitan painting was growing increasingly popular in the city and Rosa introduced collectors to the naturalistic and expressive three-quarter-length portraits of philosophers by Ribera and Francesco Fracanzano. He painted a gallery of such work; Diogenes with his lantern lit in broad daylight, searching in vain for an honest man; *A Portrait of a Philosopher* (1641), who, with the frowning brow associated with philosophy, thrusts before him a placard exhorting the viewer to a Pythagorean silence; an elderly sage (*c.* 1642–5; illus. 29), drawing attention to a learned tome. These philosophers are more dignified than those of Ribera and less flamboyantly ragged, and they seem to address the world with the harsh gaze of the moralizing satirist. In this period Diogenes and Epicurus were rapidly becoming more popular philosophers than Aristotle and Plato. Diogenes, who so cherished freedom, and with biting wit rejected all social convention, was a particular favourite of Rosa's and was painted by the artist at least eight times in Florence. To these half-length figures Rosa added scenes from the lives of the ancient philosophers, subjects rare before the seventeenth century. *Diogenes Throwing Away His Bowl*, now known as *The Philosopher's Grove*, and *Crates Throwing His Money into the Sea* were painted for Carlo Gerini, a wealthy and fortunate Medici courtier, who had perhaps attended meetings of the Percossi. Both philosophers are Cynics, intent on divesting themselves of worldly goods. Diogenes, a vivid rustic figure, seeing a boy drinking from his hands, realizes that even a drinking bowl

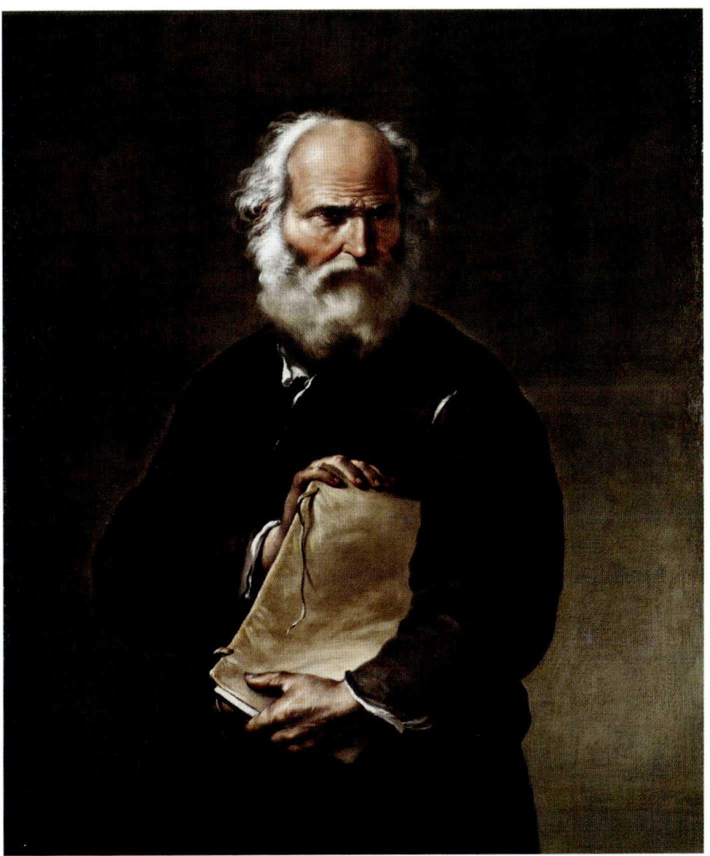

is unnecessary (illus. 30). Crates valiantly throws his money into the sea and sailors greedily jostle to catch coins while even the ancient sculpture reels back in amazement (illus. 31). The tone is humorous but erudite, creating the atmosphere of lively debate that Rosa so enjoyed in villa and academy. In *The Philosophers' Grove* the figure at the left, his black hair falling on his shoulders, is probably Rosa himself and around him his companions, each expressive and individual, talk, point

29 Salvator Rosa, *A Philosopher*, c. 1642–5, oil on canvas.

and gesture. This group is a light-hearted parody of Raphael's *School of Athens*, with a figure, like Raphael's Plato, pointing to the sky, the source of higher knowledge. Rosa continues the vein of parody and wit that had characterized Giovanni da San Giovanni's spirited philosophers in the summer apartments of the Palazzo Pitti.

Rosa's philosopher paintings were addressed to a learned public and some were perhaps portraits of his erudite friends, mementoes of a literary evening or a theatrical occasion. He would doubtless have discussed Greek philosophy with Ricciardi, but the works of two writers in particular read like fertile sources of his iconography. First comes Paganino Gaudenzio, professor of eloquence at the University of Pisa, who had written a groundbreaking history of Roman philosophy. Gaudenzio argued that scholars should study not only the thought of the ancient philosophers but their lives and deeds. His *Della peregrinazione filosofica* (Philosophical Musings;

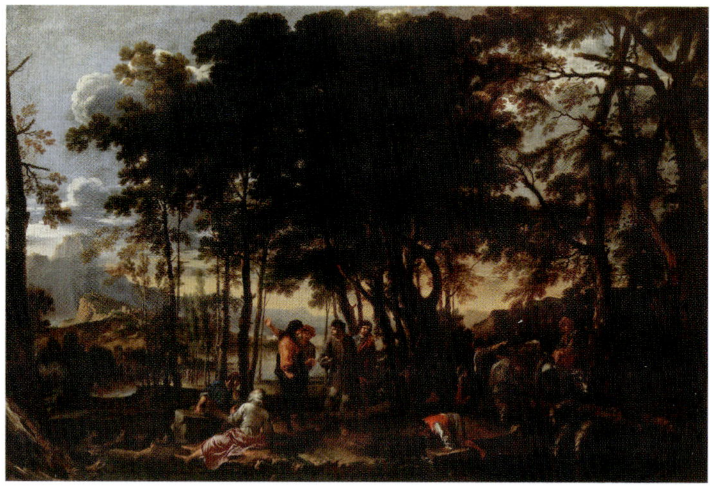

30 Salvator Rosa, *The Philosophers' Grove*, 1645–8, oil on canvas.

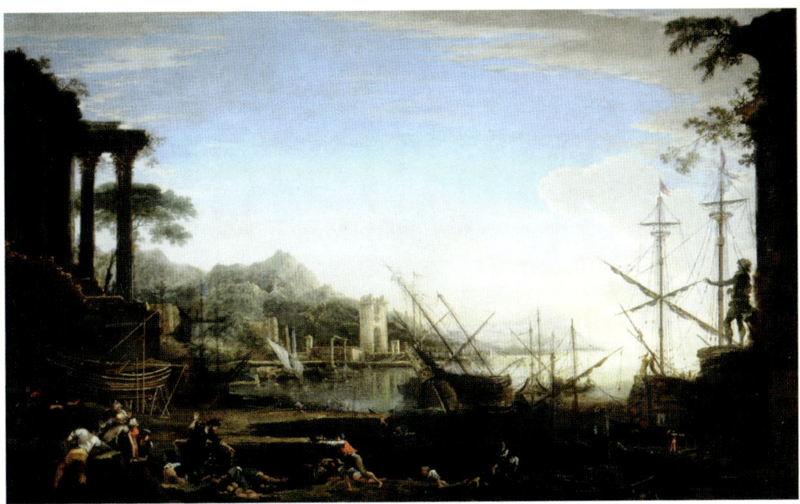

1643) is rich in the legends and superstitions that clustered around the lives of the earliest philosophers. A little later he wrote *La Galleria dell'inclito Marino* (The Gallery of the Illustrious Marino; 1648), a commentary on Marino's *Galeria*. In this collection of lyric poems, which describe paintings and sculptures, Marino had included several philosopher paintings. Gaudenzio, with an ostentatious display of pedantic scholarship, corrects, explains and expands on his remarks. Some of Marino's rarest subjects were to be painted by Rosa and perhaps he collaborated with Gaudenzio. The book closes, in a celebratory flourish, with a poem addressed to Rosa himself, 'famous painter, and poet, to whom great scholars and learned men should flock'.[54] It conveys the kind of *conversazione* that readers and gallery-goers so enjoyed, and sets Rosa at the centre of intellectual life in Florence.

At the same date Rosa and the Jesuit scholar Daniello Bartoli began to take an interest in each other's works. In 1645

31 Salvator Rosa, *Crates Throwing His Money into the Sea*, 1645–8, oil on canvas.

Bartoli, a Jesuit priest, writer and historian, published his *Man of Letters*, a small volume that enjoyed resounding success throughout Europe. The book is a celebration of humanist learning, and with it Bartoli brings a vivid immediacy to the vast heritage of classical culture. He was steeped in Diogenes Laërtius' *The Lives and Opinions of the Eminent Philosophers* and weaves through his text anecdotes, aphorisms and sayings connected with the sages of antiquity, whose lives he presents as astounding and diverting curiosities. 'Take the ancient philosophers,' he declares, 'They throw their riches into the sea, becoming beggars to avoid poverty . . . They live in barrels – more like a dog in his doghouse, than a man in his dwelling . . . Xenocrates is a marble without feelings . . . Democritus a madman always laughing, Heraclitus forlorn of hope.'[55] Such a sparkling catalogue of eccentricities would have appealed to Rosa, who mentions the book in his letters. His contemporaries were quick to draw parallels between writer and painter, and in 1645 the publisher Girolamo Signoretti, to whom Rosa had given his *Pascariello*, dedicated the Florentine edition to Rosa. 'Who better than you could portray the Man of Letters?' demands Signoretti in a celebratory epistle, lavishing praise on the liveliness and arresting immediacy of Rosa's painted philosophers, swept in with the fire of Prometheus. 'You will live', concludes Signoretti, 'through the glory of your brush, and as the subject of others' pens'.[56] Rosa tirelessly campaigned to star as the subject of others' pens. The acclaimed poet Fulvio Testi was reluctant to contribute but Baldinucci mentions that he had in his own possession many poems and letters written in praise of Rosa by the *letterati*.[57] His reputation rapidly became international, and as early as 1647 Pierre Guillebaud's

Trésor chronologique et historique mentions the Neapolitan Rosa as the flower of both painting and poetry in Florence.[58]

Rosa's aspirations grew, and he now himself longed to don the philosopher's robes, to appear, as Baldinucci tells us, 'in all his words and deeds a true philosopher', who walked beneath 'the spacious porticoes of Athens in the company of the ancient Stoics'.[59] Around the same time, in the mid-1640s, Rosa painted himself as though in the corner of a study of a learned philosopher-painter or poet (illus. 32). Here the meditative artist, his gaze downcast, a tear running down his cheek, writes on a skull the Greek words, 'Behold, whither, eventually', or 'Death is the end of all things, although we know not when.' He is sombrely yet elegantly dressed, crowned with a wreath of funerary cypress, and his thick hair flows over his shoulders. The painting is immediate and intimate, the figure set obliquely, so that we watch him as he writes. Rosa's hand is elegantly poised over the skull, with the pen caught in mid-stroke as it adds an accent to the last of the three Greek words. He seems to have just turned away from the open book behind him, while a slip of paper marks his place in a second volume, on whose spine the name Seneca is faintly visible. A crumpled sheet bears the words *Salvator Rosa dipinse nell'eremo e dono a Gio Battista Ricciardi suo amico* (Salvator Rosa painted this in a solitary place and gave it to his friend, Giovanni Battista Ricciardi). Rosa here lays claim to the learning of the philosopher, and the Greek lettering enhances this, for knowledge of Greek belonged only to the most erudite, among them Ricciardi himself. The portrait is a friendship portrait, given to Ricciardi as a memento of the days the two men had spent together at Monterufoli. The idea of exchanging painted and literary self-portraits had been well established in Renaissance Florence. Ricciardi was later to respond with a poem, 'Beneath a Cruel Star', which Rosa referred to as a 'poem of friendship'. The constant theme of Ricciardi's lyric poetry is human misery, and the consoling presence of death.

The painting remains indebted to Ribera, who frequently painted hermits or saints meditating on mortality, and the skull set on a book suggests the impotence of knowledge in the face of time. The artist sorrowfully contemplates death, echoing one of the dominant themes of seventeenth-century Florentine poetry. The volume of Seneca, whose name was later puzzlingly deleted by Rosa, suggests the Stoic's urging of a constant preparation for the inevitable end of life. Study death always, he counselled his friend Lucilius. In this way we may attain a spiritual tranquillity and freedom from fear, reconciled to our end, which will come when it will. This elegiac mood, and the poetry of the darkening sky, is close to that of the painter Guercino's celebrated *Et in Arcadia Ego*, where two shepherds, suddenly confronted by a skull in Arcady, react not with terror but with sorrow and wonder, a mood enhanced by the dusky landscape.

This self-portrait shows Rosa in solitude. In the spring of 1646 came the first hints of a rupture with the Medici court, and from 1646 to 1648 he spent most of his time between Volterra and the Maffei villas of Monterufoli and Barbaiano. He presented himself, in his increasingly angry poems, as a philosopher, 'far from the blind crowd', who yearns for the hermitage, for solitude and obscurity, aloof from the hypocrisies of the court and the disasters of war, for 'he who trusts in the world is blind and foolish'.[60] Now without the security

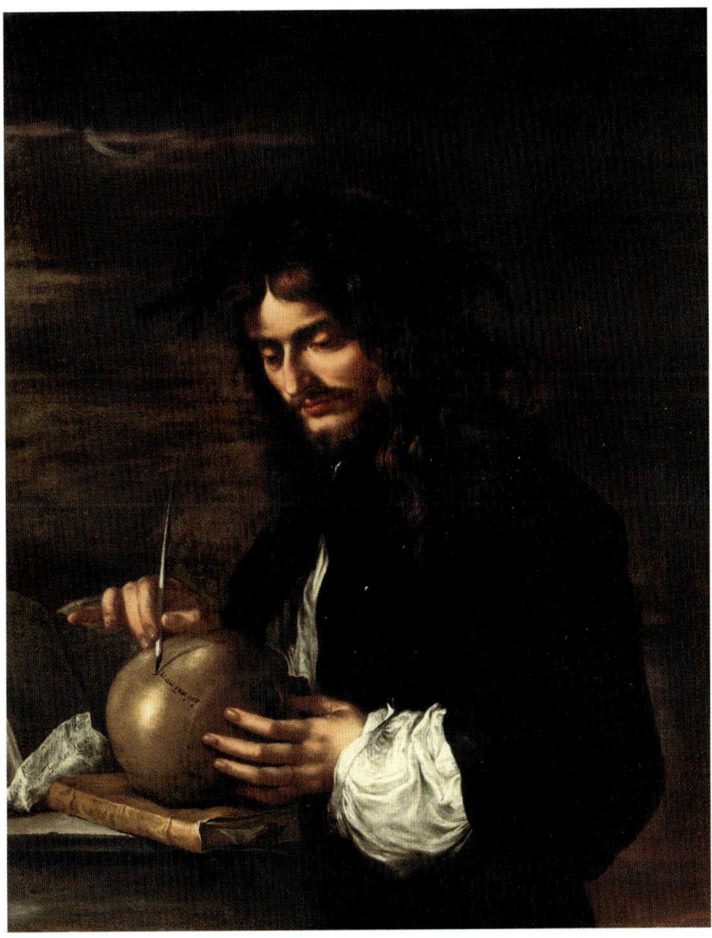

of court patronage, Rosa increasingly wooed his intellectual friends with gifts and flatteringly erudite paintings. His mood was darker, and his paintings gloomier, less sparkling and witty than in the early days of the Percossi.

Two pictures above all, which became celebrated in Florence, suggest the new grandeur of his ambition. The

32 Salvator Rosa, *Self-portrait*, c. 1647, oil on canvas.

shocking violence of Ribera's art had already impressed Florentine collectors, and Rosa now showcased, in the Medici city, a Neapolitan aesthetic of horror.[61] *Moral Philosophy* introduced a novel type of erudite painting, rooted in a Florentine taste for allegory and personification.

In the first of the two paintings the punishment of Prometheus (illus. 33), who defied the gods and stole fire

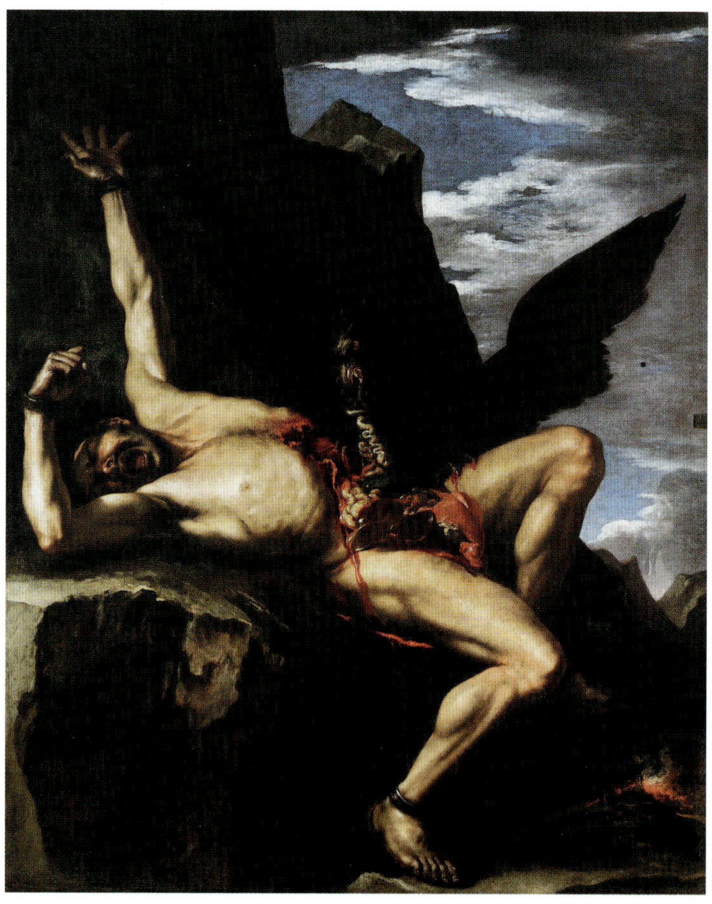

33 Salvator Rosa, *Prometheus*, 1646–8, oil on canvas.

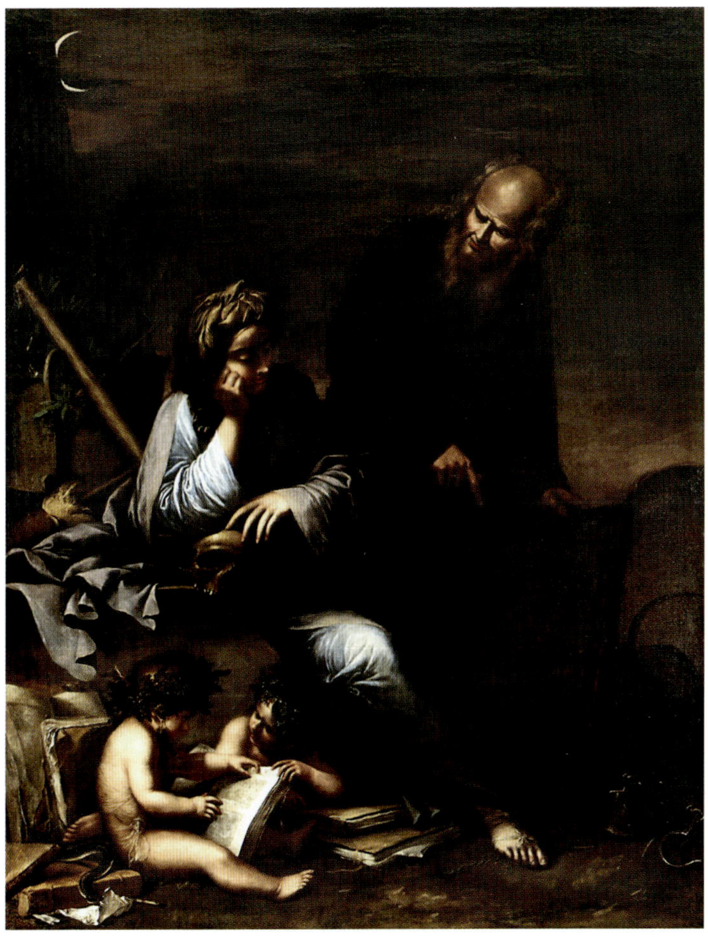

from heaven, is shown with gory detail. The titan is a more
richly ambiguous mythic figure than in Rosa's earlier *Tityus*
(illus. 7). In some accounts he is a lowly trickster, rightly punished for pride, in others a noble rebel against tyranny. The
torch could represent forbidden knowledge, or the fire of
artistic inspiration, an attribute of Prometheus as archetype

34 Salvator Rosa, *Moral Philosophy*, 1643–5, oil on canvas.

of the artist. Signoretti had indeed invoked his name to suggest Rosa's artistic power.[62]

Now far from Naples, Rosa painted a yet more Riberesque work than the *Tityus*. The painting overwhelms the viewer with its sheer scale and creates a visceral experience of intense suffering. Rosa's brutal realism surpasses all earlier representations, and he chose a new source, going directly to the Greek writer Achilles Tatius. Tatius had included, in his romance *The Adventures of Leucippe and Clitophon*, an ekphrasis of a *Prometheus Bound* by the painter Euanthes. Here the writer emphasizes, in unparalleled forensic detail, the monstrous eagle, feasting upon the belly of Prometheus, 'ripping it open, or rather already had ripped it open, its beak dipped into the wound, and it seemed to be digging about in it, looking for the sufferer's liver, which could just be seen, by the depth to which the painter had depicted the wound as being open'.[63]

No other artist follows Tatius' text so closely. Rosa brilliantly unites this ancient source with a rendering that conveys an up-to-the-minute interest in the new science. The way he presents Prometheus' abdomen suggests that he had studied sixteenth-century anatomical diagrams, perhaps Vesalius' celebrated *De Humani corporis fabrica libri septem* (Of the Structure of the Human Body, VII; 1543), and his rendering of the stomach, liver and intestines is suggestive of the Flemish anatomist's illustrations of the internal organs.[64] At the Medici court the physician Francesco Redi, a friend of Rosa's, was a little later to establish an experimental space where courtiers enjoyed discussing his dissections and vivisections, and the theatricality of Rosa's work evokes these displays.[65] Redi was later known for his experiments with rotting meat, and the circle of flies that buzz around the liver in *Prometheus* temptingly suggests that this subject had already caught his attention.

There are several literary responses to the painting that convey its appeal to an erudite audience. Most interesting are an ode and a letter by Paolo Vendramin, the Venetian ambassador in Florence and a poet who shared Rosa's love of the theatre. The ode hints that the picture was too grotesquely repulsive; 'for what delight', the poet demands, 'do you take corpses to show so lacerated a body? Perhaps a dark and cruel genius gave you so bloody a desire?' But no, he declares, elsewhere Rosa had painted canvases that were clear and serene, their subjects glorious exemplars of virtue. For him the painting has a high moral aim, for Prometheus is justly punished for his hubris.[66] In the letter Vendramin again celebrates Rosa as a painter of stern moral subjects, and Rosa finally received his longed-for consecration as a philosopher-painter, *filosofo nel dipingere*. This letter is an anthology of classical responses to an aesthetic of pain and pleasure. Before writing, Vendramin begins, he had to forget the terror of looking at the painting, so overwhelming was the bloody vision before him. This terror, he continues, echoing Aristotle's thoughts on the pleasure of distressing images, is overwhelming precisely because it arises from the painter's skill as creator.[67] Vendramin makes a valiant attempt to convey the overwhelming psychological impact of a work of art whose *enargeia*, or lifelikeness, sets the viewer at the heart of danger. He compared Rosa to Apelles, who could paint the unpaintable forms of thunder, for Rosa has painted the unseen cry of Prometheus, which we seem to hear echoing from the dark rocks before we see his torture. Underlying Prometheus' scream is the cry of Laocoön, so theatrically represented in the ancient sculpture of Laocoön and his sons, which was, throughout the seventeenth century, the *exemplum doloris*.

The *Prometheus* is an aggressively Neapolitan painting, parading Rosa's gifts as the pupil of Ribera. At the same time he delighted his friends in Pisa, several of whom were amateur painters, with his demonstrations of Ribera's technique.[68] With the *Moral Philosophy* (illus. 34) Rosa instead created a Florentine allegory, reminiscent of Giovanni Martinelli's elegant vanitas paintings, whose symbolism similarly reflects the interests of the Florentine academies. Beneath a dusky sky, with crescent moon, Rosa sets two figures: a young woman in the pose of melancholy, personifying Moral Philosophy, her hand resting on a skull; and an ancient sage, probably Socrates, pointing to the mirror of self-knowledge. The cavernous eyes and gnawing teeth of the skull, on a plinth or tomb, arrest the viewer, and remind him of the skull that speaks so harshly from a monument in Arcady. With this group Rosa dramatized two of the most popular maxims from ancient philosophy. The woman's soft hands lightly caress a phrase from Epictetus inscribed on the skull, '*Sustine et abstine*' (bear and forbear), her gesture balanced by the pointing finger of the philosopher, invoking the command, 'know thyself', often attributed to Socrates. Around them the artist sets symbols of devouring time: a pyramid, a distaff and a spent candle. The two putti, crowned with funerary cypress, evoke the closeness of the cradle and the grave, while a snake, associated with death and sorrow, tears a scroll bearing the artist's signature (a form of signature that Rosa remembered from Ribera's *Drunken Silenus*), a mournful suggestion that even art and fame shall perish. Epictetus' famed phrase had been hailed by the moralist Giovanni Andrea Viscardo as expressing all of moral philosophy, and 'happy is he who well understands and observes them',[69] while to the literary theorist Emanuele Tesauro they were 'two penetrating words that contained the whole of moral philosophy'.[70] A putto leans on a volume of Aesop; Aesop, in the seventeenth century, was often seen as a special kind of philosopher, who, through short and witty fables, presented a model of behaviour. Rosa's thought is not obscure. He liked proverbs and aphorisms; he turned to well-known emblem books for his symbols. Together his figures suggest that the contemplation of death is the proper study of philosophy. Only virtue can survive the destructive power of time, and this is attained through self-knowledge. His iconography is immediate and direct, and the painting's novelty lies in the

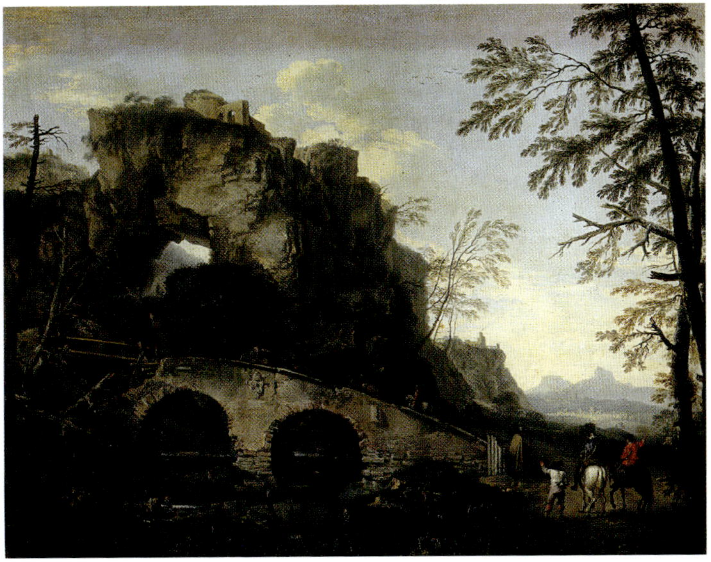

35 Salvator Rosa, *Landscape with a Bridge*, c. 1645, oil on canvas.

poetic mood, in the lament for the passing of time, which he spun so lyrically round these famous words.

Moral Philosophy was cleverly attuned to the literary debates of the Florentine academies, where the philosopher Orazio Rucellai, known as 'our own and most wise Socrates', read, at his house, a series of dialogues on the twin Socratic themes, 'This alone I know, that I know nothing' and 'Know thyself'. It was widely acclaimed in Florence, and the politician Jacopo Salviati hailed Rosa as a 'famous painter of moral subjects'. Salviati addressed a long poem to the picture, a poem entirely characteristic of the obsession with death that fills much seventeenth-century poetry, above all in Florence, where it had been encouraged by the visit of Ciro di Pers, famed for his vanitas poetry. Human misery and the brevity of life were the constant subjects of Ricciardi's poetry, and to him Rosa had sent his *Self-portrait* (illus. 32), a contemplation on the transience of life and the mystery of human destiny. To Salviati *Moral Philosophy* conveyed the fragility of life, for 'in this fragile world, death is favoured above every birth . . . The coffin stands open at our birth, and grief, like swaddling bands, grips the infant on his cradle, while virtue alone can echo from the grave.'[71]

Rosa gave this painting to Francesco Cordini, Medici courtier, actor and poet, who had a taste for philosophical subjects, and who also owned Rosa's tondo of the philosophers Democritus and Heraclitus (*c.* 1645).[72] Rosa's increasing intellectual ambition suggests that he already had Rome in his sight and his *Landscape with a Bridge* (illus. 35), probably painted for Ricciardi, is a farewell to the court and perhaps to Florence itself. It evokes the wild landscape around

Verrucola and Monterufoli, famed for its extravagant rock formations, which poet and painter had so enjoyed together. Travellers approach a bridge, uncertain as to their path. The sunny distances beckon, but on the other side horsemen lead upwards, over the perilous bridge, into the dark shadows of the looming arch of natural rock, suggesting the dangerous journey of life itself. On the bridge are the Medici arms, crumbling and in disrepair. Perhaps Rosa was rejecting the world of the court and picturing himself at the start of a hazardous journey to a world elsewhere. Dissatisfied and restlessly ambitious, Rosa left for the grander stage of Rome.

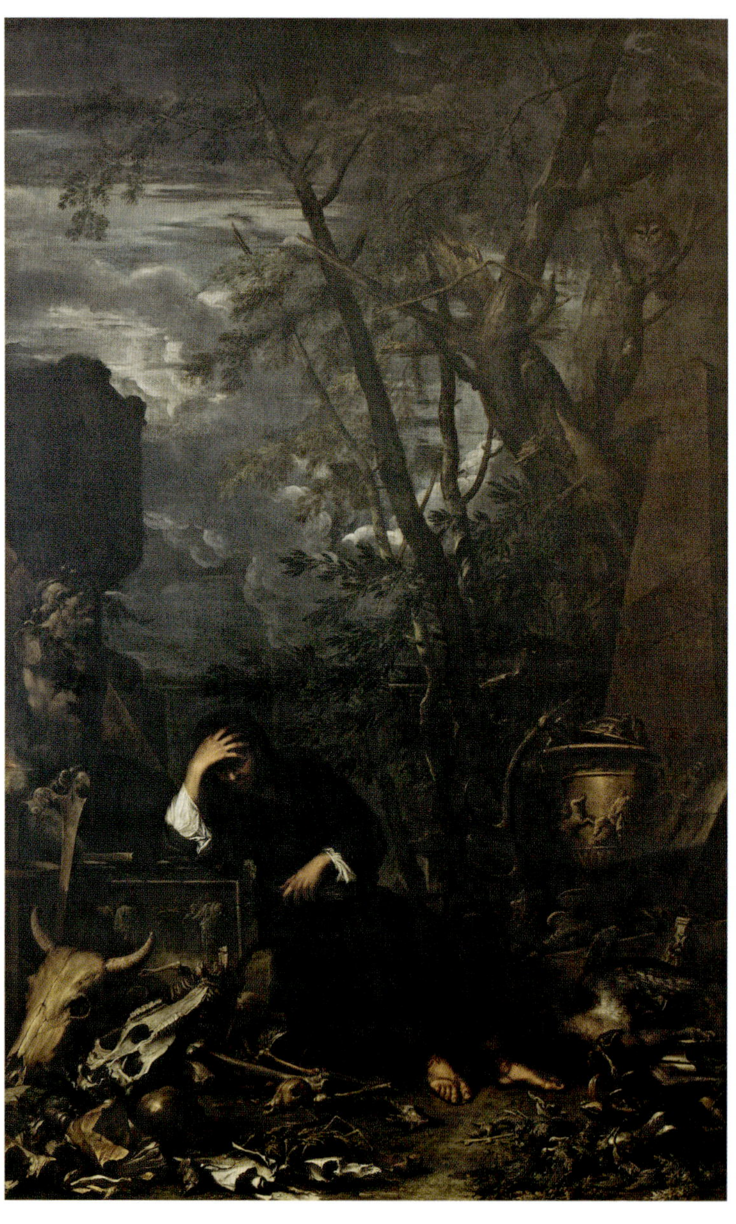

THREE

Fortune and Envy

'After a very punishing trip,' wrote Rosa, 'we've eventually found refuge in Rome, where we're presently enjoying the most cordial sight and conversation of our Signor Don Girolamo, who greets all your gentlemen and gives thanks for the cheese.'[1] Once in Rome Rosa hurried to establish his family in a house on the Strada Felice, at the Trinità dei Monti. He had received his last payments from Giovan Carlo de' Medici in 1648. He left Florence in search of a grander stage, perhaps encouraged by the prospects offered by the Jubilee year of 1650. Rosa, his friend Ascanio della Penna told Giovanni Battista Ricciardi, was infuriated by his 'little fame' in the city of the Medici and, goaded by taunts that he would not survive elsewhere, he resolved to 'win immortality' in Rome.[2]

In this nobler setting the artist cast off forever his lowly origins and remade himself as a Roman painter of erudite subjects on a new and ambitious scale. He at once won immense success, his subjects so novel, his poetry readings so captivating and his satiric persona so challenging, that he was feted throughout the city. In the next decade a series of monumental works of single figures, underpinned by ideas of philosophy, envy, vanitas and fortune, each theatrically

36 Salvator Rosa, *Democritus in Meditation*, 1650–51, oil on canvas.

provocative, new and often mysterious, suggest his constant desire to astonish a grander public. Rosa saw, in Pietro Testa and above all in Nicolas Poussin, challenging models of the learned philosopher-painter. But he was not content to mix only with the outsider artists, Pier Francesco Mola and Giovanni Benedetto Castiglione, who, interested in intriguing iconographies, gathered around his old friend Niccolò Simonelli. His ambition did not end there; he also wished to take on the challenge of the High Baroque of Gian Lorenzo Bernini, and craved for success in the public sphere so passionately that at the end of the decade he offered to decorate a Roman chapel free of charge, to display his gifts as the creator of multi-figured altarpieces. In the early 1650s Rosa glowed with success but optimism swiftly yielded to a despairing isolation, as the painter-poet became embroiled in a series of literary controversies of astonishing virulence. Rosa's angry voice echoes through his letters, and his satires of the 1650s, *Envy* and *Babylon*, are dark and bitter in mood, presenting the artist as a lonely exemplar of Stoic virtue amid an apocalyptic sea of corruption. And yet, with a series of etched figures, the *Figurine*, he flees this constraining world and takes respite from the grandeur and gloom of his large figure paintings. The *Figurine* are playful and inventive, depicting imaginary bandits both mysterious and sinister, who present a kind of freedom and a natural love of liberty, deeply attractive to the beleaguered and conflicted artist and at odds with the straitjacket classicism of his large figure paintings.

Rosa at once staged a triumphal re-entry to Rome. With truly Neapolitan vulgarity, writes Giovanni Battista Passeri, he was now dressed richly and was accompanied in the street by a liveried servant, carrying a sword with a silver sheath.[3] He sought revenge for the earlier insults he had suffered, steeply raising his prices and at the same time trumpeting his contempt for wealth. Collectors were kept in humiliating suspense as Rosa professed himself disdainful of sales. His pictures had been done for his own pleasure, he claimed provocatively, and he did not wish to part with them.[4] At once he entered the city's literary life, for his fame as a satirist and poet had preceded him. The prestigious Umoristi courted him and in January 1650 Rosa asked Ricciardi to write a preamble for a reading of one of his satires there, the tone of which should be 'noble and clear, humble but also magnificent'.[5] Cardinal Brancaccio remained an admirer and his entrée to the world of high churchmen and nobility, while his old friends Girolamo Mercuri and Niccolò Simonelli continued to offer hospitality and advice. Carlo de Rossi, the banker, art collector and merchant whom Rosa had probably known in the 1640s, also began to play a key role in the artist's life. He helped Rosa decorate his house with suitably rich furnishings and purchased works for which the artist could not find a buyer, without any condition on the price, enabling him to risk obscure and provocative subjects. De Rossi was to build up a remarkable collection of Rosa's paintings, which he displayed in his house near Sant'Andrea della Valle, along with his museum of curiosities.[6]

Rosa had now, writes Lione Pascoli, silenced his detractors and won the prestige of a great artist.[7] In the summer of 1650 he spent some months at Monterufoli with Ricciardi, and here planned a two-pronged campaign to astonish the Roman world of art and letters. First came a new satire, *Painting*, and

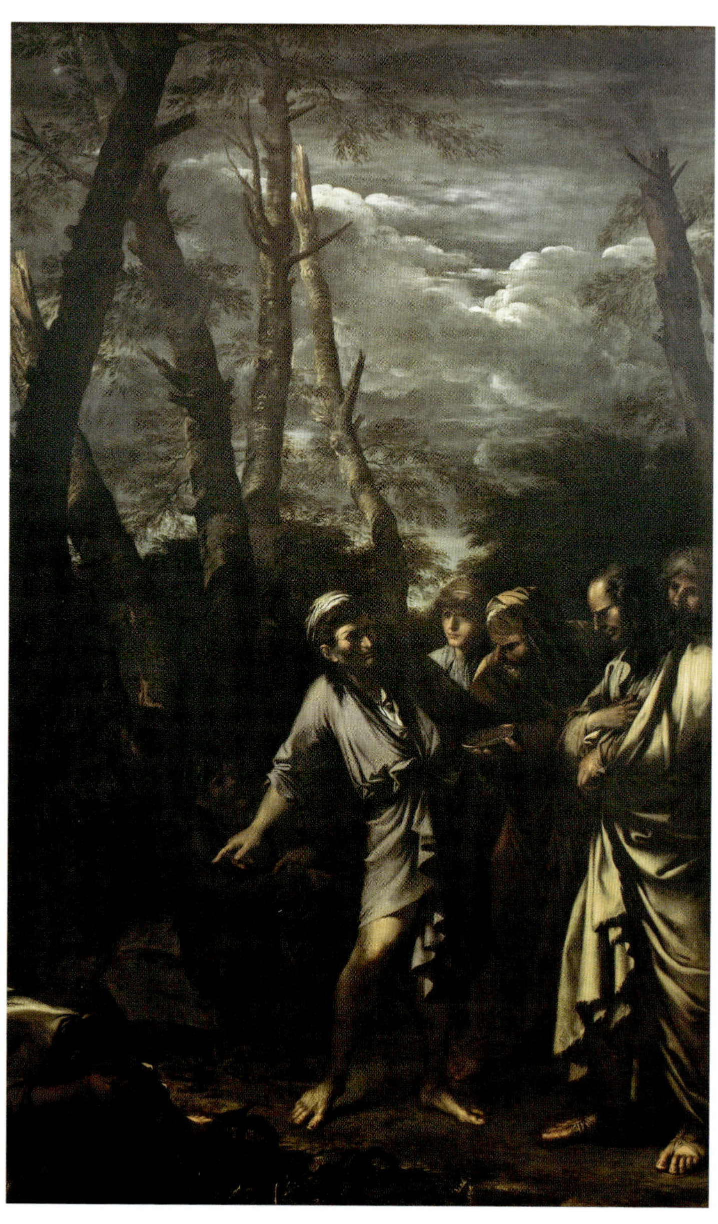

37 Salvator Rosa, *Diogenes Casting Away His Drinking Bowl*, 1651–2, oil on canvas.

second a vast canvas, *Democritus in Meditation*, which he later paired with *Diogenes Casting Away His Drinking Bowl*. The success of the philosopher paintings led to the commission for the heroic *Battle of Cimon* and with these three great paintings Rosa 'roused Rome to such a degree that you wouldn't believe'.[8]

With *Painting* Rosa was swift to ally himself with the most classicizing of Roman painters. Its opening is intensely dramatic. The gloomy artist sits pondering the decay of the world when the ghostly muse of Painting suddenly exhorts him, as the celebrated scourge of Music and Poetry, now to unleash his fury on his own art of painting. Her call to a high destiny dramatizes all the ambition of the artist, poised on the threshold of a Roman career. In her, painting and poetry come together, for she is a muse that only a painter could conceive, and Rosa, combing through Cesare Ripa's emblem book *Iconologia*, created an intensely poetic image of his artistic creed. His muse is young, with flowing hair and eyes that shine like the sun, yet her face is the aged face of Eternity and, like Fame, she has the wings of an eagle. She wears a Sibyl's turban, woven with leaves and flowers of ivy, peach and laurel, symbols of poetic fury, silence and victory. Monkey's skins line her cloak, for monkeys symbolized imitation. Beneath her arm is a globe with the image of the world and the stars, and around it swirl fantastic beings and the painter's tool. The artist takes up her challenge and establishes his credentials in an unusually long preamble. He is a Stoic content with little, who paints for glory and writes poetry for pleasure. He upholds the ideal of the learned painter, 'well versed in mythology, history, churches and religions', whose art soars beyond the material world to 'everything that is incorporeal and that is possible' (*Painting*, ll. 171–7).

This high aim established, there follows a vivid and lively picture of the failures of the contemporary art world, as Rosa garrulously denounces almost every kind of painting, including the lasciviousness of mythological art and the insane virtuosity of baroque church art. Above all he forever turns his back on the *bamboccianti*, and his long description of their disgraceful subjects, and their sordid lifestyles, forms the backbone of the satire. Rosa shows himself as being entirely abreast of contemporary aesthetic debate. In a languishing art market the financial success of the *bamboccianti* and their despicably small paintings were envied by classicizing artists. Voices had already been raised against them; Pietro Testa, in his complex allegorical prints of the 1640s, had imaged these artists as dirty monkeys or the apes of nature, as Rosa does in his satire. In 1651 the painters Andrea Sacchi and Francesco Albani exchanged letters in which both heaped abuse on the *bamboccianti*, though it is not clear whether this discussion preceded Rosa's satire. Rosa himself now virulently rejects these northerners with whom he had earlier competed. Most unusual is his attack on noble collectors, who, he claims, abhor in real life what they like to see in a painting and delight in the picturesque rags of the poor, though soon the poor will lose even their skins (*Painting*, l. 259). As a backdrop to this bitter denunciation of the contemporary art world Rosa sketches in the virtuous lives of the painters of antiquity, his own role models. These include Metrodorus, a philosopher and painter skilled, as Rosa aspired to be, in correcting both morality and colours (l. 157); and the great Apelles, who liked to exhibit his paintings to the public and, keeping himself hidden, overhear and profit from any criticism. Another, Zeuxis, intriguingly, stands condemned for arrogance (l. 415). He believed that his works were beyond price and so gave them as gifts. Rosa perhaps remembered Zeuxis when he later plotted his own pricing strategy.

Satire paved the way for Rosa's campaign, and in the same months of that year Rosa painted *Democritus in Meditation* (illus. 36), followed, in 1652, by *Diogenes Casting Away His Drinking Bowl* (illus. 37). Philosopher paintings were popular in Rome and during this time Democritus and Diogenes were beginning to replace Aristotle and Plato as the most popular of the ancient sages. Rosa's two vast works, perhaps conceived as pendants from the start, throw out a challenge to Raphael's Plato and Aristotle, the noble centre of his frescoed *School of Athens.* Around these new icons clustered lively debates as the new science questioned scholastic certainties, and the ethics of poverty engaged philosophers.

Rosa had earlier painted *Democritus and Heraclitus* following a well-worn tradition of pairing the cheerfully mocking Democritus with the weeping Heraclitus. By the early 1650s the coupling of Democritus with Diogenes had become as common as, and more powerful than, this now formulaic pairing. Rosa now shows Democritus as melancholic, dressed in black, outcast and alone, in a threatening landscape. The painting is a vanitas and the great scientist, for whom the world was composed of atoms moving without purpose through a boundless space, grieves over the futility of intellectual achievement. The god Terminus dominates all and Rosa piles up around him emblems of mortality, a learned variety of the relics of ancient civilizations — a tripod, an urn, a sarcophagus, stele

– and a macabre collection of skeletons. And yet the painting is not only a lament for the transience of all things. Rosa's later etching of the same scene bore the inscription '*Democritus omnium derisor*' (Democritus who scoffs at all things) and his picture is, rather, a harsh denunciation of folly, an overwhelmingly dark and pessimistic vision of humankind. The boisterous laughter of Rosa's earlier Democritus has become a sneer of contempt, for, as Juvenal had written, 'To condemn by a cutting laugh comes readily to us all.'[9] For this despair Rosa's source was a famous letter, then ascribed to Hippocrates, which tells of Democritus' defence of his apparently indiscriminate laughter. He laughs, he explains, at 'one thing only, man, irrational, with no virtue, puerile in all his projects, suffering for no reason endless ambitions, pushed by his immoderate desires to journey to the ends of the earth'. Democritus' tirade is a Cynic diatribe, harassing and repetitious and hammering in the pointlessness of human hope and ambition, 'of lust for money, insatiate greed, enmity, plotting, scheming and chicanery'. This letter informs the atmosphere of Rosa's painting, where the finer achievements of man are excluded, and the skeletons are those of base animals. A human skull mingles on equal terms with ox and ass, and a boar's head takes on a mocking macabre vitality. Rosa's tumbled obelisk, an iconographic detail lifted from Pierio Valeriano's *Hieroglyphica* (1567), where it is entitled *Humanae vitae conditio*, is a clever visual equivalent to Democritus' lament that 'the whole of man is a disease from birth'. It suggests the swift passage from infancy to old age, with hatred and discord overcoming what is divine in man, and culminating with the hippopotamus, whose meaning is violence, discord and death.[10] Rosa's late satires share this black nihilism.

For Ricciardi, too, who was surely involved in the making of the picture, Democritus was a biting satirist. In a short invocation to the philosopher he entreats him to return from Hades and bewail the present age, an age that outshines all others in vice. 'Return,' he cries, 'and teach our lips a new form of laughter.'[11]

In sharp contrast to the solitary Democritus Rosa's *Diogenes* gives vivid life to Diogenes the teacher. Diogenes believed that virtue could be taught and can be achieved only through words and practice. He enlightened others through concrete acts and here, through gesture and expression, he emphasizes to his listeners the meaning of his casting away his bowl. One philosopher leans forward in amazement but the stately figure in the foreground remains unmoved. This is perhaps intended as Plato, and Diogenes was well known for his impatience with Plato's theoretical ideas. The painting suggests the lively discourses of the Roman academies and looks back to the *Philosophers' Grove* (illus. 30), where Rosa had included himself among Diogenes' audience. He no longer pokes fun at Raphael but with these two works suggests the concerns of a new age.

Both paintings were exhibited, in successive years, at the annual exhibition at the Pantheon, which, in the 1650s, became the highpoint of Rosa's year. He may also at this moment have begun to exhibit at the yearly exhibition at San Giovanni Decollato, which was to become increasingly important to him. The display of the *Democritus* was carefully choreographed; Rosa worked in secret, and no one, apart from Simonelli, was allowed to see the painting in advance. The picture thrilled the Roman art world and the artist reported that he had 'astonished all of Rome at the feast day of the

Pantheon'.[12] Cosimo Brunetti, a lawyer, poet and man of letters, and a close friend of Rosa's in the 1650s, reported its dazzling success in some detail. Cardinals, princes and ambassadors flocked to see it; artists were ready to die before it and even the great Pietro da Cortona professed himself 'enchanted'. Rosa's public debated its meaning: did it display the disasters of humankind or the teachings of Stoicism, or perhaps the words of Ezekiel ('Dry bones hear the word of the Lord')? Connoisseurs admired the invention, 'so strange and curious', and the puzzling expression of Democritus, 'so jovial and contemplative', an expression variously seen now as one of wry melancholy or a derisive sneer.[13] Their praise reveals how cleverly Rosa had pleased his audience; they liked the desolate landscape, the ostentatiously erudite and varied relics of Roman antiquity, and the display of bones, which were calculated to interest the antiquarian and scientific circles around the collector and scholar Cassiano dal Pozzo. His leaving the iconography open, rejecting well-worn topoi, also encouraged pleasurable *conversazione*. At some level too Rosa, for this his debut, intended to present intriguing self-images, of the lonely outsider, or the harsh satirist, the stern moral mentor of his age. He himself joked, when he could not sell the *Democritus*, that maybe this was due 'to the affinity this philosopher has with a Stoic like me, or because of the antipathy philosophy has always had to being locked up in the palaces of the rich.'[14] Rosa hoped for 1,000 scudi for this painting alone, however the Venetian ambassador, Niccolò Sagredo, sent him wine and other delicacies and in the end bought the *Democritus* and *Diogenes* at a disappointing price of 300 ducats, but with such tact and flattery that Rosa saved face and was pleased.[15] A month later he regretted this, when he was offered 500 scudi by Monsignor Caetano, who intended to send the paintings as a gift to the king of Spain. 'Am I not advancing in glory, is not my art growing in reputation and consideration?' he wrote exultantly to Ricciardi.

From this success sprang a highly important commission. Cardinal Neri Corsini, the nuncio to France, requested a painting to be sent as a gift to King Louis XIV. Rosa was thrilled that his fame would spread to France and proud that his virtuoso speed of execution, a quality that many seventeenth-century artists valued, had in part won so glamorous a commission.[16] It is not clear who chose the subject – though its immense ambition suggests that it may have been Rosa himself – for he went on to paint one of the greatest military exploits of the Athenian statesman Cimon, who won two victories, on sea and land, on the same day. The double battle was an extraordinary challenge to the artist and an opportunity to surpass all other painters. Here, for perhaps the first time, he painted a historic conflict, *The Battle of Cimon* (illus. 38), and competed with Pietro da Cortona's recent *Battle of Alexander and Darius* (1644–50), reaching beyond this to an echo of Giulio Romano's *Battle of Constantine* fresco of 1520–25. No earlier painter had created so vast a scenery of mountain, sea, land and sky, against which seethes a dense mass of ancient warriors and horses, full of movement and expression. The Roman ruins link past and present and the frieze of figures, their gestures tautened by the shallow space, evokes the violence of an ancient bas-relief, the stony, almost monochrome colours heightening the sculptural effect. To this Rosa added a harsh Neapolitan realism. He conveys no sense of heroism but presents an overwhelming variety of brutal motifs, of expressions of horror and anguish, of amputated limbs, bulging eyes and grasping, pleading hands. Cosimo Brunetti sent a remarkable and detailed ekphrasis of the work to Ricciardi. Brunetti identifies the subject, adding that the learned Ricciardi would of course recognize it, and praises this variety. He wonders at the splendour of the setting, adding that the mountain was thought to be one of Rosa's noblest achievements. He described the play of light and shade of the clouds that pass, and the mix of air and dust, adding the amusing, Plinian, anecdote that a viewer thought the dust was real, and stepped forward to clean a cloud. This description of the dust, and other passages in his letter, such as his listing of the prominent array of foreground objects, are close to the notes in Leonardo's 'Way of Representing a Battle', which Rosa probably knew of in Florence. However, there was also renewed interest in Leonardo at this moment, for in 1651 the first printed edition of his *Treatise on Painting* was published and had been the subject of intense research in the library of Cardinal Francesco Barberini, which gathered scholars from all over Rome. Nicolas Poussin had done drawings for it. It seems likely that Brunetti and Rosa himself were interested in this project, and the strong accent on cruelty and horror reflects an interest in Leonardo. To Brunetti the painting was 'sublime, noble, beyond everything marvellous' and the spectator, at the sight of the burning ships on the sea, was 'stupefied, transported'. Here Brunetti began to use the language of the sublime and Rosa's painting is consonant with this nascent aesthetic, reflected also in the growing interest of the Umoristi in Longinus' ancient treatise *On the Sublime*.

The painting has an astonishing visionary quality, setting the puniness of man against the eternal grandeur of nature. This contrast of a sublime nature with the violence of human-kind is close to that expressed by Daniello Bartoli, with whose writings Rosa's art had many conceptual affinities. In his *Man of Letters* Bartoli, in a paraphrase of a celebrated passage from Seneca's *Natural Questions* (AD 62–4), imagines looking down from the highest sphere of the heavens, 'where the mind conceives ideas higher than the world below', to contemplate the tininess of the earth, to possess whose kingdoms' men

> have invented manifold battle arts and arms for murdering . . . Sieges, assaults, conflagrations, batteries, pitched battles, ruins of whole nations done in no time that that have so often made widowed nature weep, filling the air with the stench of rotting carcasses, damming rivers, and dyeing the corpse – laden sea red with great pools of human blood? Such are the incredible wonders of human madness? Our vastest desires are wasted on a dot.[17]

The painting enjoyed overwhelming success and, Brunetti tells us, all Rome came to see it.[18]

Rosa, on a wave of success, jubilant that his pictures were sought after in the courts of Europe, increasingly presented himself as a philosopher-painter, above all worldly concerns. He was perhaps emulating the Stoicism of Pietro Testa and was also ever aware of the ideal philosopher-painter, embodied by Poussin, who chose themes and a mode of living that suggested his belief in the doctrines and morality of the

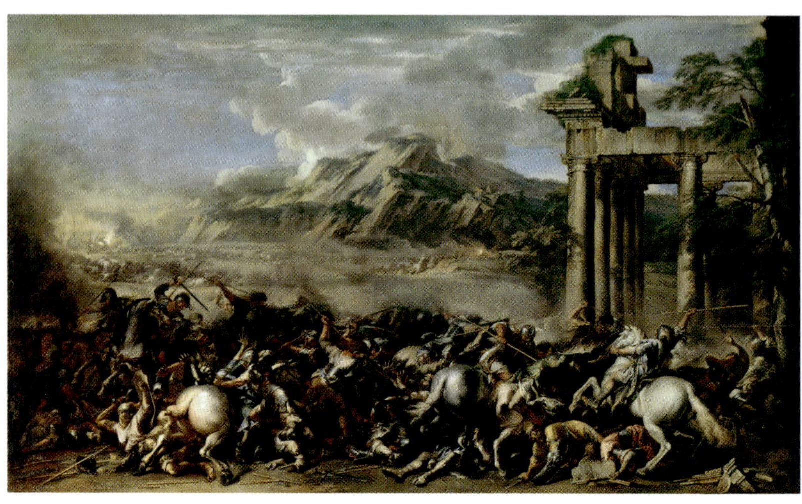

ancient Stoics. Poussin's house was small and modest, his life frugal, his days disciplined. In sharp contrast Rosa's house became a theatre in which he staged his ambitions, welcoming his guests with beauty and comfort, but reading the satires in a starkly simple setting, befitting his Stoic pose. Ricciardi was astonished to find an expensive silver bowl in his bathroom, a lavish gift that the artist had received from an admirer, which was now an irreverent symbol of his Stoic contempt for wealth. Ricciardi, surprised and amused, hurried to tell all his friends that in this way Rosa claimed to be 'the true heir of the genius and customs of the wisemen of antiquity'.[19] Cardinals, nobles and high churchmen flocked to Rosa's studio. Carlo Dati visited, both to see the *Democritus* and to hear the satire on *Painting*. On one occasion three eminent cardinals, Brancaccio, Omodei and Ottoboni, came to hear the satires and Rosa received them with astonishing informality, in his slippers, as though they were ordinary people, and delighted them with his

38 Salvator Rosa, *The Battle of Cimon*, 1652, oil on canvas.

bizzarrie and wit.[20] Rosa's Stoic persona was flamboyant. It contrasts sharply with the true simplicity with which Poussin himself carried a candle to light Cardinal Camillo Massimi to his door. When the cardinal pitied his lack of servants, Poussin replied that he pitied the cardinal for having so many.[21] The visits of the great and powerful were important, a validation of Rosa's social rise and central to an artist who, as Passeri tells us, needed constant acclaim and adulation. Every evening Rosa put on a display at the Trinità dei Monti, near his house, gathering around him a following of literary men, musicians and singers, all avid to form part of so fashionable a spectacle.[22] He was perhaps again consciously emulating Poussin, who walked on the Trinità dei Monte in the mornings, engaging his friends in 'curious and learned discourses'.[23] In the evenings the French artist mixed with the foreigners who gathered in the Piazza di Spagna, discussing art with men of intelligence, displaying his wide learning and being generous with his company.

Rosa's circle of distinguished admirers, from both Florence and Rome, now conducted an extraordinary publicity campaign on his behalf, sending him eulogistic letters and poems that were intended to be copied and shared in scholarly circles and read in the academies. Baldinucci emphasizes the importance of the letters sent from Florence and added that he himself had a large collection of the originals.[24] Brunetti, as we have seen, wrote an important description of *The Battle of Cimon*, an account that was circulated, and which he probably followed up with a public encomium, to be read in an academy.[25] Rosa was proud of a laudatory sonnet by the great Ciro di Pers, which he flaunted in public 'as though it were a sacred thing'.[26] In 1650 Daniello Bartoli published a new book, *Contented Poverty*, and included an ekphrasis of a recent painting, *Marius Meditating among the Ruins of Carthage*, which he must have seen in Rosa's Roman studio. So close in date are painting and book that it seems Bartoli perhaps added his description after the book had gone to press. Rosa hastened to buy the book as soon as it came out, commenting that it was 'entirely Stoic';[27] surprisingly, he does not mention the ekphrasis.[28]

Most interesting of these many poems was Ricciardi's *Beneath a Cruel Star*, a long philosophical poem that, shortly before 1651, circulated through Rome. The poem was addressed not to a picture but to Rosa himself, 'the great king of the brushes', and proud wearer of double laurels, and perhaps Ricciardi was moved to present the poem to Rosa in gratitude for the self-portrait that Rosa had made for him (illus. 32).[29] It opens with many of the images of vanitas poetry. Unhappy man, bound in his swaddling clothes, already weeps, and the path to the tomb is short. Fortune bears towards him a stony breast, life offers neither peace nor joy, no single day of happiness; nothing of man will remain but a shadow. It is a black vision, and one shared by Rosa's *Democritus*, but it develops into an exhortation to courage, to seek tranquillity among the dangers and sufferings of life. The poem includes a roll-call of the iron-willed heroes of antiquity and of the early philosophers, who have lived free from hope and fear, and whose fame resounds throughout the world. Among them,

A constant Socrates
turns hemlock into an antidote to death

and to erect statues in the midst of hatred
Atilius changes nails into so may chisels.

Rosa will follow in their steps and himself become an illustrious exemplar for, to his great gifts as painter and poet, he adds,
more lovely still to Ricciardi's eyes, the 'spotless splendour'
of his virtue.

At precisely the same time that Rosa was displaying his
skill as a painter of erudite philosophical subjects, his paintings
Marius Meditating among the Ruins of Carthage, *The Death of Atilius
Regulus* and *The Death of Socrates* echo the themes of *Beneath a
Cruel Star*. Rosa set himself in the philosophical and antiquarian
circles of Pietro Testa and Nicolas Poussin. His *Death of Socrates*
(illus. 40) is suggestive of Testa's print of the *Death of Cato*
(1648), while *The Death of Atilius Regulus* (illus. 39), despite a
Riberesque stormy violence, emulates the storytelling and
the study of gesture and expression of such a dramatic and
realistic history painting as Poussin's *Death of Germanicus* (1627).
A small group of works around the *Death of Socrates* from the
early to mid-1650s present strikingly stark and pared-back
compositions, almost monochromatic and reminiscent of
shallow bas-reliefs. With these grave and stony works Rosa
created an intensely personal form of Roman classicism.

The triumph of these first happy Roman years was short-
lived. Rosa's sharp and satiric tongue, his endless boasting
and cultivation of groups of offensively rowdy supporters
began to attract enemies and the overwhelming success of
Democritus and *The Battle of Cimon* roused deep envy. Initially
his detractors focused on the satires and as early as 1650 Rosa
told Ricciardi of a 'slew of stupid criticisms levelled at my

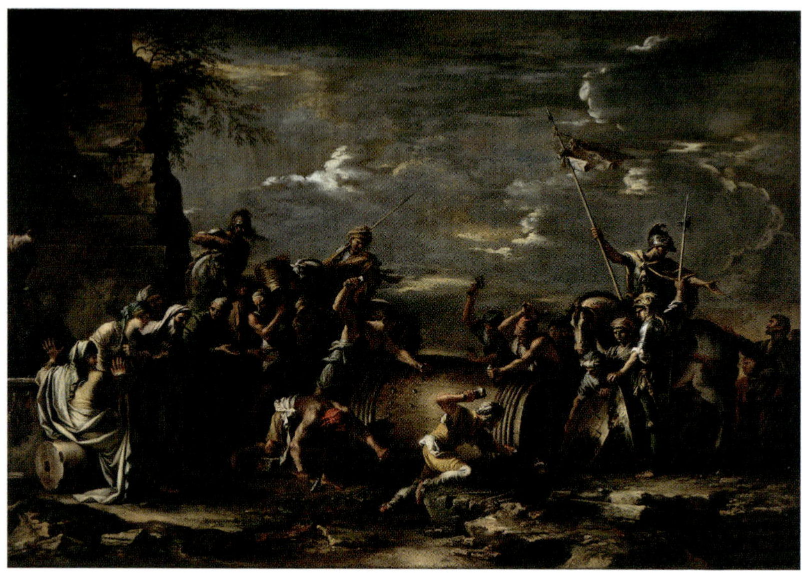

satires that will make you laugh'.[30] Brunetti mentions these criticisms, optimistically seeing them as raising Rosa's profile and so surrounding him with respect.[31] But the campaign, led by Agostino Favoriti, secretary to Flavio Chigi and the author of some pedantic Latin verses, was to escalate with extraordinary ferocity and in 1652 the Umoristi considered expelling Rosa.[32] He was belittled as a figure painter and it was suggested that he had not written his satires but stolen them from his brother or from Ricciardi, or from the now safely dead priest Reginaldo Sgambati.

With his fifth satire, *Envy*, written between 1652 and 1653, Rosa boldly confronted his detractors. This satire is unusually personal. It includes a virulent pen portrait of Favoriti and is also uncharacteristically focused. Rosa resists temptation to wander off into generalized denunciations of corruption.

39 Salvator Rosa, *The Death of Atilius Regulus*, c. 1650–52, oil on canvas.

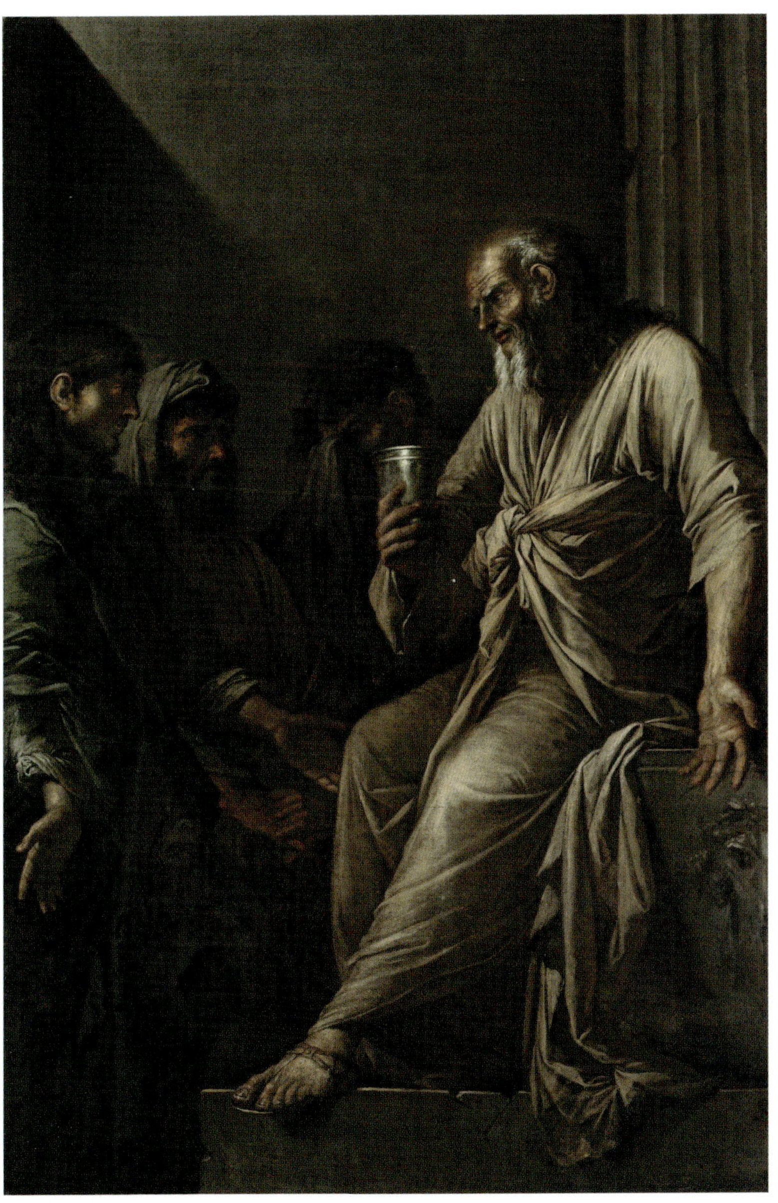

40 Salvator Rosa, *The Death of Socrates*, early 1650s, oil on canvas.

Envy was a central theme in ancient and Renaissance art and literature and in his satire Rosa wove together highly personal details and a traditional iconography, applauding emulation as a positive quality but positioning himself as the noble heir to a long line of persecuted artists and writers. It was, above all, as artist-writer and philosopher that he sought vindication and he constantly mentions brush and pen together. The satire opens dramatically, in the stillness of night, as the painter dreams that the fearsome figure of Envy, 'with livid breast, squint eyed, bristling hair' (l. 54), has barred his ascent to the Temple of Immortality. Envy, he declares, has provoked the Umoristi to deride him, just as in the past she had created shameful rivalries between the great writers of antiquity. She has sent her supporters to mock his paintings at the Pantheon (l. 515), so that this year he had shown only a vast painting of a rock (l. 540), on which the barking dogs of Envy might break their teeth. It is not clear whether this painting ever existed or if Rosa was writing metaphorically but it is possible that he displayed at the Pantheon a large rocky landscape.[33] He contemplated a painting of Envy (l. 505), and described in detail Apelles' celebrated painting the *Calumny of Apelles* (ll. 463–507), a satirical self-defence by the ancient Greek artist. This work was described by Lucian in his dialogue *De calumnia* and popularized in Leon Battista Alberti's *On Painting* (1435). Above all Rosa exalts the concept of the learned painter. Fame, in every time and through all the world, has spread such artists' fame (ll. 640–41), he declares, and since antiquity painters have been not only poets, 'but grand philosophers, and demons in seeking out the secrets of nature' (ll. 655–6). Rosa sets himself in this glorious tradition. The great Michelangelo, poet, painter and sculptor, is his illustrious predecessor, as are many about whom he had read in the pages of Vasari's *Lives* of 1550 (l. 654), where the theme of artist-writer, and that of Envy, are often intertwined.[34]

Envy provoked a volley of abusive pamphlets and satires against him, in both verse and prose, and Rosa lamented that he would have done better to break his neck rather than embark upon so ill-conceived an undertaking.[35] Emilio Sibonio's *Purgatory*, the only text to have survived, presented Rosa in conversation with the priest Sgambati, adding weight to the notion that Rosa may have stolen his words from the priest.[36] Another was so vicious that it elicited censure from 'their own comrades-in-malice, thereby producing more credit for my work';[37] yet another presented Rosa at the gallows, waiting to be executed for his crimes. This satire denigrated Rosa's entire life, deriding his lowly Neapolitan origins and mocking his career in Florence as a frivolous actor and stealer of silverware, an odd recurrence of the accusation levelled against him by Ottaviano Castelli in the boastful year of 1639.[38] The details of Rosa's humble background in Naples were correct and must have pained the artist. His response is characteristically self-dramatizing: 'have I not become the Socrates, the Tasso, the Guarini of my time?'[39] However, a note of real fear soon began to touch his accounts – he often broke out into cold sweats and thought of taking refuge with Ricciardi – and his critics moved from attacking his poetry to a dangerous assault on his moral character.[40] Above all Rosa dreaded the involvement of the Holy Office, for he lived with a married woman – in 1656 he felt it wise for them to separate for a time, and sent Lucrezia and his son Rosalvo to his brother in Naples.

The cause of the astonishing violence of the attacks on Rosa is not entirely clear. His lowly origins perhaps played a large part. Roman *letterati* found it hard to accept that a young Neapolitan, badly educated and with little Latin, could excel in both painting and poetry. His presumption and desire not only to belong to the literary academies but to dominate them created many enemies. The crowds of sycophants who transformed the Pantheon into a platform for Rosa's self-display enraged others, and Sibonio specifically complained that he 'made cliques at the Pantheon'; Rosa was infuriated when a carefully timed pamphlet came out on the day of the exhibition at the Pantheon, 'when I usually triumph'.[41] In part these feuds were an occupational hazard, common in the Roman literary academies, which were constantly riven by poisonous feuds. Rosa believed that slander and acrimony had caused the death of the dramatist Giovan Battista Filippo Ghirardelli, whose prose tragedy, *Constantine* (1653), had attracted similar attacks; Rosa had defended the poet against the attacks of Favoriti, and designed a frontispiece for his play, which, through fear, he left unsigned.[42]

Now, having declared his triumph as a painter of ethical and heroic subjects (*Envy*, l. 527), Rosa took up the theme of Envy in painting and prints, vindicating his gifts in startlingly different works. From the mid-1650s comes his great *Belisarius* (illus. 41), a monumental Roman history painting. Belisarius, we read in the sixth-century historian Procopius' *Persian Wars*, was an invincible general, the incarnation of ancient Roman heroism and Christian virtue, and above all of the virtue of unswerving loyalty. Medieval legend added that Justinian, envious of his general's popular appeal, blinded and persecuted

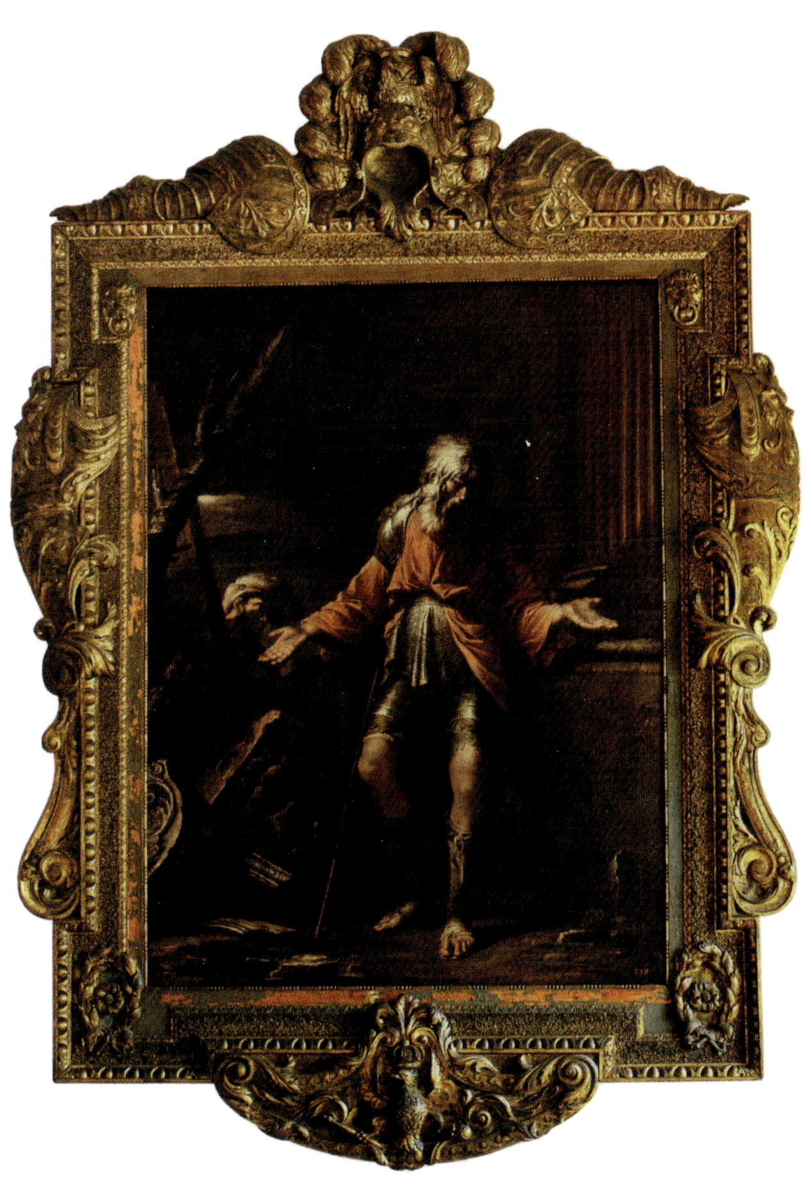

41 Salvator Rosa, *Belisarius*, mid-1650s, oil on canvas.

him and he was reduced to the sad life of a wandering beggar. This legend, doubted by many historians, had been legitimized by the Catholic historian Cesare Baronius, who had hailed him as a kind of Christian martyr, the victim of Envy, 'that wild beast, and robber, revelling in downfall and persecution . . . [similar to] dragons, poisons, lethal herbs, which conquer with grief and pain'.[43] Rosa's immediate source may have been Giambattista Marino's *Galeria*, where Marino described his imaginary portrait of Belisarius, a few pages on from his description of Atilius Regulus in his barrel. Here the great commander stands before the reader as a beggar, the champion of freedom, and yet blinded by an envious ruler. In Rosa's own literary circles the subject was common. His friend, the prolific and venerated dramatist Giacinto Andrea Cicognini (d. 1651), had written a play entitled *The Fall of the Great Captain Belisarius in the Reign of the Emperor Justinian*. Volunnio Bandinelli, a member of the Accademia dei Percossi, described Belisarius as the champion of a heroic past, whose fame had released the power of envy, rendering him yet more glorious as an object of compassion.[44]

The subject was, however, entirely unknown in painting. Rosa set the general, who 'had a fine figure and was tall and remarkably handsome',[45] against a darkening sky, evoking the end of an era, for he was often named the 'last of the Romans'. Belisarius' eyes are unseeing and his head is lowered, his outstretched arms making a mute appeal to the spectator. He wears Roman armour, conveying his once high rank, and the rich highlights and colour contrast with the beggar's or blind-man's staff, which divides light from dark and concentrates our gaze on the general's head. Around him are the remains of a vanished but glorious past, the pyramid, the fallen columns and the Roman relief together suggesting the vanity of all human aspirations. The fallen general is a moving object of compassion and his pose has overtones of Christ on the Cross, or Christ before Pilate. His tragic gesture appeals directly to the spectator and we, before the painting, identify with the three viewers who come upon him from the distance. He is totally unaware of them and they enhance his dark solitude. The Roman relief, adapted from a celebrated sarcophagus in the Medici gardens, shows a sacrifice.[46]

The story conveyed, above all, the bitterness of Envy and the vanity of all human achievement, topics that held, at this moment, an all-absorbing personal resonance for Rosa. The fall of great rulers was a common theme of contemporary tragedy. His friend Ghirardelli's *Constantine* finished with the most powerful man in the world, alone on the stage, fallen from the heights and having become the plaything of fortune. Rosa's frontispiece showed the tragic hero, frontal and close to the spectator as is Belisarius, accompanied by figures who express the tragic emotions of pity and fear. An astonishing and hubristic sonnet, probably from this date, suggests how the artist felt his persecution as a martyrdom of his great genius. Like Peter, he is denied, and by Judas betrayed; 'Why,' he proudly declares, 'because I am called Salvator, does everyone cry out "Let him be crucified"?'[47] Very little is known about the early history of the *Belisarius*. It was in the collection of Girolamo Pannesio, a Genoese poet and dilettante, who also owned pictures by Guercino and Pier Francesco Mola. The picture has something in common with Mola's splendid *Barbary Pirate* of 1650, a single monumental figure set so boldly against a dramatic sky. It may be that Pannesio commissioned it, but nonetheless the painting remains a theatrically self-dramatizing work.[48]

Rosa had harshly rebuked his detractors in verse and in a monumental painting presented the terrible onslaughts of Envy. Now he turned to etching, a medium he had rarely used, but one that offered an opportunity to display to a wider public his gifts of spontaneity and invention. The times were harsh, plague threatened and painting was neglected. Rosa hoped to make some money and it became a common pattern to turn to etching at such difficult moments in his career. He did not, as many Italian printmakers did, associate himself with a publisher and it is his name alone that appears on his etchings.[49] In the mid-1650s Rosa created a suite of 62 etchings of soldiers and of genre figures, both male and female, which he called the *Figurine*. The frontispiece bears the inscription, 'Salvator Rosa dedicates these prints of playful leisure to Carlo de Rossi as a pledge of outstanding friendship' (illus. 42).

This frontispiece looks back to the opening of his satire *Envy*, where the artist, intent on engraving his name on the altar of the Temple of Immortality, is barred by the fearsome figure of Envy. In the frontispiece all is reversed. A youth in a flamboyantly feathered hat, elevated and dominating in poise, proudly points at the name of Salvator Rosa, which is engraved on a tablet that bears the symbol of immortality, a smoking urn. Envy, traditionally represented with withered, hanging breasts and snakes for hair, is vanquished and fades powerless into the abyss. The youth is derived from Cesare Ripa's emblem for Capriccio in his *Iconologia*.[50] Ripa's illustration

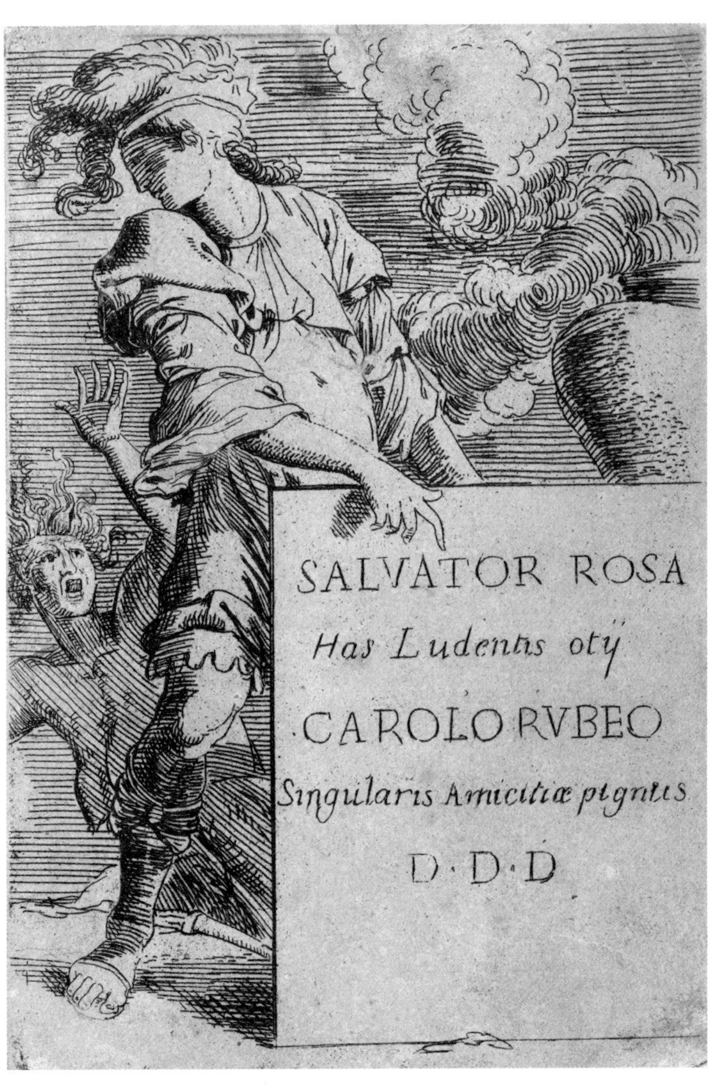

42 Salvator Rosa, frontispiece to the *Figurine* series, *c*. 1656–7, etching.

shows a jester, in sprightly pose, wearing a feathered hat and with a charmingly rueful expression. With his right hand he blows air from a bellows into his face, while with his left he dangles a spur by its strap. Ripa's accompanying text is worth quoting at length, so revelatory is it of Rosa's intentions. Capriccio, writes Ripa, is

> A young boy, dressed in various colours, wearing a hat, on which there are various feathers, similar in colour to his clothes. In his right hand he holds a bellows, in his left a spur. People who are called 'capricious' are those whose actions are governed by ideas which differ from the ordinary ideas of men, but who change from one idea to another of the same kind; and, by way of ana-logy, ideas that in painting, music or elsewhere appear out of the ordinary are termed 'caprices'. Inconstancy is shown in the age of the child, variety in the diversity of colours. The hat with the various feathers shows that this extraordinary variety of actions have their seat chiefly in the fantasy. The spur and bellows show that the capricious man is ready to praise other people's virtue or to prick their vices.[51]

Rosa would have appreciated the ideas 'which differ from the ordinary ideas of men' and the stress on variety and fantasy; but Ripa does not abandon the concept of the high calling of art, for spur and bellows are the weapons of the satirist and moralist. A unique impression of the print shows the bellows between the youth's legs clearly, though in the final state they were reduced to a nozzle.[52]

There follows a masterful display of figures of a variety of mood and pose and a range of gestures and groupings. They were bound together in a small book and may have been partly intended as a pattern book for later artists. The *Figurine* tell no story and yet, as the viewer leafs through them, they seem to suggest a tense drama, one that is never quite defined. Rosa shows single warriors, often alone on mountain tops, looking down on the clouds, windswept and brooding against a stormy sky; others sleep or wander in dark grottoes, melancholy in a wilderness of trees and rocks. These warriors delight with a wealth of rich detail, some blending ancient and exotic dress with Renaissance and classical armour, while others are plumed and turbaned, redolent of an exotic eastern world. Some show groups of figures often seated on walls or rocks, very close to the picture plane, poised to enter the world of the viewer. This closeness intrigues, and invites us to weave a story around them, perhaps evocative of the romances of Torquato Tasso and Ludovico Ariosto, as they point, gesticulate, grieve and fear. They seem involved in tense and mysterious dramas, always beyond our grasp.[53] The genre figures – old men, beggars, fishermen, women, some contemporary, some nude and classically idealized – provide a counterpoint to the romance of the warriors. The prints are light in touch and spontaneous, seeming to bring the viewer close to the artist's fantasy. With these etchings, in the midst of his anger, Rosa displayed his skill as a figure painter and gave free rein to his inventiveness and imagination.

In the 1650s Rosa created a sequence of landscapes enriched by such warriors. He and Ricciardi were connoisseurs of wild landscape, a pleasure stimulated by their stays in the

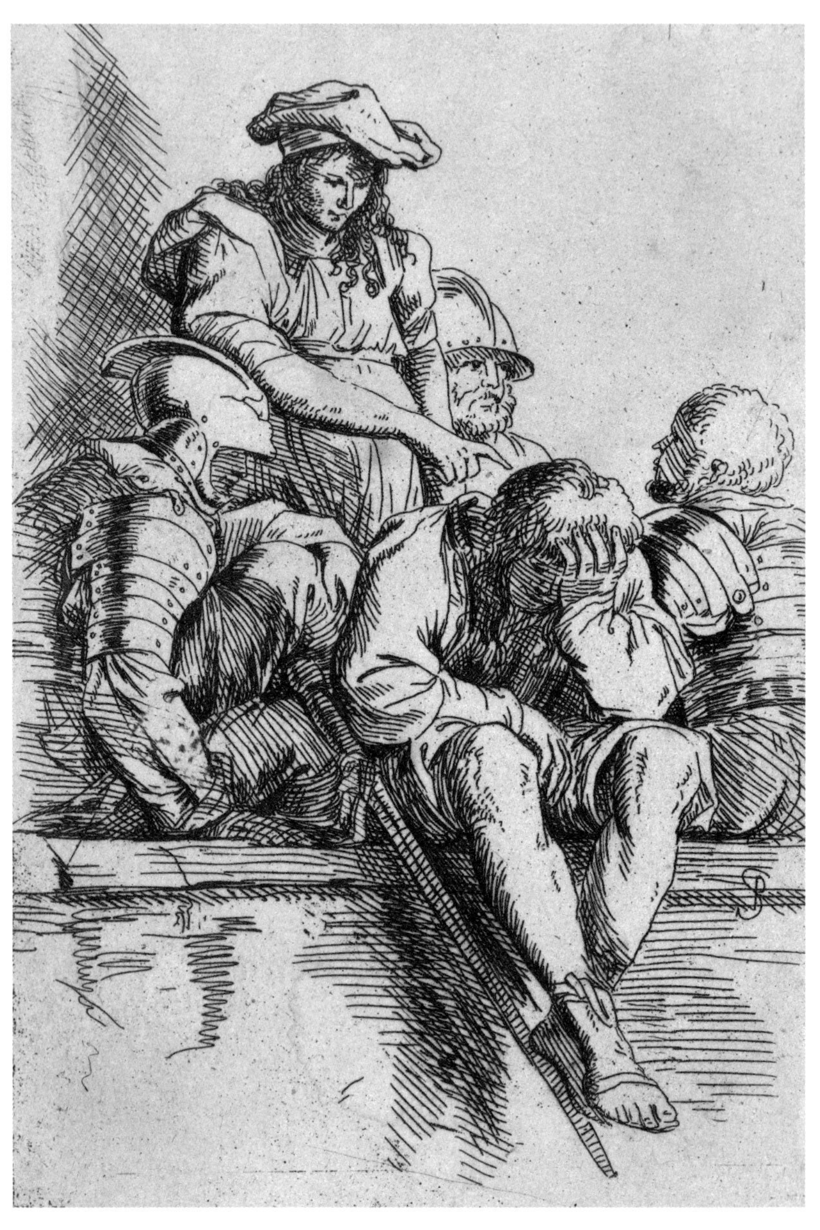

43 Salvator Rosa, 'Four Warriors and a Standing Youth', etching in the *Figurine* series, c. 1656–7.

countryside around Volterra. Rosa enjoyed Ricciardi's account of a visit to the mountainous Garfagnana, in the northern-most reaches of Tuscany, 'so congenial to our nature';[54] and he praised the 'savage quality' of Monte Verruca, a strangely shaped mountain near Pisa.[55] A medieval fortress above the small hilltop town of Verrucola di Fivizzano was associated with the sixteenth-century legendary bandit Michele delle Verrucole and in the castle were two poetic inscriptions by Ricciardi.[56] Rosa's rocky landscapes with bandits of the 1650s recall the friends' pleasure in the wildness and myths of this countryside (illus. 44). Bandits – the bold, outlawed men who haunted the rugged terrain of the Abruzzi or the Garfagnana – were feared by the traveller but Rosa's warriors, archaizing and romantic, are imaginary figures who evoke the myth of the noble bandit. Very much alive in the seventeenth century, the noble bandit, who led an adventurous life of personal freedom, was the star of ballads and popular accounts, and Rosa may well have heard recitals of the daring deeds of the southern brigand Marco Sciarra on the wharves of Naples. Rosa, for a brief moment, escapes from his consuming desire to be known as a Roman history painter and instead delights with these capricci, which, for him, become emblems of the freedom of the artist.

The mid-1650s were challenging years. Lucrezia returned from Naples to Rome, but in 1656 Rosa's son Rosalvo and his brother died there of the plague. A little later Rosa received the false news that his sister and all her family had died. Rosa's response to these miseries is revealing, and his despair and helplessness enrage him: 'And I let myself believe I was the first man of the century? A person with the most beautiful genius,

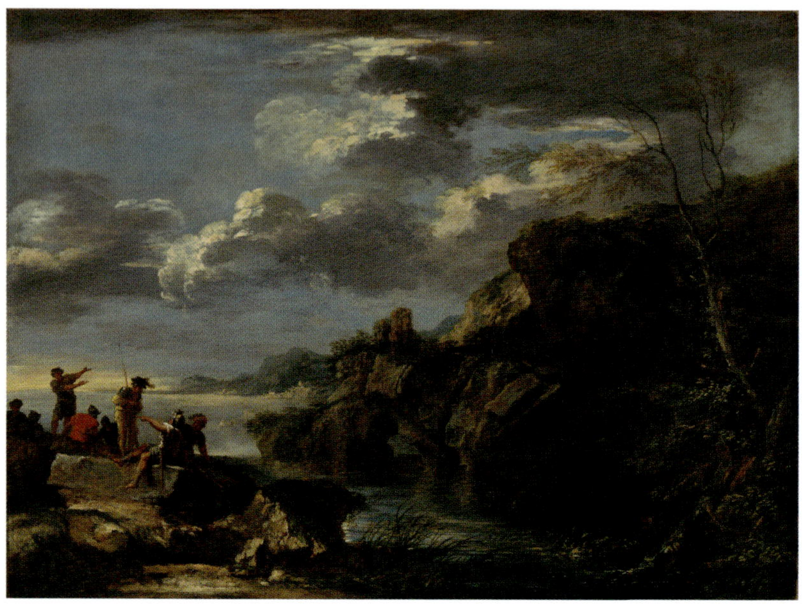

extraordinary prudence, and skilled shrewdness? Pshaw. I'm an idiot, an ass, an enormous dickhead.'[57] He cannot attain a Stoic calm in adversity, though he stands firm in his belief that he was in no way inferior to the great role models of antiquity, whose virtues he now doubts; 'We should have met these Socrateses, Zenos, Aristippuses and Catos, and not remain steeped in these centuries-old accounts like sheep who run one after the other with an utterly stupid credulity.'[58]

Nonetheless Rosa's status was rising and at this moment he entered Chigi circles. His old friend Niccolò Simonelli had, after 1655, become the *guardaroba* to Cardinal Flavio Chigi. Simonelli advised the cardinal on his collection of erudite paintings, among them works by Angelo Caroselli and Pietro Testa, and on his creation of a celebrated cabinet of curiosities,

44 Salvator Rosa, *Bandits on a Rocky Coast*, 1655–60, oil on canvas.

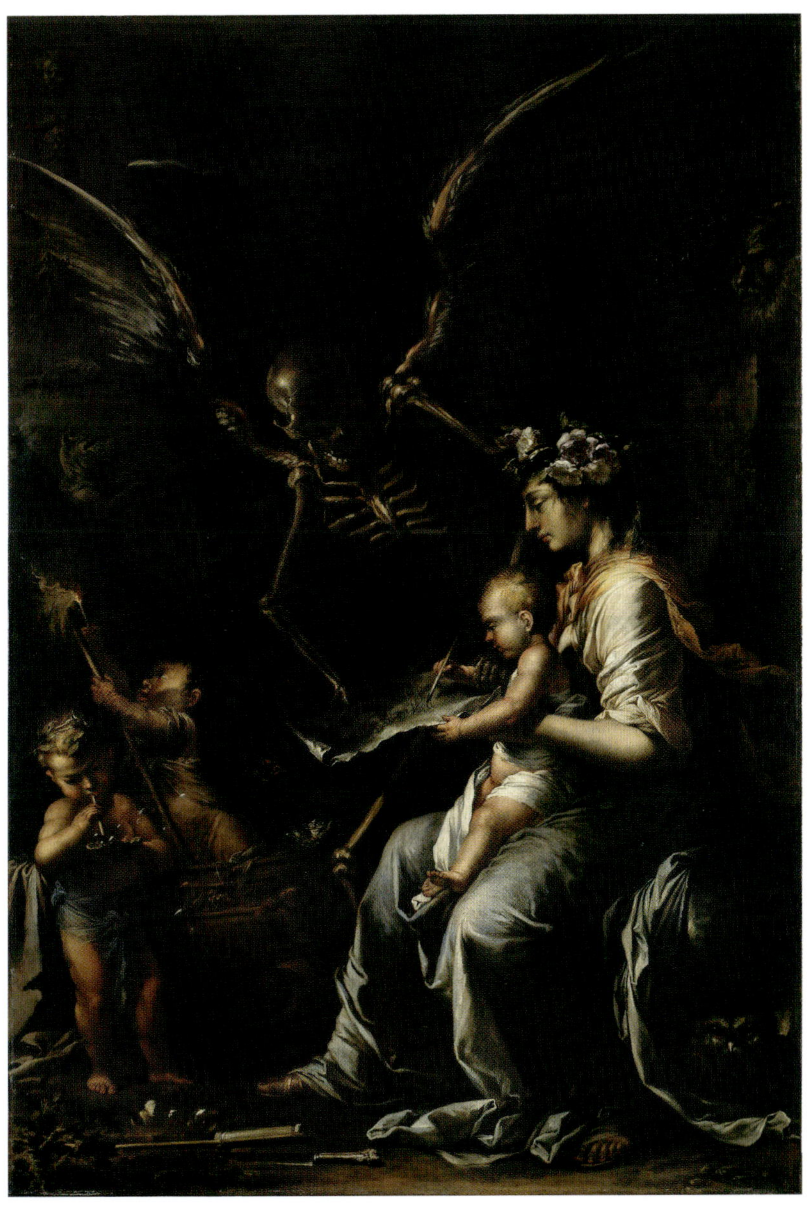

45 Salvator Rosa, *The Frailty of Human Life*, c. 1656, oil on canvas.

displayed in his palazzo overlooking the Quattro Fontane. Flavio Chigi liked complex allegorical painting and it is very likely that he commissioned from Rosa *The Frailty of Human Life*, a macabre work, redolent of the cabinet of curiosities, which was in his collection by 1658.[59] Its imagery would have pleased the pope, Alexander VII, who constantly meditated on death.

The Frailty of Human Life (illus. 45) is a memento mori, an allegorical painting that unites fear and grief and poignantly laments the precariousness and brevity of human life. In a sombre night-time setting the cold hand of grinning Death guides the sickly baby, who, gravely intent on his task, writes the words '*Conceptio culpa, nasci pena, labor vita, necesse mori*' (conception is sin, birth is pain, life is toil, death inevitable). These rework the Latin of the medieval poet Adam of St Victor, and recall the opening of Ricciardi's *Beneath a Cruel Star*.[60] The child is tenderly observed by the melancholic woman, who, seated on the glass sphere of Fortune, is impassive, meditative and submitting to Death and Time, as her pallid crown of roses fades. Beneath her skirt a sinister owl, bird of night and ill omen, confronts the spectator. The owl links the picture to the Democritus and Rosa re-uses some of this vanitas imagery. An obelisk, whose hieroglyphs, as we have seen, symbolize the brevity of life, and a cypress-crowned Terminus, god of Death and boundaries, frame the gigantic and fearsome winged skeleton, so dramatically poised to seize the baby. This macabre apparition has the paradoxical vivacity and sardonic grimace that had begun to characterize scientific illustrations in this period, when the motif was enjoying extraordinary success. Rosa would have known the winged and flying skeleton in Bernini's *Memorial to Alessandro Valtrini*, a funerary monument in the church of San Lorenzo in Damaso, and he may well have been aware that Bernini was planning to adorn the tomb of Alexander VII with a similar feature: a sinister skeleton brandishing an hourglass.

Around the figures Rosa wove symbols of the transience of human life. A putto blows fragile bubbles, butterflies flutter into the dark, a spent rocket lies beside a knife – all motifs that evoke the idea of severance, or death. Rosa has brilliantly united aspects of the northern genre of *danse macabre*, or Dance of Death, where gleeful skeletons brutally assault the living, with the perfect visual equivalent of very many seventeenth-century lyrics that plangently lament the brevity and transience of all life. This was a favourite theme of Marino and his followers and, as we have seen, Ricciardi and many Florentine poets wrote vanitas poetry. They conveyed the closeness of birth and death, of the swaddling clothes and the shroud, and of the cradle and the bier. They suggested that life itself was, like smoke, bubbles or a play of shadows, merely an illusion. The great poet of the vanitas was Ciro di Pers, of whose appreciation Rosa was so proud. In the *Death of a Friend* Pers wrote of the bitterness that colours all the sweetness of life; we do not live here, he laments, for this our life is but an illusion, a shadow that vanishes as it appears.[61] *The Frailty of Human Life* is close in feeling to these baroque lyrics. Death is poised to take the baby, and the cradle in which one putto stands, lighting a brief flare of burning straw, suggests the closeness of death and birth, the cradle being 'the small bark' that will carry him swiftly to the end.[62] Above all it is the eerie night-time setting that creates the mood. Figures and objects reveal themselves slowly in the mysterious darkness; the play of dark and light draws the viewer in and the painting evokes the illusory nature of life. It is in a sense a collection of emblems, easily deciphered and understood, yet Rosa creates a powerfully poetic image of the precariousness and insecurity of man. His imagery looks back to the *Democritus*, however the mood is no longer harsh but rather a haunting blend of fear and melancholy.

Rosa's success was growing. He was admired by the Chigi family and in 1659 they presented him with a silver ewer and basin.[63] In the same year Alexander VII recorded in his diary that he had gone to see Rosa's paintings. Through their protection his circle of patronage widened to include members of families within their orbit, among them Monsignor Giovanni Battista Costaguti and Cardinal Jacopo Nini. In 1652 the success of the *Democritus* had won him a commission from Cardinal Omodei for an *Assumption* for the Milanese church of Santa Maria della Vittoria and, probably at the same time, *St Paul the Hermit*, which was paired with a *St John the Baptist in the Desert*, a collaboration between Pier Francesco Mola and Gaspard Dughet.[64] His *Assumption* is a stiff, anxious work, based on Annibale Carracci's *Assumption* in Santa Maria del Popolo, revealing Rosa's uneasy desire to conform to the great traditions of classical figure painting. His success in the public sphere in Milan did not satisfy him and he longed to win a commission in Rome itself, so passionately that he offered to paint, for free, five paintings for Carlo de Rossi, intended for his chapel in Santa Maria in Montesanto, one of the twin churches in the Piazza del Popolo. It seems that Rosa worked on these paintings in the second half of the 1650s, though the project sometimes halted owing to lack of funds and in

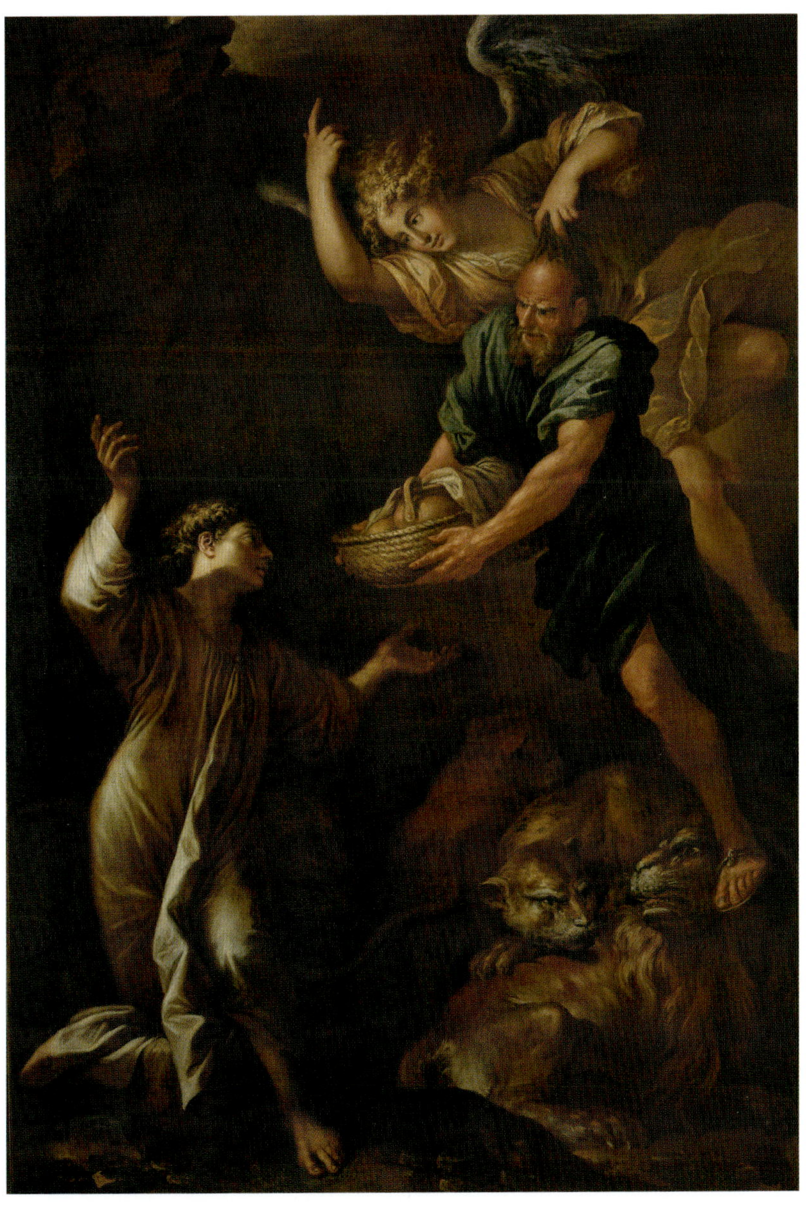

46 Salvator Rosa, *Daniel in the Lions' Den, c.* 1660, oil on canvas.

the end the paintings were not installed in the chapel until after the artist's death.[65] His intention was to display, in a church in the centre of Rome, his gifts as a painter of religious art and to attract commissions for similar works. Rosa pitted himself against his great contemporaries and, in what are perhaps the first of these works, *Daniel in the Lions' Den* (illus. 46) and *The Angel Leaving the House of Tobias* (both *c.* 1660), his debts to Bernini and to Pietro da Cortona are clear. The church of Santa Maria in Montesanto faces the church of Santa Maria di Popolo, where, for the celebrated Chigi chapel that was built for an ancestor of Alexander VII, Bernini had carved two works, *Daniel in the Lions' Den* (*c.* 1655–7) and *Habakkuk and the Angel* (*c.* 1656–61). The themes of Rosa's paintings – resurrection and salvation – echo those of the Chigi chapel and Rosa's *Daniel* seems to unite Bernini's two sculptures and emulates the strange serpentine pose of his Daniel. Rosa was competing with Bernini or perhaps paying homage, both to him and to the Chigi, in a bid for other prestigious commissions.

The paintings brought Rosa some measure of success. In 1662, probably again through Cardinal Omodei, he won a commission for a *Madonna del Suffragio* for the church of San Giovanni Decollato alle Case Rotte in Milan.[66] For this he was unusually well paid, suggesting that his fame as a painter of sacred histories flourished in Milan.[67] Rosa was thrilled with his success, writing jubilantly to Ricciardi 'by the grace of fortune, and in spite of whoever thinks I'm only good at other things, it was seen by all the best painters of Rome, and – reaching Milan – it's turned the city topsy turvey'.[68] Passeri, amusingly, wrote rather carefully about this success: 'The cardinal was satisfied with it. As for whether or not it pleased

Milan, there was no news in Rome.'[69] Rosa was to wait for some years before receiving such a commission in the papal city.

Rosa, now favoured by the Chigi, was enjoying considerable *réclame*. However, still enraged by his detractors, he came perilously close to throwing it all away. In 1659 he exhibited, at the annual exhibition at San Giovanni Decollato, a stunningly provocative *Allegory of Fortune* (illus. 47), showing Fortune pouring her gifts on a stolid group of farmyard animals. Two prelates, Volunnio Bandinelli and Cesare Rasponi, had seen the painting at Rosa's house, where they had enjoyed a reading of the satires. Delighted and amused, as they left they met Don Mario Chigi, the pope's brother, and told him they had both seen and heard a satire. Don Mario was intrigued at the idea of seeing a satire, and enjoyed Rosa's 'bel concetto'.[70] The painting's fame began to spread around Rome and Rosa, encouraged by this, decided to display it at San Giovanni Decollato. This was a bad move, and Roman painters, collectors and patrons were all insulted. Rosa was only saved from imprisonment by the intervention of Mario Chigi, and was made to write an apology.

With this painting Rosa placed himself in a tradition of angry artists enraged by the bitter enmity of their rivals and the ignorance of their patrons. His most famous precursor was the lost ancient work the *Calumny of Apelles*, which Rosa had described in his satire *Envy*, adding 'I shall myself with my brush create a fine joke' (l. 505). He may have known a print after Lorenzo Leombruno's *Allegory of Fortune* (c. 1523), which shows Fortune, on a raised platform, dispensing money, sceptres and crowns to the Vices, while Penitence and Truth are disgraced. He would have known, too, Federigo Zuccaro's

Calumny of Apelles (c. 1569–72), made famous through prints, and the scandals around his satirical *Gate of Virtue* (1581), for which Zuccaro had been expelled from the Papal states.

Rosa's closest precedent was the painter Guido Reni's *Fortune*, known in two versions (1637), and through engravings and drawings. Here the goddess, naked and fair, glides through the cerulean skies above the globe. She is a positive image, poised to bring wealth and power, and she has turned so that the little Cupid or genius may catch her by the forelock, or seize the moment. Beneath a starry sky Rosa's Fortune, her nudity and flowing blonde hair echoing that of Reni's goddess, sits precariously on a glass globe, a symbol of instability. However, in sharp contrast to Reni's ethereal and benevolent Fortune she is brought low, close to the animals, intent on her task. Traditionally Fortune's cornucopia is upright but here she holds an exaggeratedly long horn, which seems to twist and turn in her hands. From this she pours, with wild generosity, grain and fruits, sceptre and crown, a cascade of coins and jewels, both the fruits of nature and the accessories of rank and power. This Fortune is not blind; she looks down gleefully and aims her riches with care. Before her are a group of farmyard animals, stolid and unaware, representing all that is most feeble and degraded in humankind. Rosa's message is very clear: Fortune showers her gifts on those that least deserve them.

Mario Chigi had enjoyed seeing a satire and this is Rosa's most Juvenalian painting, recalling the Roman satirist's obsession with Fortune and his scathing attacks on the contemporary world. Juvenal had written bitterly of the great household of the patron Numitor, where the pet lion was lavishly fed and

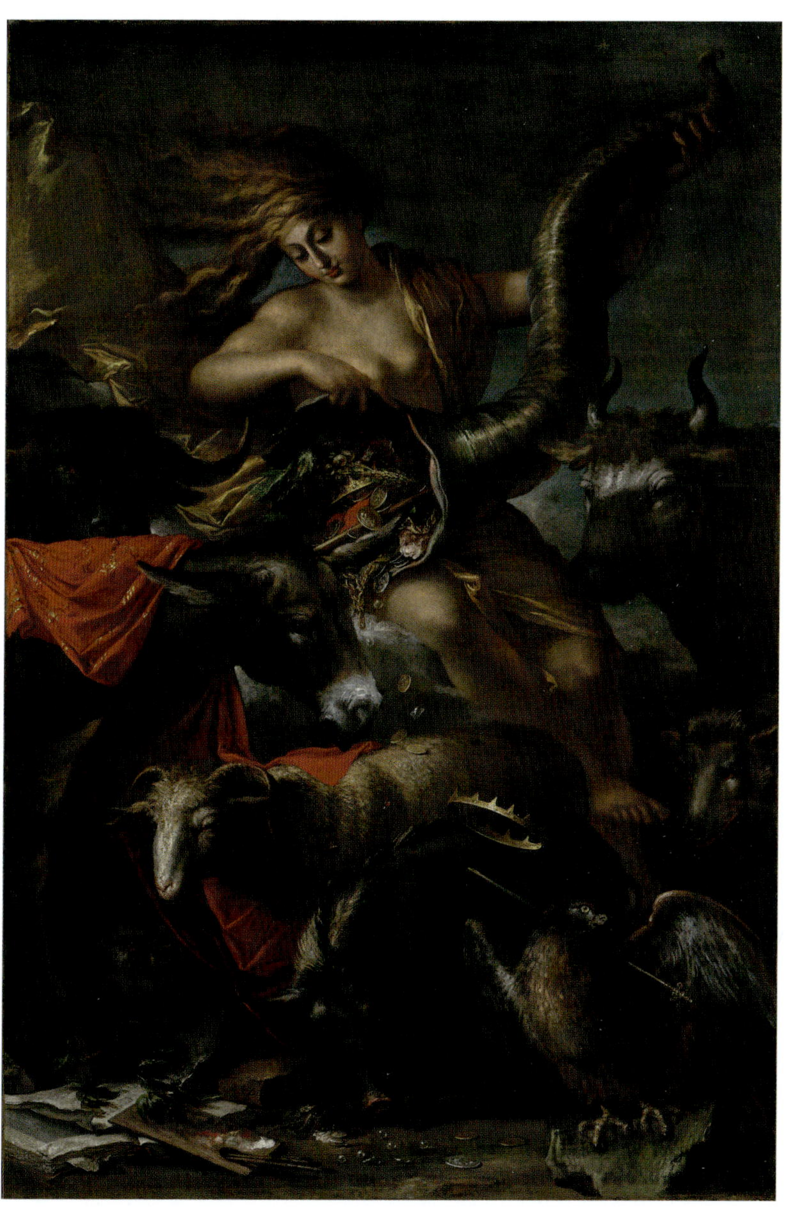

47 Salvator Rosa, *Allegory of Fortune, c.* 1658–9, oil on canvas.

men received nothing. Animal imagery was a traditional rhetorical device in the classical world and it runs obsessively through all Rosa's satires, from the opening lines of the first satire, *Music*, where the poet describes how asses take the first place at court and, for very many lines of tiring wordplay, weaves together images from the Bible and classical literature to evoke a world overrun by a startling array of asses. In a preparatory study for the painting Rosa shows Fortune standing among the animals, gesturing upwards to the stars of the zodiac (illus. 48). Rosa perhaps took this idea from Bartoli's *Man of Letters*, which had opened with Bartoli's demand,

> Should the houses of the great be turned into temples
> where the heads of monkeys are adored, and buffoons
> are honoured, while Men of Letters are outcasts . . .
> A Scorpion, a Dog, a Hydra, a Goat, a Bull, they are
> placed over our heads with names of the zodiac, while
> an Achilles, an Orpheus, and all the chorus of the
> demi-gods are consigned to below our feet.[71]

The brilliance of Rosa's painting lies in his ability to unite, as he did in the satires, the high and the low and the erudite and the popular. Bartoli's image – of a world upside down, where only the beasts ascend to the stars – is one that was well known in popular poetry and the motif also delighted popularizing poets; Giulio Cesare Croce, in *The World Upside Down*, had marvelled at how 'the ass bestrides the saddle, while the poor citizen hoes the earth'. Rosa blends his imagery with the language of proverb and maxim for, in the foreground, the boar sniffs at pearls on the ground, evoking

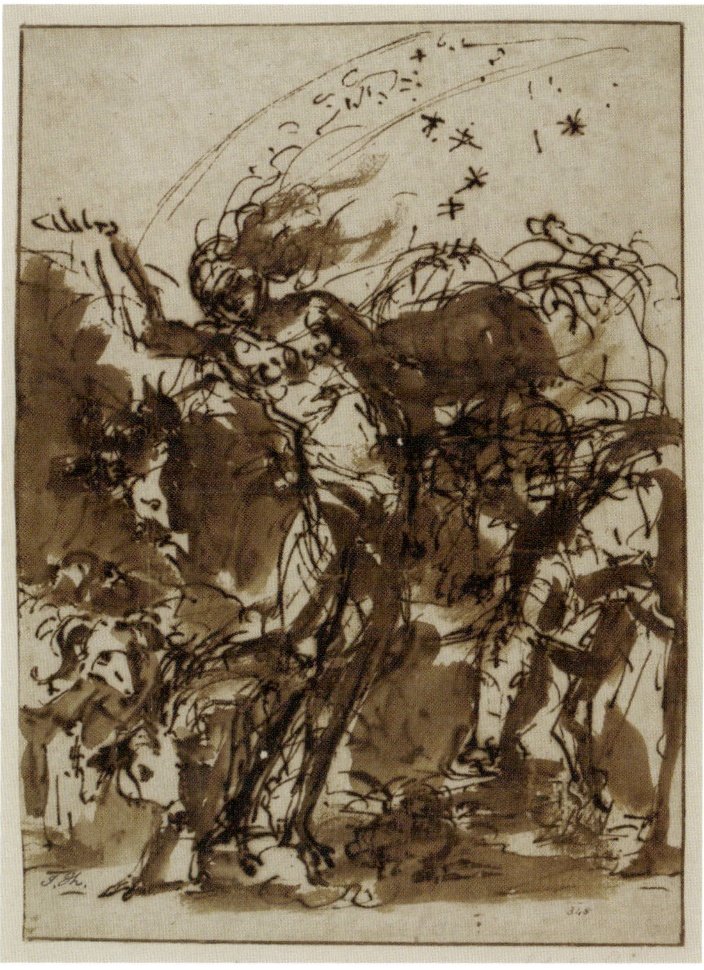

the well-known expression 'casting pearls before swine'. It
tramples on fresh roses (suggesting the artist's name), which
lie beside a book bearing his signature, and brushes and palette are together symbols of Rosa's twin glories in poetry and
painting. And Rosa would have known Giovanni Battista

48 Salvator Rosa, *Study for an Allegory of Fortune*, 1650s, pen and ink and wash.

della Porta's *Della fisionomia dell'uomo* (The Physiognomy of Man), and his comparisons of the profiles of animals with human portraits, reflecting a widespread interest in comparisons between human consciousness and animal behaviour. Della Porta describes the ass as 'most sensual, free from every thought', and the sheep as 'most obtuse, cruel and evil', and over ass and sheep Rosa drapes the sumptuous red cloth of the cardinal.[72] Rosa blends Fortune with Circe, who had changed Ulysses' followers into beasts, and he would have known Castiglione's print and paintings of Circe, where the enchantress is surrounded by macabre animals. Circe was associated with the imagery of the court, where the ugly ambitions of men lead to bestial behaviour. Towards the end of the century this imagery of animals and disease reached a climatic finale in Francesco Frugoni's satire *Dog of Diogenes*, where Frugoni describes how Circe lured men into the court, there to abandon liberty and to become as wild beasts in a world where the monkey adores the prince, the parrot repeats him and the world flatters him.

At the same date Rosa was writing his satire *Babylon*, and many of the same images recur. But where the painting amuses with its lively wit and is a reminder of how good an animal painter Rosa was, the satire is marked by a new obsessive quality. It is a denunciation of the corruption of Chigi Rome and Rosa's anger exploded into an apocalyptic vision, of a sickening degradation that filled him with horror. His language is newly violent – 'So many sorts of ordure, horrid vermin of putrefied vice, have found us to be bait to satisfy their desires' – he laments (ll. 307–9), and in a city where all that is noble is overrun by degradation, mallows and nettles overrun the roses (l. 493). He sets this black vision against an unusually lengthy literary self-portrait, culled from Roman satire, in which he laid claim to the virtues of the early Stoic philosophers – sincerity, frugality, silence, poverty, freedom from hope and fear – in passages that read like an anthology of all their best-known sayings. The satire's defensive mix of vanity and pride with disgust and despair suggest how deeply the tribulations of the 1650s had affected him.

The story around the *Fortune*, which was acquired by Carlo de Rossi, remains mysterious. The painting, and *Babylon*, were attacks on Chigi Rome, and yet Mario Chigi generously saved the artist from imprisonment. Rosa had come perilously close to ruining his career. The next few years were to be immensely productive, as he strove to rise again, and to yet greater heights.

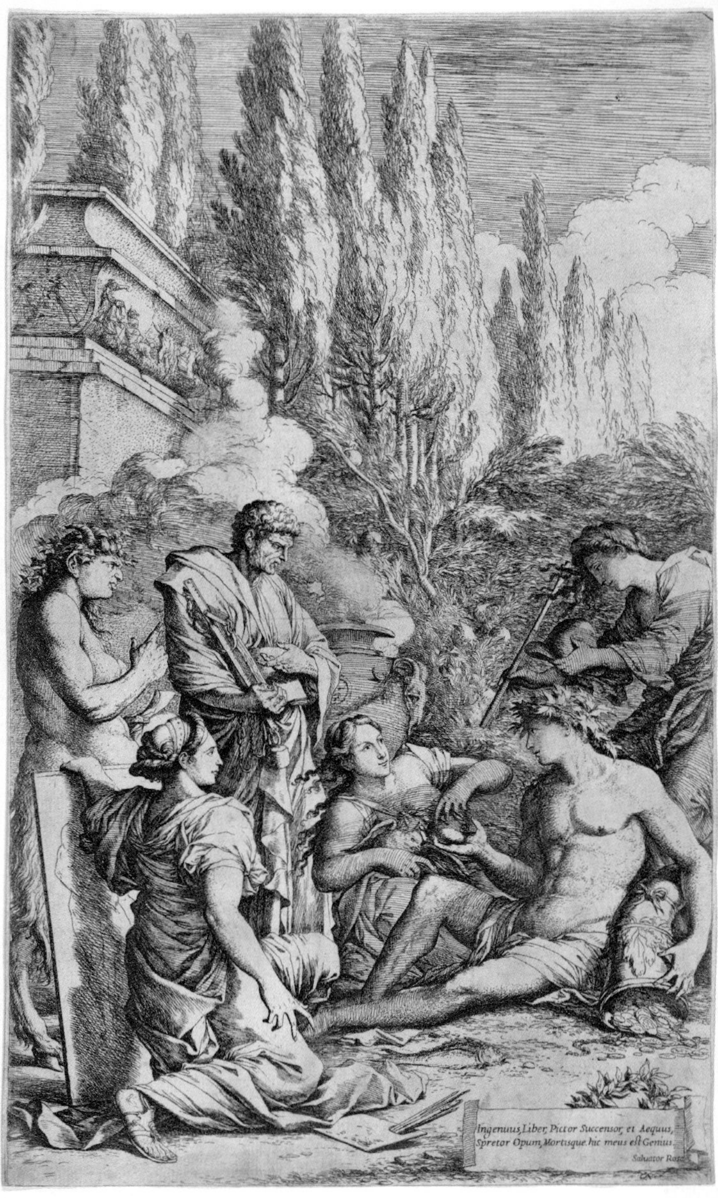

Ingenuus, Liber, Pictor Succensor, et Aequus,
Spretor Opum, Mortisque, hic meus est Genius.
Salvator Rosa

FOUR

Magic, Prophecy and Terror

As the new decade opened Rosa was one of the three or four most celebrated painters in Rome, famous throughout Europe and admired as painter, poet and intellectual. Mattia Preti, describing the state of art in Rome in 1665, dismissed the artists Ciro Ferri and Maratta as derivative, but praised Rosa for his originality.[1] Yet times were harsh. The long-term effects of the plague of 1656 lingered on, and malaria and depopulation were feared. As war with the French threatened, and the public debt grew, the old aristocratic families suffered. 'Everyone here talks of nothing but reforms and savings, with people secluding themselves, tightening up, exercising restraint, and frightened,'[2] Rosa lamented, while his paintings 'trudge along with feet of lead, being sold off little by little. This is the result of the current troubles, together with those of my austere destiny.'[3]

In response Rosa, ever on the search for new sales, displayed a dazzling variety of subjects and styles. Fresh strains of thought and feeling were forming in the 1660s and Rosa, with panache, placed himself at the centre of new intellectual worlds. The scientific community had fallen silent after the condemnation of Galileo in 1633, but now an atmosphere of lively debate was reborn, and Rosa was attracted above all to

49 Salvator Rosa, *The Genius of Salvator Rosa, c.* 1662, etching.

the scientific world that flourished around the flamboyant Jesuit Athanasius Kircher. Kircher's fame was reaching new heights and both his provocative and beautiful writings, such as the lavishly illustrated *Subterranean World* (1665), and his public lectures and magic lantern displays at the Collegio Romano enthralled a European public. Queen Christina, famous convert and passionately interested in alchemy and astrology, formed another centre. She held her own academies, where amateurs, cardinals and dilettantes gathered to enjoy lively philosophical discussion. The scientific world and the creative power of experimentation now fascinated Daniello Bartoli, who no longer wrote on ethics but became the poetic champion of empirical science. His *The Wise Man's Recreation* (1659) conveyed the poetry of the vastness and beauty of the Galilean universe and looked back to the ancient aesthetic of the sublime to find a language that could express its *meraviglia*, or wonder. This new world was underpinned by knowledge of the ancient world and Rome was a city of art and learning, rich in collections of books, paintings and fragments of Greek and Roman antiquities. To the antiquarian Giovan Pietro Bellori, these collections presented 'a portrait of the ancient world', and his researches culminated in his profoundly influential address in 1664, *L'Idea*. Here he elaborated his concept of ideal beauty, an ideal inspired by nature, but nature perfected and enriched by the study of ancient sculptures and of the most perfect Old Master painters, Raphael and Titian.[4]

In this new world of spectacle and drama, Rosa put himself on display, intriguing potential buyers with his bizarre and difficult persona and choosing startling and rare subjects. He echoed the showmanship of Kircher himself, searching for striking images and displaying a gift for topical and popular themes, prodigies, enchantments and prophecies, often am-biguous and puzzling and calculated to provoke pleasurable discussion. At the same time he was intent on appealing, to the point of pedantry, to the learned connoisseur and to take his place in the tradition of great history painting, producing often stiffly classicizing works. The 1660s present the ongoing drama of the public exhibitions, where Rosa electrified his public with a series of grand monumental works, impressive both in their scale and their astonishingly novel iconography. Despite the grandeur of this ambition, he found it difficult to shake off his reputation as an artist who excelled in both small paintings and in landscape. 'He decided fixedly never again to paint small pictures, even if he were offered large sums of money for them,'[5] Giovanni Battista Passeri tells us, and throughout the decade Rosa was ever more dissatisfied and deeply conflicted. At times he seemed to himself like the misanthrope Timon of Athens, a lonely outsider, eccentric and even feared, yet at others he boasted of his studio as the social hub of Rome, frequented by cardinals and diplomats, and he longed for his pictures to be included in the great Roman collections. Above all he craved public success, an aim deeply at odds with his pleasure in painting for a small circle of intellectual friends who enjoyed his rare iconography.

In the slow art market Rosa again turned to printmaking. By 1663 he had completed a series of large etchings, which formed an ambitious publicity campaign intended both to make money and to spread knowledge of his art throughout Europe, and at the same time to attract new commissions. Printmaking, by its nature free of the demands of patrons, allowed the artist an unusual liberty, and Rosa's model was perhaps the intensely personal iconography of Pietro Testa's large prints. At the centre of the series is *The Genius of Salvator Rosa* (illus. 49), a celebration of his genius, that is, his inclination or talent. The print is inscribed and signed on the scroll, 'Sincere, free, fiery painter and equable, despiser of wealth and death, this is my genius.' In a grove of funerary cypress rustling in the wind, with evanescent smoke curling upwards before a lofty tomb, the allegorical figure of the artist reclines in the pose of an ancient river god, with echoes of Michelangelo's Adam. He turns from a cornucopia spilling coins and offers his heart to Sincerity while Liberty places a cap on his head. Before him stand three symbolic figures: Painting, a clear reference to a famous figure in Raphael's *Transfiguration*, who holds a drawing of a male nude; a Satyr, representing satire, who seems to encourage the artist to rise and berate human vice; and a Philosopher, who holds a book and balance, for the philosopher should be composed and tranquil. His images are closely paralleled by those that Rosa used in his literary self-portrait in his satire *Babylon*. Both satire and etching suggest that he had combed through Cesare Ripa's *Iconologia* for easily recognizable imagery and in the etching each of the figures is clearly identified in the inscription. The almost pedantic clarity of his self-celebration is unexpected. In the letters he claimed extravagant invention and often referred to his fiery spirit but there is something plodding about this print, each point hammered home and far removed from the poetry and mystery of Castiglione's *Genius of Castiglione* (c. 1645/8), which perhaps was his initial inspiration. It is a response to the moment, for Rosa here aspires to a genius that will place him

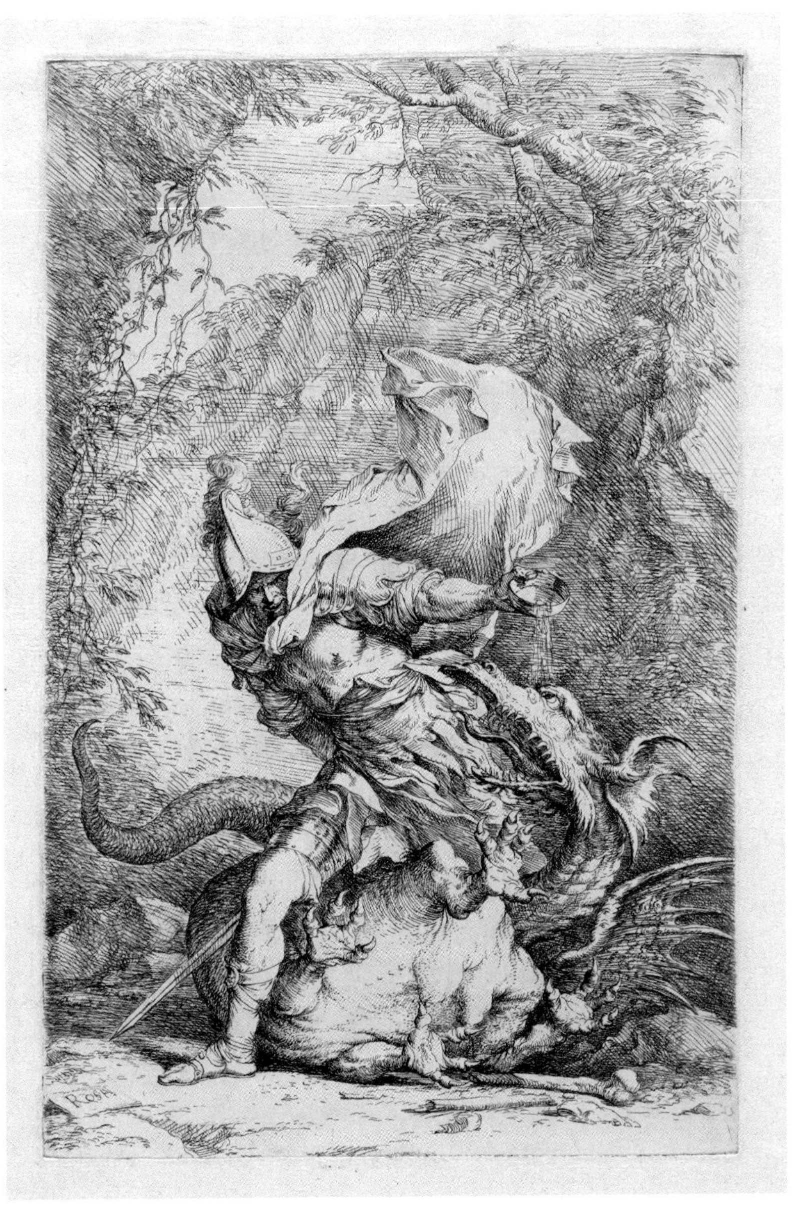

50 Salvator Rosa, *Jason and the Dragon*, c. 1663, etching.

among the classicizing artists of the early 1660s, and squarely at the side of Nicolas Poussin. His etching has a classical clarity of composition, and the references to Raphael, the nude and to Roman art recall Bellori's concept of ideal beauty.

Around this programmatic statement Rosa's etchings presented a showcase of his many-sided talents. He displayed his skill in large, multi-figured compositions, and the vividness of his rendering of the *affetti* (emotions), his *novità* and *invenzione*, and a variety of styles, ranging from stiffly classicizing to baroque fantasy. The prints after his famous paintings of *Democritus* and *Diogenes* look back through his career, and are a reminder of a time when all Rome had discussed their intriguing novelty. The final prints, *Jason and the Dragon* (illus. 50) and *The Rescue of the Infant Oedipus* (1663), are resonant of the new passions of the 1660s, for magic and monsters, and for wild nature. The etchings all bear inscriptions, both stressing their moralizing purpose and the closeness of painting and poetry. Some bear personalized inscriptions to close friends and the dedications suggest the close intellectual circles in which Rosa moved. Rosa wished to attract new commissions and explained to Ricciardi that he had inscribed his etchings '*Salvator Rosa Inv. Pinx. Scul*' (Salvator Rosa composed, painted, engraved) even when no painting existed, in the hope of stimulating demand. His strategy sometimes failed and, he lamented bitterly, 'Not even an invention like the giants sufficed to move anyone's desire for a painting of it.'[6] Generally, however, he was pleased by the success of the prints. By 1662 they were popular in Flanders and Paris, increasing in price 'as well as in veneration'. Most excitingly, Alexander VII valued them, commenting that they 'have poetry and extraordinary eccentricity'.[7]

In the 1660s Rosa was newly attracted to philosopher paintings. His interests had changed; he no longer painted moral philosophers, the Cynics and Stoics, whose witty repudiation of court and city had so appealed to him, but instead focused on the pre-Socratics and natural magicians. In his satire *Envy*, Rosa had declared 'Not only were painters poets, but great philosophers, and spirits inspired in their search for the great secrets of nature' (ll. 655–7). Pythagoras, Thales of Miletus and Archytas were intriguing figures who preserved the secrets of the ancients and towered over the origins of human knowledge. Rosa now saw in these mysterious philosophers parallels to his own creativity. The 'secrets of nature' fascinated the scientists who gathered around Queen Christina, and her librarian, the libertine philosopher Gabriel Naudé, had, in 1625, published his *Apologie pour les grands hommes soupçonnez de magie* (Apology for Wise Men Unjustly Reputed Magicians), in an attempt to peel away the many legends of spells and magic that had blackened the reputations of the early philosophers. In Athanasius Kircher's museum a vast array of magical machines displayed the technical feats and secrets of ancient times. Very many books of secrets were published and Domenico Auda's *Breve compendio di maravigliosi secreti* (A Brief Compendium of Marvellous Spirits; 1655) had by 1663 reached its fifth edition.

Rosa showed two of his philosopher paintings, *Pythagoras Instructing the Fishermen* (illus. 51) and *Pythagoras Emerging from the Underworld* (illus. 52), at the exhibition at San Giovanni Decollato in 1662. This year the exhibition gave him an unusual opportunity. It was organized by the Sacchetti family, who were patrons of Pietro da Cortona, and Cortona's works,

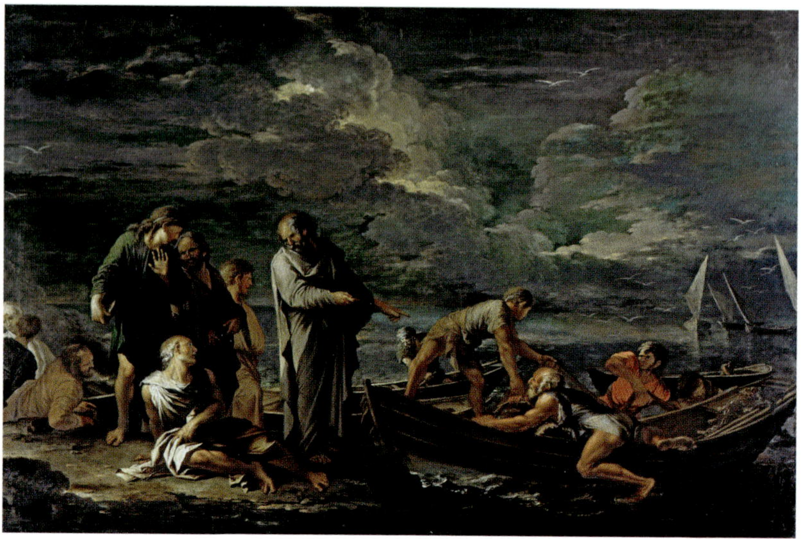

to Rosa's displeasure, dominated. The Sacchetti filled the exhibition with paintings from their own collections and added to these Old Master paintings the flower of the most celebrated galleries in Rome. This was perhaps the first time that Old Master paintings had been shown with contemporary pictures and, for Rosa, it was a challenge. Unusually he displayed five large paintings, though only three were painted specifically for the occasion, and he chose subjects of startling rarity. His two *Pythagoras* paintings are gravely ambitious, and the frieze of sculptural figures and the emphasis on the language of gesture emulate the noble classicism of Raphael's tapestry cartoons and the late figure paintings of Poussin. Rosa, aware of the competition offered by the Old Master paintings displayed that year, claimed his place in the classicist tradition of figure painting, whose ideals Bellori was articulating at the time.

51 Salvator Rosa, *Pythagoras Instructing the Fishermen*, 1662, oil on canvas.

The *Pythagoras* paintings are of rare subjects, and Rosa described them to Ricciardi as 'completely and utterly new . . . Never treated before by anyone'.[8] *Pythagoras Instructing the Fishermen* is taken from Plutarch, who, in the *Moralia*, describes how Pythagoras once bought a netful of fish and then ordered them to be cast off. He was a vegetarian and he saw fish as friends, cruelly captured, and perhaps containing the souls of relatives.[9] His text implies a belief in metempsychosis, or the transmigration of souls. Rosa may also have known Iamblichus' *Life of Pythagoras*, which tells how Pythagoras, on his arrival in Croton, appeared to some fishermen who were drawing from the sea nets heavily laden with fish. The philosopher miraculously guessed the number of fish in their catch and then ordered them to be returned to the sea, a feat accomplished without the death of a single fish. The miracle won him fame

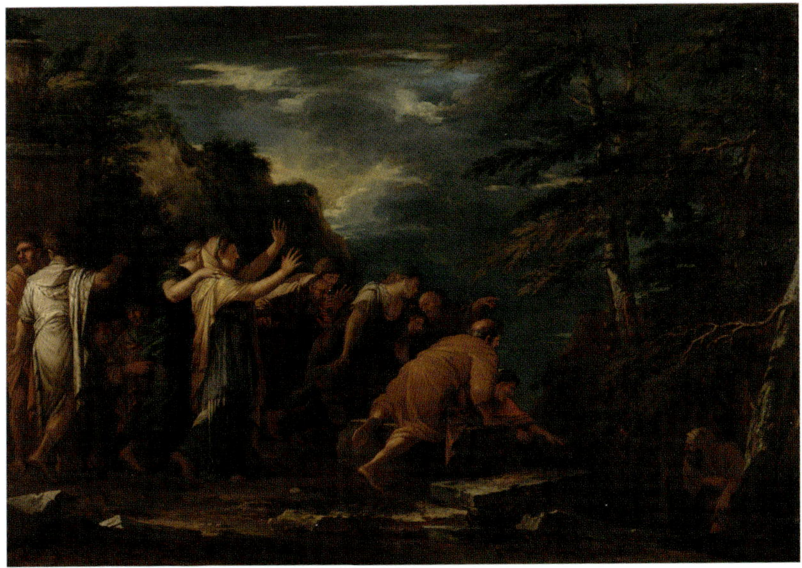

52 Salvator Rosa, *Pythagoras Emerging from the Underworld*, 1662, oil on canvas.

and followers, who rushed to see his godlike countenance. The tale suggests a parallel with the Christian story of the miraculous draught of fish (Luke 5:1–11) and Rosa was aware of this. His composition recalls Raphael's tapestry cartoon of this subject and his Pythagoras, a noble figure in his white robes, seems a precursor of Jesus on the shores of the Sea of Galilee.

Pythagoras Emerging from the Underworld shows the philosopher's supposed descent to Hades, an anecdote told by Diogenes Laërtius. Pythagoras hid below ground for a year, employing his mother to keep him informed about events from above. He then ascended, 'withered and looking like a skeleton . . . And declared he had been down to Hades.' His followers wept and wailed and called him divine. They sent their wives to him for instruction, and they became known as the Pythagorean women. Here he emerges from the cave with a truly wicked grin on his face, in sharp contrast to the grand figure in the companion piece.[10]

Together the paintings show Pythagoras' double reputation as sage and the grandest of all Greek teachers, and as conjuror, magician, cheat and imposter. The subjects were rare but not obscure and both were drawn from well-known and much-discussed anecdotes. The themes were suggested by Queen Christina and closely reflect the interests of the philosophical circles in which she moved, both in the fate of the human soul and metempsychosis and in trickery and imposture as tools of social control.[11] It is tempting to think that the accent on the Pythagorean women in the second painting, a group so evocative of classical sculpture, may suggest an input from the queen herself. Rosa's admirer Paganino Gaudenzio had, in his *De Pythagorea animarum transmigratione* (The Pythagorean Transmigration of Souls; 1640), commented on Pythagoras' belief in abstinence and vegetarianism and his supposition that if the soul moves from body to body then it is dangerous for men to kill animals. What folly, Gaudenzio concludes, is this belief, for we Christians believe that the world has a beginning and an end. Christina herself had commissioned a commentary on the Pythagoreans from Johannes Schaeffer; published in 1664, it was very close in date to Rosa's pictures and lay emphasis on metempsychosis. Gaudenzio had also recounted, in his *Della peregrinazione filosofica* (Philosophical Musings), the well-known story of Pythagoras coming out of the cave, although he concluded that it was probably an invention. However, the idea of a ruse, of claiming divinity by a trick, was often mentioned by libertine philosophers and religion as imposture or deceit is a traditional topos of libertine philosophy. Gabriel Naudé, in his *Apologie*, likened Pythagoras to other great religious tricksters such as Mahomet, who was reputed to have hidden one of his companions down a well and then, through a sarbacane (a small ear trumpet), caused him to yell, 'Mahomet is the great prophet sent by God on earth.'[12] In one painting Pythagoras recalls Jesus on the shores of the Sea of Galilee, but in the second the idea of a feigned resurrection seems to debunk the very concept of resurrection. The unexpected but comprehensible iconography and the provocative parallels would have interested the circles around the queen. In the end she never received them, for she baulked at the high price, and they were acquired by another admirer of philosopher paintings, the Sicilian Don Antonio Ruffo.

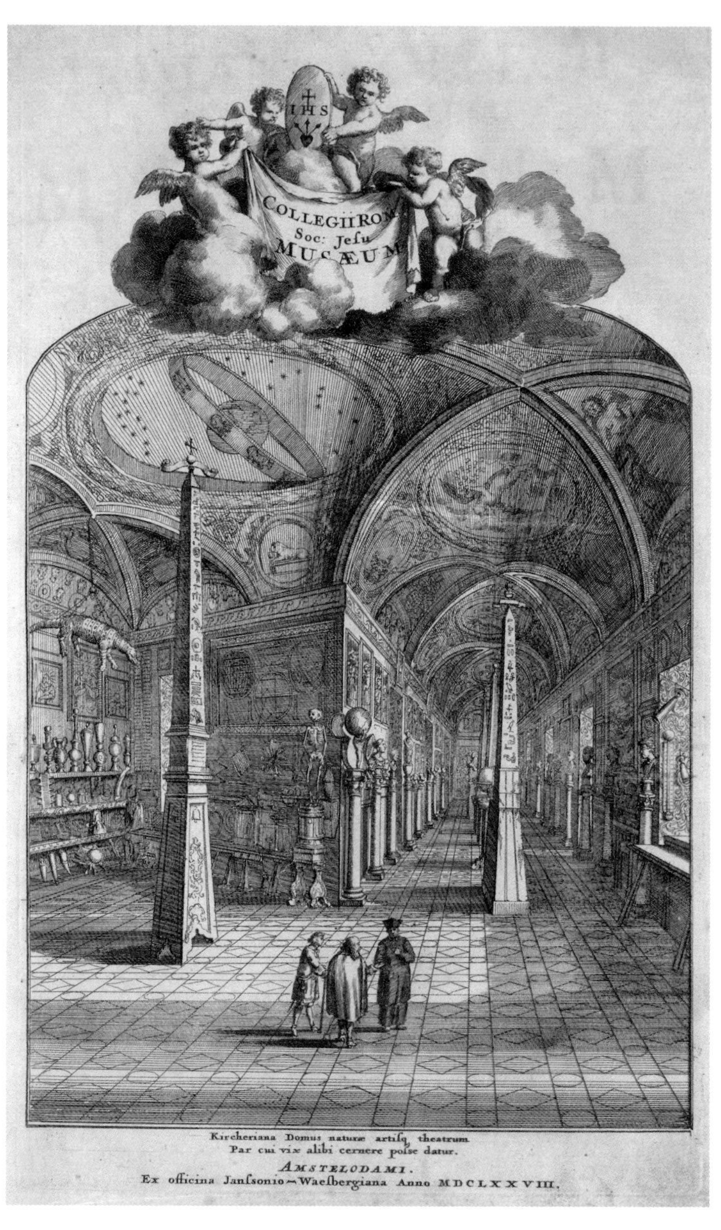

53 Museum of Athanasius Kircher, frontispiece to Georgius de Sepibus and Athanasius Kircher, *Romani collegii societatis Jesu Musaeum celeberrimum* (1678).

Pythagoras' sly grin and his furtive emergence from an eerie underground grotto suggest Kircher's cult of tricks and practical jokes, and from the mid-1660s Rosa drew closer to his world. Kircher's Museum at the Collegio Romano had become one of the essential sites of Rome, drawing visitors from throughout Europe (illus. 53). Here the scientist, a provocative showman and lover of spectacle and *meraviglia*, presented an astonishing 'workshop of Art and Nature', a mix of rare and mysterious animals and natural specimens, Egyptian obelisks, classical and Etruscan art, technological artefacts and magnetic displays. A vast array of magical machines overwhelmed the viewer, including one of 'the dove of Archytas reaching towards a crystalline rotunda and indicating the hours by its flight', another 'a large crystalline globe full of water representing the resurrection of the saviour in the midst of waters'.[13] The 'great magician' entertained and instructed with live presentations that used jokes and sound effects to demonstrate the structure of the universe or the tiny world so miraculously revealed by the microscope. Kircher linked the new science with an older world of magic and alchemy; science became an examination of the marvellous and above all a pleasurable activity. Two of Rosa's philosopher paintings, *Thales Causing the River to Flow on Both Sides of the Lydian Army* (illus. 54) and *Archytas of Tarentum*, strongly evoke this culture. Thales, renowned as the father of philosophy, in a scene very rare in art, divides the Halys river in two so that the Lydian army may pass over. This was a feat so spectacular that it seemed magical. It would have enthralled the scientists around Kircher, who were fascinated by hydrology and by the engineering feats of modern times, such as the hydraulic

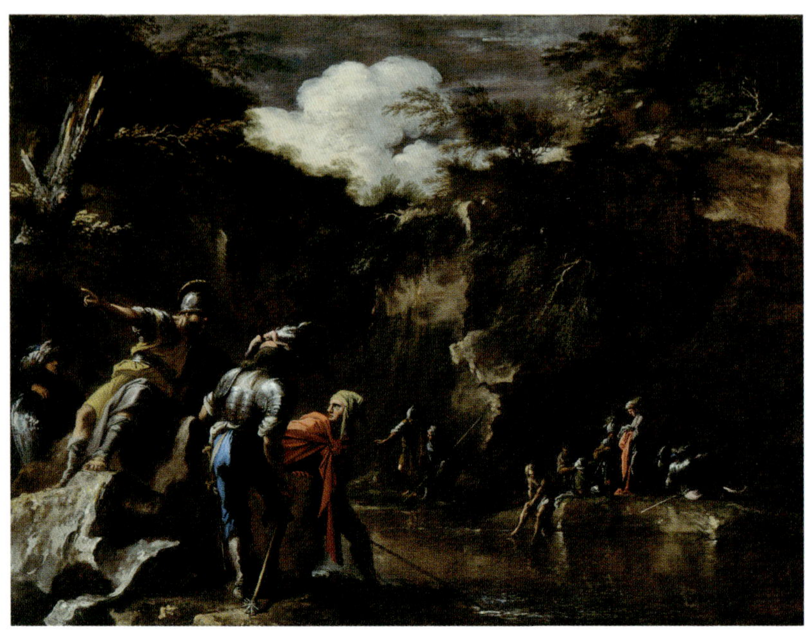

machinery that caused the water to gush through the hollowed rocks of Gian Lorenzo Bernini's *Fountain of the Four Rivers* in the Piazza Navona. Archytas (illus. 55) was famed for his wooden dove, which flew and was the most celebrated automaton of ancient times. In the 1650s and '60s it had reached new heights of celebrity, as part of the baroque culture of special effects that lay at the centre of Kircher's museum, and an international elite enjoyed hearing of such devices. Kircher illustrated a design for a miniature version of the dove, which was displayed in his museum, in his book *Magnes sive, De arte magnetica tripartium* (The Magnet; or, The Art of Magnetics; illus. 56), first published in 1641; Rosa's inspired *Archytas* is a newcomer to seventeenth-century galleries of ragged Cynics and Stoics but, as the historian Anthony Grafton has written,

54 Salvator Rosa, *Thales Causing the River to Flow on Both Sides of the Lydian Army*, c. 1663–4, oil on canvas.

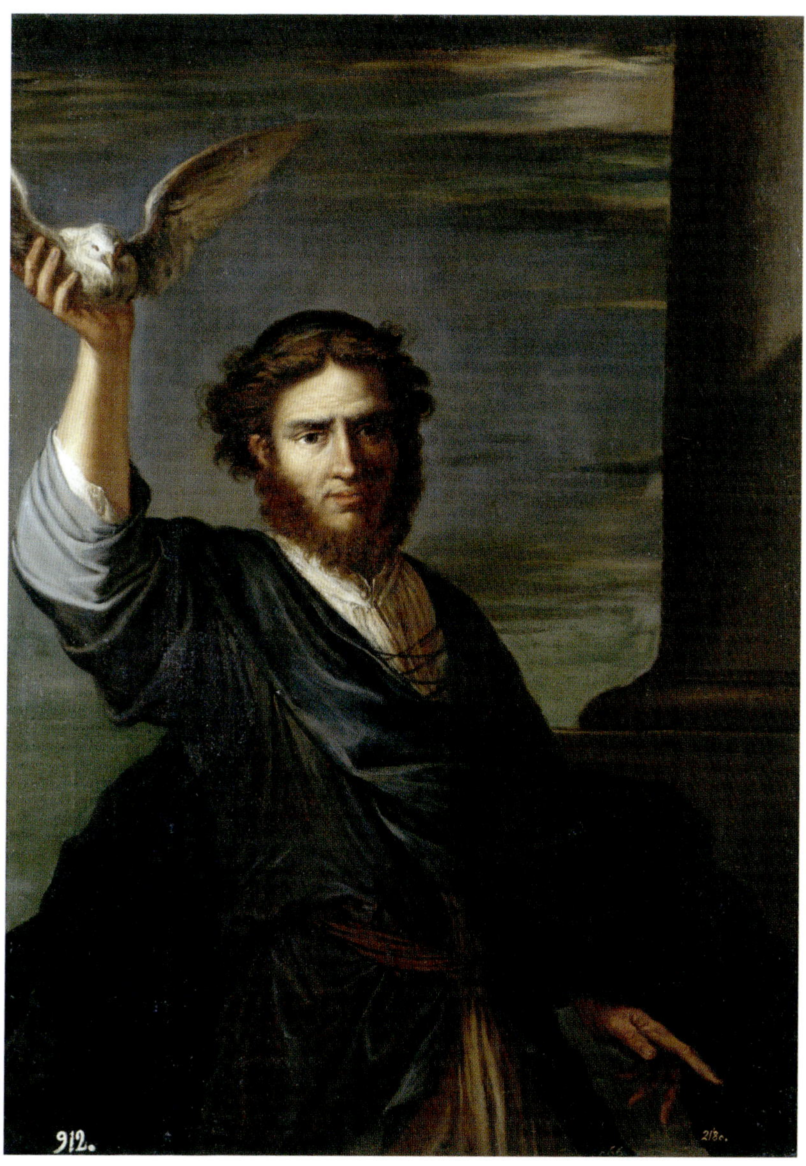

55 Salvator Rosa, *Archytas of Tarentum*, 1668, oil on canvas.

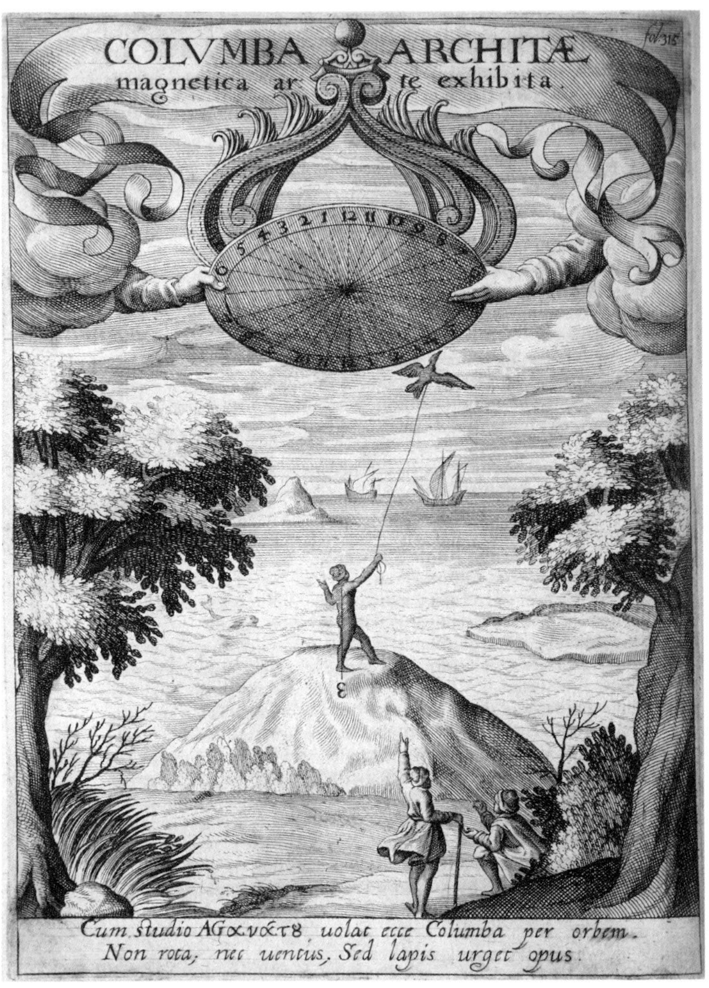

the philosopher 'made a natural hero for moderns dreaming that philosophy could give man power'.[14]

Rosa's later philosopher painting, *The Death of Empedocles* (illus. 57), evokes the strange mysteries of Kircher's *Mundus Subterraneus* (1665), where demons, spirits, dragons and giants

56 Athanasius Kircher, 'Archytas of Tarentum', illustration from *Magnes sive, De arte magnetica tripartium* (1643).

inhabit the whirlpools, caverns, mountains and volcanoes of a mysterious underground world, and modern science and medieval bestiary seem to go hand in hand. Kircher, who perhaps saw himself as the heir to the philosopher Empedocles, had travelled extensively in the seismic zones of southern Italy. He had himself lowered into the crater of Vesuvius and, in the preface to *Subterranean World*, described this perilous descent,

> When I reached the crater, horrible to relate, I saw it all lit up by fire, with an intolerable exhalation of sulphur and burning bitumen. Thunderstruck by the unheard-of spectacle, I believed I was peering into the realm of the dead, and seeing the horrid phantasms of demons, no less. I perceived the groaning and shaking of the dreadful mountain, the inexplicable stench, the dark smoke mixed with globes of fire which the bottom and the sides of the mountain continuously vomited forth from eleven different places, forcing me at times to vomit it out myself.[15]

He illustrated his text with a dramatic scene drawn from his own sketches. In 1669 Mount Etna erupted and in 1670 Giovanni Alfonso Borelli, who had also studied the volcano at first hand, published a scientific account of this, his *Historia et meteorologia incendii Aetnaei anni*, with splendid illustrations of the smoking volcano. Already well known in Rome, Borelli was to become a favourite of Queen Christina in the 1670s and in 1675 he discussed the eruption of Etna at the queen's Accademia Reale. Rosa had died two years earlier, but his painting nonetheless suggests this circle's interest

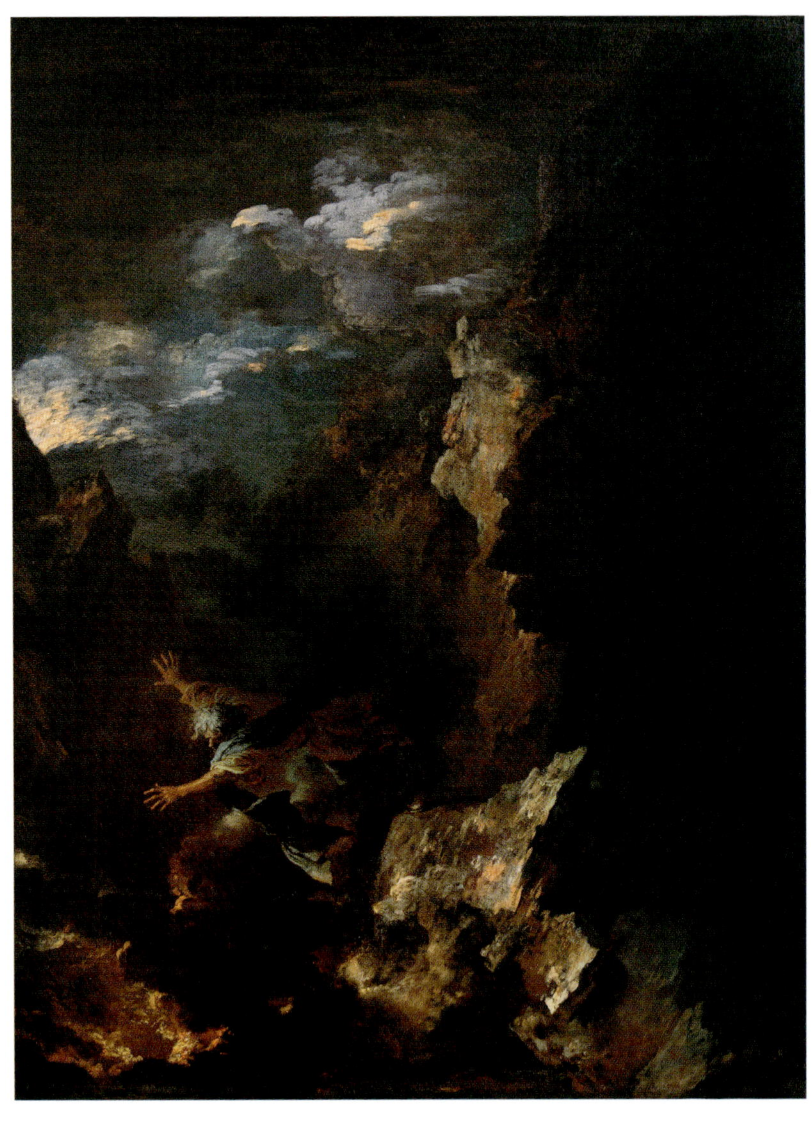

57 Salvator Rosa, *The Death of Empedocles*, 1665–70, oil on canvas.

in volcanology. Queen Christina owned some preparatory drawings for Rosa's painting and it is just possible that the picture post-dates the 1669 eruption and suggests an awareness of Borelli's yet unpublished work. It may even be that Queen Christina herself again suggested the subject.

Empedocles, who evolved the theory of the four elements, was widely admired as a natural philosopher, poet and magician, and grew to believe that he was a god. His puzzling death is described by Laërtius in his *Lives and Opinions of the Eminent Philosophers*: Empedocles, 'to confirm the report that he had

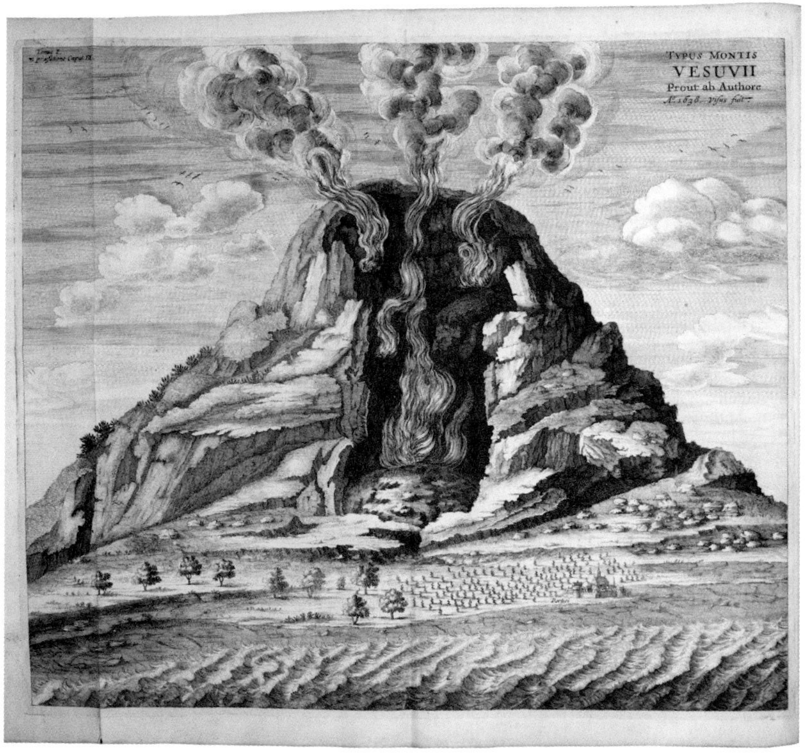

58 Athanasius Kircher, 'Vesuvius', illustration from *E Soc. Jesu Mundus subterraneus, in XII libros digestus* (1664).

become a god' (VIII: 69), plunged into the fiery craters of Mount Etna, reasoning that, when his body vanished, his compatriots would think he had gone to the heavens to join his fellow gods.[16] His golden sandal was caught on a branch and the truth became clear.

The philosopher had been an ambivalent figure from ancient times, both admired and ridiculed. Laërtius said briskly that Empedocles had simply fallen into Etna. Horace, in the *Ars poetica*, included him in an account of the madness of poets, craving fame even in death. His belief in the transmigration of souls and his claim to have been a fish were mercilessly mocked by the Church Father, Tertullian – why not a tasty melon, he quips – and he laughs at his choice of Etna for his grave, where he truly roasted like a fish.[17] In Rosa's time the general tendency was to vindicate him. Gabriel Naudé, in his *Apologie* of 1625, defends Empedocles as he had done Pythagoras, writing that if he had indeed perished in this way it was because he wished to examine too closely the marvels of nature. From here it was a short step to praise him both as a precursor to Pliny, whose fascination with the eruption of Vesuvius caused his death, and as forerunner to the heroic scientists of modern days. The deaths of natural philosophers formed a special category in the art and literature of the seventeenth century. It was widely believed that Aristotle, like Empedocles, had died as a result of his search into the causes of things. Paganino Gaudenzio, in his early essay *Considerazioni accademiche* (1631), had written, 'Pliny, the author of the *Natural History*, who, to observe the flames of Mount Vesuvius, brought about his own death. Aristotle, not finding why the Euripus ebbed and flowed, threw himself in it.'[18]

Gaudenzio often refers to Empedocles in his writings, suggesting the kinds of discussions that Rosa's circles enjoyed. In his *Della peregrinazione filosofica* he condemned the leap into Etna as an act of astounding vanity. In his *Nuovo poema in sonnetti*, however, Gaudenzio addressed three poems to the philosopher, which together convey the ambiguities of his reception. First, Empedocles is a god among the wise men of old, who has sought truth and studied the secrets of nature. Second, he is a poet, worthy heir to Lucretius. But a final poem, entitled *Empedocles, Wishing to be thought a God*, ridicules the philosopher's overweening folly, as Tertullian had done in *De anima*.

Empedocles had much in common with Pythagoras, for 'one dies to be reborn, one descends into the depths in order to ascend.'[19] Both were tricksters, claiming a false divinity, and both were ambiguous: Pythagoras both noble sage and charlatan; Empedocles both fearless scientist and mad poet. So powerful is Rosa's painting that it is hard to see it as negative. He daringly rejects all lingering traces of a classical structure, creating instead an all-over pattern of rocks and flame – shifting, fragmentary and unstable. The jagged edges of the crater seem to tumble down the painting, thrusting towards the spectator, drawing him into the dark centre that is soon to engulf Empedocles. Yet Rosa does prominently show the golden sandal and perhaps there is something comic in the sprawling figure, reminiscent of the earlier Crates' ungainly throwing of his money into the sea, and still in the spirit of Bartoli's amusement at the ridiculous antics of the ancients. With this painting Rosa brilliantly placed his art at the centre of many stimulating discussions in the contemporary Roman world of art and literature.

Empedocles, who so daringly confronted the cosmic violence of the elements, embodied the new aesthetic of the sublime that had begun to attract artists and writers of the 1660s. Longinus' treatise on rhetoric, *On the Sublime* (mid-first century AD), well known since the mid-sixteenth century, was increasingly interesting scholars and *letterati* at the Accademia dei Umoristi.[20] For Longinus the sublime is a rhetorical phenomenon that uplifts the soul and, through its intensity and expression of vehement passion, transports its audience with wonder.[21] He said little about nature in its own right, though, in a famous passage, he suggested that whatever is divine in humankind longs for the infinite. We admire, he writes, not small streams but 'the Nile, the Danube and the Rhine, and even more than these the Ocean'; not the household gods but 'those of the heavens, shrouded in darkness, and the craters of Etna',[22] a catalogue of wonders celebrated at the Umoristi by the poet Alessandro Tassoni. In the 1660s this Longinian sublime and the nature poetry of late antiquity began to chime with the new emotions of awe and wonder before the vastness and mutability of the newly revealed Galilean universe. Daniello Bartoli, a fervent admirer of Galileo, in the 1660s created an eloquent aesthetic of the sublime. Bartoli was drawn to the spectacular and overwhelming and to the rough and irregular, and throughout his writings he presented the natural world as a sequence of theatrical marvels, of shipwrecks, waterfalls, the Nile and Etna, the sun, mountains, immense forests and heroic trees. Very often Bartoli plays on the union of horror and delight, a topos rooted in ancient writing, and for him the cascades of the Nile, 'frightening and delightful', cause 'awe and horror mixed with an equal pleasure'.[23] Marinisti poets abandoned the harmonious landscapes of pastoral poetry and began instead to create thrilling scenes of mountain terror. The poet became a lonely wanderer in the precipitous wildernesses of mountain crags. Claudio Achillini's sonnet to the *Heights of the Apennines* opens with a painterly glimpse of the mountains touching the blue of the sky;[24] and the poet Carlo de Dottori, in his *The Apennines*, described a sense of freedom and rebellion, and of the liberation of the imagination in a rocky landscape where the precipice dropped sheer and the mountainous cliffside reached its naked back to the sun. Rosa's great friend Paolo Falconieri, a collector and intellectual from a noble Florentine family, who moved in Galilean circles, himself wrote evocative descriptions of thick forests, deep shadows and 'wild horrors that please', and was a fervent admirer of Rosa's wild landscapes.[25]

In 1662 Rosa himself travelled in the Apennines, for around fifteen days, and a letter to Ricciardi written on this journey makes it clear that he was in search of extravagant motifs. It is an unusual letter, which has something of the quality of a set piece. Rosa writes with rapture of the variety of landscape and the mixture of 'savage wilderness and domestic scenery, of plains and precipices', evoking that harmony of contrasts that had pleased ancient poets. He longed to share his pleasure with his friend, commenting that the wildness of the Apennines far surpassed that of Verrucola, where Ricciardi often stayed. At Terni Rosa saw the Cascata delle Marmore, the famous waterfall of the Velino river, one of the most celebrated elemental sites in Italy. Virgil had here imagined the Fury Alecto plunging into the infernal regions, where a crashing torrent roars over rocks and a dark forest presses in upon it (*Aeneid,*

VII: 66–71). The waterfall, Rosa wrote, was a 'thing to delight every dissatisfied mind with its savage beauty: the sight of a river dashing down from a mountain half a mile high, hurling its foam up to almost the same height'.[26] Here Rosa articulates an aesthetic close to that of Bartoli and echoes the mountain scenes of the poets. The formula of 'savage beauty', or *orrida bellezza*, had long been associated with anchorite landscapes, but now it is secularized, conveying new emotions of pleasure and delight in the wilderness.[27]

Rosa's landscapes of the 1660s — rivers, deep forests, mountains, caves, the sun — have striking conceptual affinities with the Bartolian sublime. In the circles around Bartoli and Kircher scientists and men of letters felt the wonder of the Galilean universe, and at the same time looked back in awe to the dawn of human knowledge; they were fascinated by ancient mysteries hidden in both the relics of antiquity and strange natural forms. Rosa was closely involved with the erudite antiquarian circles who gathered around Kircher, among them his long-time supporter Cardinal Brancaccio and a newer admirer, Cardinal Jacopo Nini. Kircher, in particular, was interested in what he called 'primeval theology', or *prisca theologia*, and in the thoughts of Egyptian wisemen, Persian magi and Chaldean philosophers. At this date he was interested in the ways in which the Etruscan civilization looked on to the Romans and how together they prophesied Catholic Rome.

Rosa's *Augurers* (illus. 59) places him in this nexus of antiquarian and scientific thought, and displays again his gift for choosing an unexpected but intensely topical subject that appealed to a small erudite circle. The painting shows Etruscan priests studying the will of the gods in the flights of birds. It is a subject very rare in art, though it is possible Rosa knew Giovanni Battista Fontana's print of *Romulus and Remus Resort to Divination to Determine the Site of Their New City* (c. 1575). An interest in Etruria had come to the fore in an enthralling controversy which, in the 1630s, had erupted around the young and erudite nobleman Curzio Inghirami, who was a close friend of Raffaele Maffei (a cousin of Giulio Maffei), and both were friends of Rosa. Inghirami claimed that he had discovered a cache of Etruscan manuscripts in the rugged countryside around Poggio Scornello, near Volterra. He published this astonishing discovery in 1636 in a lavishly illustrated volume, the *Etruscarum antiquitatum fragmenta*. Here, with theatrical flourish, the supposed author, one Prospero of Fiesole, introduced himself as a novice in training, studying to become an augur; 'I, Prospero, was instructed in the art of divination

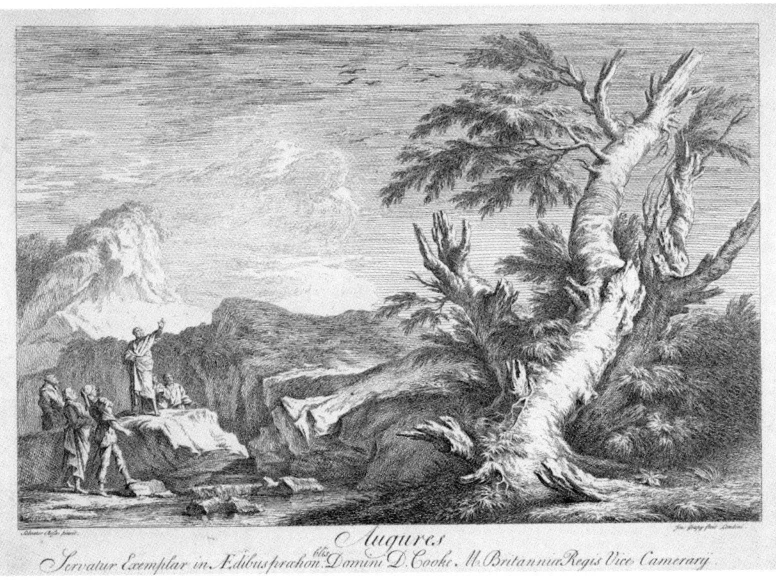

59 Joseph Goupy after Salvator Rosa, *The Augurers*, 1724, etching..

by my father, Veselius, as is the custom among the Etruscans, so that from the records of the nations I came to believe in the coming of the great king, after whom the years shall be numbered.'[28] Inghirami described the stark terrain in which the discovery had been made: a landscape 'uncultivated, precipitous, full of bushes, massive trees, stumps . . . above the documents were undergrowth, the massive roots of oaks, elms and other ancient trees'.[29] It is possible that Rosa went with him to this site, so familiar was he with the intellectual world at Volterra. These discoveries were in fact stunning forgeries and controversy soon raged around them. Paganino Gaudenzio agitated against them; the theologian, librarian and member of the Umoristi Leone Allacci condemned them savagely, while Kircher initially stood carefully to one side. In the 1660s, however, there was a renewal of interest in the manuscripts and Raffaele Maffei tried to interest Kircher in their rehabilitation, despite the fact that they had been, as he sadly put it, 'damned as apocryphal by the whole universe of the *letterati*'.[30] Kircher himself, through the 1660s, was interested in speculative prehistory and in the archaic memories evoked by a wild and prophetic landscape. In 1671 he published *Latium id est* and in the last thirty years of his life worked on his *Iter Etruscum* (now lost), a study of the marvellous landscape and antiquities of Etruria. *Latium* includes an illustration of the Temple of the Tiburtine Sibyl, a site associated with the Sibylline prophecies, which were then interpreted as referring to the coming of Christ.[31] Here the temple is framed by a rock arch, and the dizzying fall of water, brought very close to the spectator, seems to plunge below the earth and, as Kircher commented, it was a 'horrid spectacle, you might call it the jaws of hell'.[32] The passage recalls Rosa's description of the Falls at Terni.

Rosa's *Augurers* stands at the centre of these interests. He perhaps intended his augurer, or prophet, to be Prospero of Fiesole, and in a sense the flamboyant seer Kircher was himself a modern-day Prospero. Rosa's landscape, a setting for the archaic art of augury, is starker than earlier works and he presents a sequence of sublime objects: a mountain, a setting sun and, above all, a heroic tree. The heroic tree, inspiring both reverence and wonder, is an image deeply rooted in Latin literature and was resonant in the seventeenth century. Pliny the Elder, in his *Natural History*, describes a holm oak on the Vatican Hill, older than the city, which bore a bronze tablet with Etruscan letters. He tells of a grove of celebrated trees near Tusculum, one a vast holm oak, which sent out 'what look like ten separate trees of remarkable size, and forming a world of itself'.[33] The trees were cultic objects, whose rustling branches and roots that stretched down to the Underworld united heaven and earth and had oracular power. Daniello Bartoli's prose is often redolent of this nature poetry of late antiquity and he devoted many passages to the grandeur of trees. To him the primeval forest evoked the first days of philosophy. Bartoli exclaimed in wonder at a Plinian *'selva nell'aria'*, or forest in the air, where

> Those great trunks of wild and vigorous trees, and their vast branches, every one of which is itself an entire and large tree, all together they make a forest in the air springing from one trunk; and of these same trunks those that are most ancient, hollowed out and

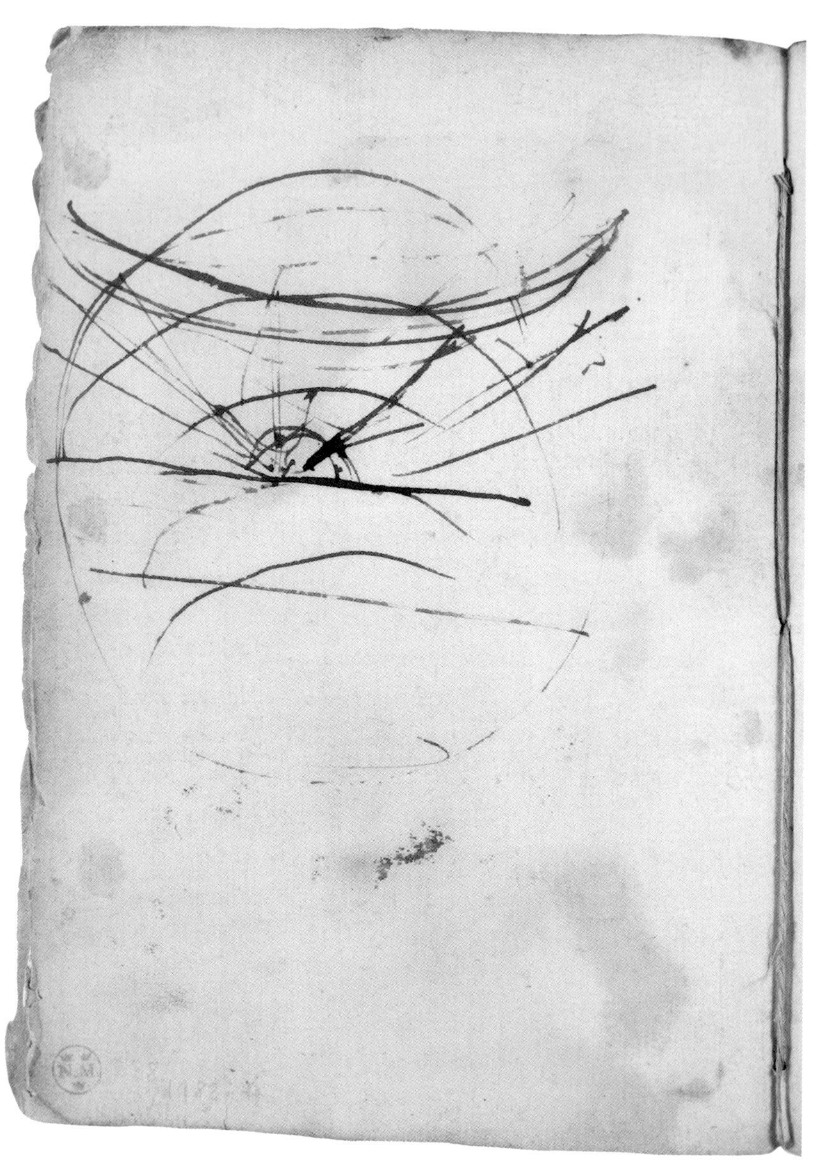

60 Claude Lorrain, *The Sun*, n.d., late sketchbook drawing, pencil and brown ink on paper.

cavernous; and those shadows over shadows of trees over trees and finally that eternal silence, that holy wilderness, that majestic horror.[34]

His is an image of infinity, of the mind seeking to soar beyond the boundaries by which we are circumscribed. In a similar spirit Rosa created an awe-inspiring mythic landscape, a primordial world in which the aged tree evokes the mysteries of ancient religious practice.

As we have seen, the success of Rosa's small landscapes irritated the artist. However, his interest in a Kircherian landscape – of torrents, rocky mountains and underground caves – won him fame in the literary and scientific world. Carlo de Rossi owned *The Augurers* and Valerio Chimentelli, who in the 1640s had written *Report on Peace*, now praised the sublime landscapes of the 1660s. Probably around 1668, he addressed a lengthy poem to 'Sig. Salvator Rosa . . . *pittore ingegnosiss.o*' in praise of a 'sun, most beautifully painted'. 'What greater marvel, o painter, do you offer to the sight?' he exclaims, and he praises Rosa's incredible effects of light, of the rays of the sun, so magically represented that the viewer wonders more at the painted than the real sun. It is not clear whether Chimentelli is describing a painting of the sun alone or of effects of sunlight in a land- or seascape, but his description has echoes of the discoveries of Galileo, and Rosa united the new science with the ancient aesthetic of the sublime.[35] Rosa had not painted such Claudean effects since Florence, but perhaps this work was now done in rivalry with the French artist, who, in an astonishing drawing, had filled a whole page with an image of the rising sun (illus. 60).[36]

In the same years, Rosa was creating landscapes of horror, populated by monsters, dragons, snakes and spectres, scenes that recalled Kircher's subterranean world where fire-breathing dragons lurked. He became increasingly fascinated by the dark side of Ovid, where Jason drips poison onto the head of a dragon or the scaly body of Glaucus erupts menacingly from the waves. In the dark, almost monochrome landscape of *Cadmus and the Dragon* the shrieking boy, wrapped in the monster's coils, is a homage to the *Laocoön Group*, deepening the terror that resonates through the landscape.

These Ovidian paintings were popular, attracting a public enthralled by a Kircherian world of magic and spells. In his grander exhibition pieces, too, Rosa, ever in search of a rare iconography, pleased the connoisseurs with learned subjects. In 1663, at the exhibition of San Giovanni Decollato, Rosa displayed his *Oath of Catiline* (illus. 61), a dark painting of the inverse sublimity of crime, redolent of seventeenth-century Senecan theatre and plays of crime and blood, guilt and fear. Rosa may have known Longinus' praise for Aeschylus' description, in the play *Seven Against Thebes*, of a moment when seven warrior captains brush their hands with bullock's blood and swear an oath 'by War and Havoc and Terror, the lover of blood'.[37] Emanuele Tesauro likened the oath of Catiline to a thunderbolt, a metaphor common in the rhetoric of the sublime.[38] The subject was taken from Sallust's *Catiline's War*, a riveting historical account of the Catilinarian conspiracy of 63 BC, and Sallust commented that he had been drawn to this subject by 'the novelty of the crime and the danger arising from it'.[39]

The infamous Catiline was an ambivalent figure, of great vigour of mind and body but profligate and depraved.

His insatiable mind 'craved the excessive, the incredible, the impossible',[40] and yet guilt weighed upon him and his countenance was pale, his eyes ghastly. His Rome was a cesspit of corruption, of avarice, luxury, greed and excessive licence; Catiline played on this degradation to ferment discontent among a gang of rebels, 'guilty of many shameful crimes'. One night in June, in 'an out of the way room' in his palace, Catiline roused their rebellious spirits, and they swore to overthrow the Roman Republic. 'At the end', it was rumoured, he 'passed around bowls of human blood mixed with wine', binding the

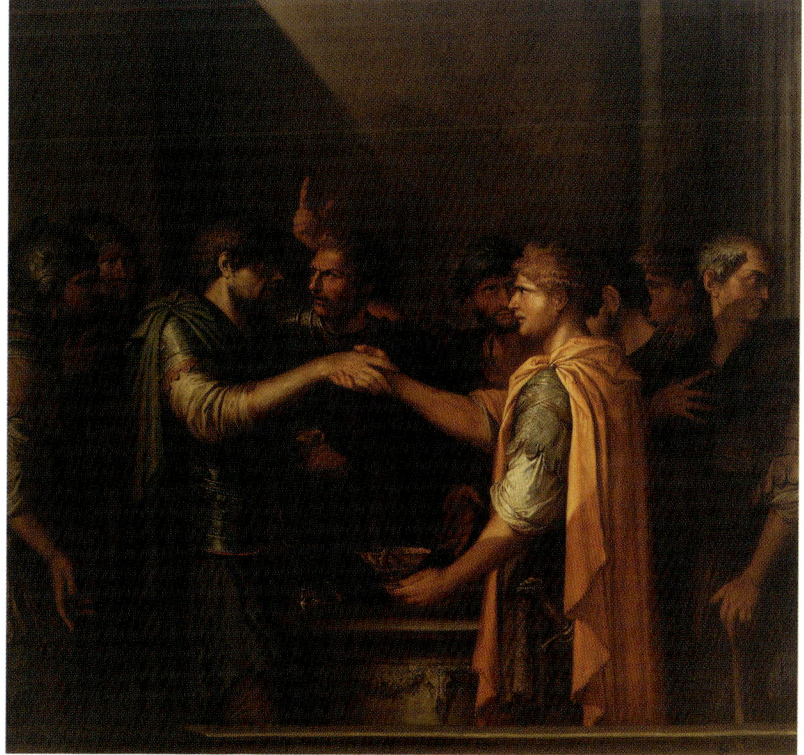

61 Salvator Rosa, *The Oath of Catiline*, 1663, oil on canvas.

participants in an oath, 'each sharing the guilty knowledge of so dreadful a deed'.[41]

The painting was well received, and Rosa boasted to Ricciardi that 'the experts, in particular, were extraordinarily pleased with it'.[42] It is a scholarly work and Rosa gave it an aura of antiquity by a composition that suggests a Roman bas-relief, and the inclusion of a marble altar and drinking bowl. The sharp profile heads and postures were studied from ancient sources, such as sarcophagi and coins. Rosa was clearly aiming to compete with the great Roman history paintings of Poussin and Pietro da Cortona. Above all the painting astonished with its vividness and its new and disturbing psychological intensity. At this date there was a renewed interest in the portrayal of the *affetti* and the Neapolitan Giovanni Battista della Porta's *Della fisionomia dell'uomo* enjoyed a new popularity; Rosa may have appreciated della Porta's description of staring eyes, 'pallid, dry and bloodshot', which convey 'malevolence, iniquity, diabolical malignity, and obtuseness'.[43] The poet and scientist Lorenzo Magalotti wrote an ekphrastic description of the painting, intending, as Paolo Vendramin had earlier done with his essay on the *Prometheus*, to spread Rosa's fame. Like Vendramin he praised Rosa's *enargeia*, or overwhelming lifelikeness. We do not need to know the story, he writes, to appreciate the danger and fear aroused by the intensity of the eyes and the faces.[44] The painting is among the most theatrical of Rosa's works. We seem to look through a window, or across a balustrade, at a moment of high drama, the figures posed on a stage as the evil ceremony is about to unfold. Blood drips from a conspirator's arms and Catiline, about to drink, clasps his hand above the ancient altar at the painting's centre. Light falls from above and the featureless room has the murky atmosphere of a prison or dungeon, a hiding place 'where one conceals treasures, hides criminals, to undertake some great enterprise in secret'.[45] Light falls most strongly on the faces of the principal players, while the play of light and dark enhances the sense of evil mystery. At the left two soldiers, perhaps the military veterans of Sulla, look on in fear; on the right a figure turns away in disdain. He, separate and a little older, may perhaps be intended as Cicero, since the head resembles Roman portrait busts of the statesman. Cicero would not have been present during the conspiratorial meeting, but here he represents the future: he exposed the plot, and Catiline was forced to flee Rome. The five conspirators were executed. The painting would have appealed to a seventeenth-century viewer's liking for the bloodthirsty horrors of contemporary theatre, for such works as Carlo de Dottori's *Aristodemo*. And perhaps it contained a warning to contemporary Rome, whose corruptions and excesses, so apocalyptically denounced in the satire *Babylon*, might raise again the fearful spectre of Catiline. Sallust's account was well-known and became the model for seventeenth-century accounts and plays of rebellion.

The exhibition of 1668 offered Rosa the perfect opportunity to create a yet more sensational work and again to astonish all Rome with all the melodrama and horror of seventeenth-century theatre. The circumstances were particularly challenging for the exhibition was organized by five members of the Rospigliosi family, the brother and nephews of Pope Clement IX. They decided to show only Old Master paintings from the most distinguished collections of Rome, including that of Queen Christina, whose paintings alone, Rosa commented, 'would be enough to frighten the Devil himself'. They intended to exclude contemporary painters but 'that spurred me even more to enter myself to take part in it'. To Rosa it was a wonderful occasion to compete with the great artists of the past and he somehow arranged to be included, declaring with jubilation that he 'alone of all living painters would be allowed to measure myself against all the dead'.[46]

At this prestigious exhibition Rosa presented two very large and grand canvases, *Saul and the Witch of Endor* (illus. 62) and *St George and the Dragon.* The Witch of Endor's story is told in the first book of Samuel (28:3–25). Saul had banished spirits and wizards from his land but, on the eve of his battle with David and the Philistines, he felt fear so intense that he asked a medium at Endor to raise the prophet Samuel from the dead to tell him what to do. She, afraid of punishment, reluctantly complied and told Saul she saw 'gods ascending out of the earth . . . An old man cometh up; and he is covered with a mantle.' Saul recognized the dead prophet, and bowed to the ground before him, but Samuel was angry at the disturbance and ruthlessly declared that the Lord had truly abandoned the disobedient king and that tomorrow 'shall thou and thy sons be with me'. On the following day Saul's sons were killed in battle and Saul himself committed suicide.

The subject is rare in art but in the sixteenth century, the era of the witchcraft trials, it became established in northern prints, especially in German illustrated Bibles, and the woman of Endor became a witch, old and scraggy and practising her magic rituals among an elaborate paraphernalia of objects and techniques.[47] Rosa's witch, an old crone with hanging breasts, waving flaming branches, follows this northern tradition and

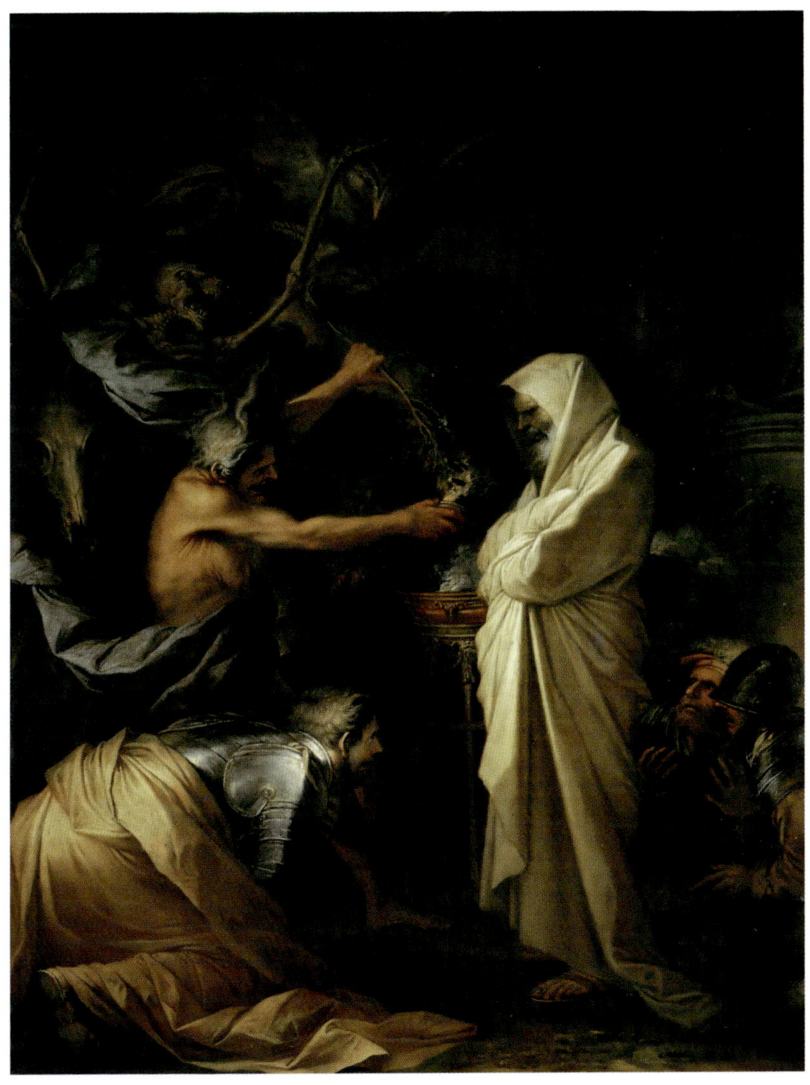

62 Salvator Rosa, *Saul and the Witch of Endor*, c. 1668, oil on canvas.

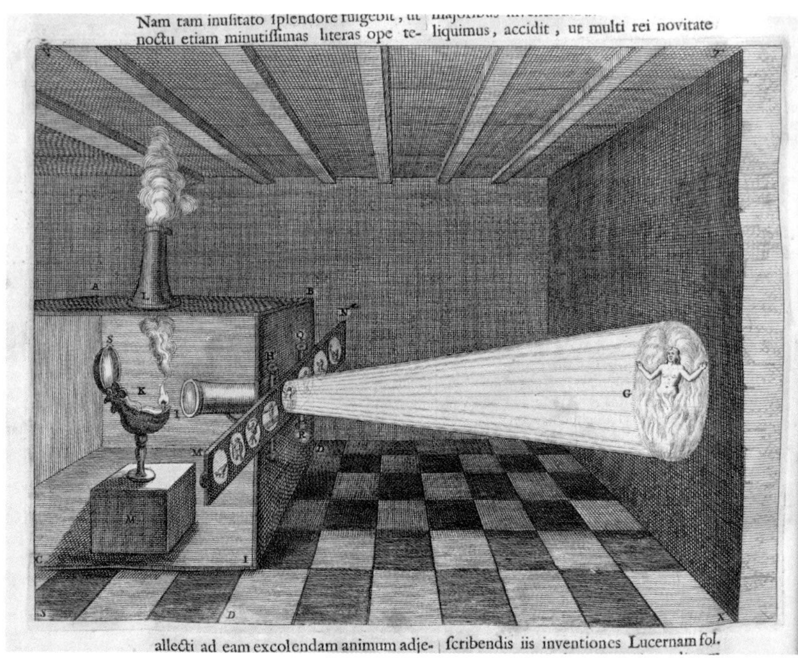

the graveyard atmosphere creates a setting for necromancy.
The subject was common in the theatre and Rosa enjoyed the
baroque culture of special effects. He would have seen Kircher's
magic lantern shows at the Collegio Romano, where the scientist showed devils dancing in the light and dark and a soul
burning in the flames of purgatory (illus. 63). In *Ars magna lucis
et umbrae* (1646) Kircher described the fearsome spectres and
flights of ghostly figures that could be summoned up from
the darkness.[48] The sudden and shocking entrance of a ghost
on stage had been a feature of ancient drama and Longinus
mentions the heroic image of the shade of Achilles appearing
above his tomb to those who sail away, a scene vividly depicted
by Simonides.[49] Ghosts and spectres were also plentiful in

63 Athanasius Kircher, 'Magic lantern and burning soul', illustration from
Ars magna lucis et umbrae (1671).

seventeenth-century theatre. Necromancers, stage magicians, fireworks and devils abound in the *commedia dell'arte*. They occur frequently in Renaissance drama, inspired by the ghosts and horrors of Senecan tragedy, which exerted so strong an influence throughout this period. In Seneca's tragedies seers conjure up the ghosts of the Underworld and his set pieces describe an infernal landscape of sinister and supernatural elements, such as snakes and furies, which create a vivid and gloomy setting for the most hideous crimes. Scenographers enjoyed developing techniques to represent ghosts on stage. They discussed the use of fireworks and flames, and special effects of light to create luminous white drapery, such as Rosa's Samuel wears, for the 'sheeted dead'. Nicola Sabbatini, in his *Pratica di fabricar scene e machine ne' teatri* (1638), devoted a whole chapter to spectres on stage.

Rosa's sensational painting evokes all the melodrama and Senecan horror of seventeenth-century theatre. It is a moving work, conveying the terror of this ambiguous and tragic story of frailty and fear and of the desperate night-time journey of the disguised king and his two companions. Saul is utterly humiliated before the medium he had himself banished and, hoping for good news, he falls in anguish before Samuel as the prophet delivers the shattering sentence of death. Rosa chose to depict the highest moment of dramatic action, as Samuel speaks, and all around – in the graveyard setting, in guilty night – swirl macabre and terrifying skeletons and prophetic spirits and birds conjured up from the Underworld. Billowing smoke and flames create the immediacy of a vision, of a world caught in the light for a moment but poised to fade into darkness. The biblical scene is presented as an astonishing theatrical spectacle. The overwhelming scale of the canvas and the strong verticals draw the viewer in, and the figures around Samuel seem themselves like spectators. The prostrate Saul leads the gaze to the stark confrontation of the witch and the prophet Samuel, where the two worlds of 1660s Rome seem to meet. Samuel is a statuesque classically draped figure, accompanied by the antiquarian detail of smoking altar and tripod; but the frenzied old crone, with her swirling drapery, and the macabre skeletons, come from another world, one of prophecies, necromancy and magic. Here, for the last time, Rosa looked back to the skeletons and spectres of Filippo Napoletano's small hellish scenes and yet created a grandiose witchcraft scene with tragic weight.

Rosa's painting would, like his *Democritus*, have stimulated debate and controversy, for the nature of this ghostly apparition had been long and fervently discussed. Hamlet's famous line 'art thou a spirit of health, or goblin damned' suggests the contemporary fascination with the ambiguities of ghosts and spectres and the ghost of Samuel roused intense controversy. This focused on the question of whether a necromancer could have power over the soul of a prophet; was Samuel really conjured up or was his appearance a diabolic illusion? Some believed that, without doubt, the spirit of Samuel had returned. Others thought that it was a demon or the Devil in person, and others still that his appearance was a trick of the pythoness, who had the gifts of a ventriloquist. The debate fascinated scholars in Rosa's immediate circle. In Rosa's Tuscan years Paganino Gaudenzio had argued that the story of Samuel's prophecy after death was clear evidence for the immortality of the soul.[50] The Church Fathers had written copiously on the subject and the Greek scholar and Vatican librarian Leone Allacci, a member of the Umoristi, had discussed, at immense length, the opposing views of Origen and Eustathius of Antioch. He finally came down on the side of Eustathius, who believed the spirit was a trick of the Devil.[51] Rosa's frenzied witch, surrounded by demons, is surely evil; Baldinucci had no doubt and described the pythoness tricking the king with the false appearance of Samuel.[52] Like his *Pythagoras* pictures, and his *Empedocles*, the painting explored the ambiguities of trickery and imposture and its splendid visual drama would have stimulated pleasurable discussion, perhaps reawakening debates that were losing their fire.

Rosa had enjoyed immense success at the exhibition of 1668, and it was probably on this occasion that his supporters noisily rallied support for him, declaring 'Have you seen the Titian, Correggio, Paolo Veronese, Parmigianino, Carracci, Domenichino, Guido Reni and Signor Salvatore? In fact Signor Salvator is not afraid of Titian, of Guido, of Guercino, and of anybody else.'[53] But melancholy and illness coloured his final years. The glory he craved forever eluded him; increasingly he felt like an outsider, angry, alone and unrecognized. His letters are full of nostalgia for the happy days he had spent with Ricciardi, 'all those walks, all those jokes',[54] but his mood gradually darkened. He was anxious to put on a brave face, to avoid the fate of Pier Francesco Mola, whose livelihood had been ruined by both illness and rumours of illness, but months would pass without his painting. This may explain his extraordinarily rude behaviour to Don Antonio Ruffo, a major patron from the early 1660s, to whom he declared that he could not paint for him, 'because I don't paint in order to make money but for my own satisfaction, I must allow myself to be carried away by the impulses of enthusiasm and take up the paint-brushes only when I feel myself rapt.'[55] Rosa here, anxious to delay his commission, presented himself as an intriguing personality and spoke the language of Platonic inspiration. Plato had described the poet as 'winged and holy . . . Unable to compose until he is possessed and out of his mind, and his reason is no longer in him.'[56] In the end, however, Ruffo did get his painting, the *Archytas of Tarentum.* But Rosa, depressed and ill, remained in darkness. In July 1672 he wrote a touching letter to Ricciardi, a blend of nostalgia for the happy days at his friend's family villa at Strozzavolpe and gallant attempts at humour over his health. All is well, he declares, except for his teeth, his eyes and his head; his mind too is well, except that 'I'm daily transfixed by a hatred of everything, and with such a wild disgust of mankind that, if it were not for fear of my life, I'd have surrendered myself to the most Timon-like lamentations.' He was kept in Rome by his work on a painting but in future resolved to 'banish even that little tinge of ambition that plagues my mind, recognizing such things to be vain in comparison to the eternity of the centuries that devour everything'.[57] In the harsh winter of 1670 the artist feared death. He could not work, and his

> canvases are turned against the wall and the colours are all dried up . . . The passion that once blazed within me has entirely vanished . . . on the sunny days I walk alone like a maniac, visiting all the solitary spots of this city. And during the bad weather I remain locked up in the house, pacing about like a lunatic, reading some

book or listening to the conversation of others, rather than talking myself.[58]

Two works, a satire, *Tirreno*, and a painting, *Job and His Comforters*, together convey the bitterness and isolation of these final years and both are, in a sense, portraits of the artist as angry outsider, protesting, as he had done from the start, at a world upside down. *Tirreno* is now printed as the seventh satire but its date is not entirely clear. It is just possible that it was written before *Babylon* but there is no doubt that Rosa intended it to act as the sad epilogue to the book of satires that he was then planning. The satire has no contemporary target but is an autobiographical monologue, confessional and yet proud, as the artist looks back in old age at his high calling as a poet. At the opening Tirreno, who is the artist himself, stands alone on the Pincio, his face full of pain, his brow downcast, and bitterly denounces the folly and danger of writing satire. Tirreno's sad figure became the image of all Rosa's sense of isolation in these final years. Through an overwhelming catalogue of the vices of a corrupt age he wove long passages of literary self-portraiture, renouncing with breathtaking vanity his role as satirist. The wicked have laughed at his sayings and now he will leave it to God to castigate vice. Rosa echoed many passages from his earlier satires, creating a sense of closure and for the last time claiming his place in the fiery tradition of Juvenal and Lucilius (ll. 192–4). An array of maxims adorns his claim to be the proud heir to the Stoics and Cynics of antiquity; he is 'pure from his feet to his flowing locks' (l. 448); 'no particle of hope touches his heart; all desire for gold has been forever vanquished' (ll. 447–9). With overwhelming and

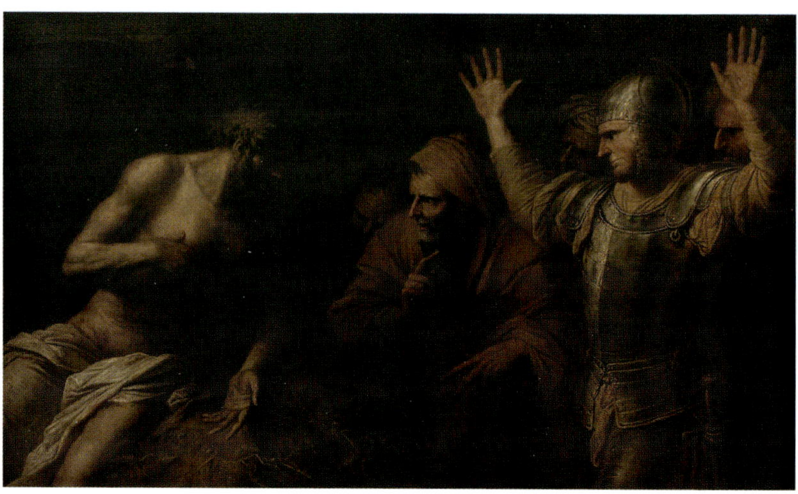

extraordinary confidence, Rosa set himself on high, as though on a pedestal; he is the poet who has brought truth to poetry and has created a model for Italian satire (ll. 600–602). Oddly, the last nineteen lines repeat directly the last lines of his earlier satire *Poetry*. This, too, had ended with a grandiose farewell, as he declared, 'Music, Poetry, Painting, I shall be silent' (l. 861). Perhaps now, with this last repetition, and thinking of publication, he intended to draw the satires together as one work, finally concluded, with both melancholy and pride.

To Rosa Old Testament prophets and monastic saints had long represented, side by side with the philosophers of antiquity, a world of ancient virtue in sharp contrast to contemporary Rome; St Francis of Assisi became to Rosa 'Zeno of Assisi' (l. 394). In *Tirreno*, more prominently than in earlier satires and alongside the harshest ancient philosophers, biblical prophets of doom and the anchorite saints of early Christianity

64 Salvator Rosa, *Job and His Comforters*, late 1660s, oil on canvas.

berate humankind. 'I yelled like Jonah and I screamed like Joel' (l. 121), Rosa exclaimed, and many times he longed for a landscape of retreat, of mountainous ridges and the caves and deserts of the hermits, 'hell to the evil, but paradise to the just' (l. 393).

These subjects are paralleled in his paintings and from the late 1660s come dramatic and savage paintings of anchorite saints, among them *St Onuphrius* and *St Paul the Hermit*, ecstatic, penitent, in turbulent visionary landscapes. In the same years Rosa painted a compelling *Job and His Comforters* (illus. 64), close in feeling to the harsh and angry mood of *Tirreno*. The painting was in Rosa's studio at the time of his death and perhaps Rosa identified with this outsider, a just man, brought low and understood by few. In an earlier ode Job had prompted a bitter meditation on Rosa's favourite theme; why the unworthy prosper while the virtuous suffer adversity. God, the poet exclaims, must be a tyrant.[59]

The biblical story is a blend of lament, proverb and dialogue. God allowed Satan to test the obedience of the virtuous Job, who, stripped of riches and fame and smitten with sore boils, sits alone, in grief, on a mound of earth. In the painting Job, the winged devil above his head, confronts his three friends, in exotic eastern turbans, who have come to comfort him. These comforters blame him, accuse him and treat him with contempt and sarcasm. Job, combative and defiant, asserts his individuality, and exclaims 'Miserable comforters are ye all' and, as a kind of Hebrew Diogenes, 'I cannot find one wise man among you' (Job 16:2). Rosa, unusually, chose the moment when Elihu, who had been listening to this discourse, his wrath kindled, rose from the onlookers to berate them all. Young, fiery and armour-clad, he challenged the wisdom of the aged and established. The heads of the three friends create a rising arc behind him, evoking the crescendo of accusation that had filled their speeches, while, just glimpsed in the background, lurks one of the listeners. *Job* is a grave, austere painting, dark and almost monochrome, where each head and eloquent gesture, which pattern the surface, play a precise role. Job, questing, and touching his chest in wonder that he above all should so suffer, seems to reach out in some kind of acceptance to the isolated Elihu. Job, both rebel and martyr, had the provocative ambiguity that often attracted Rosa.

Amid this gloomy resignation Rosa won new fame in Rome. He wrote to Ricciardi that the Florentine Signor Filippo Nerli, treasurer of the pope, had 'determined to vanquish my cruel destiny' and had commissioned an altarpiece for his new chapel in the church of San of Giovanni dei Fiorentini. The task was urgent, since the painting was needed in time for the celebrations of the canonization of Maddalena dei Pazzi. Rosa, jubilant, exclaimed, 'Ring out the bells! At last, after thirty years of living in Rome, with a never-ending hope filled with continuous lamentations — both to the heavens and mankind — I have now, finally, succeeded in offering the public one of my altarpieces.'[60] This altarpiece, the *Martyrdom of Sts Cosmas and Damian* (illus. 65), showed saints particularly venerated in Florence. They were early Christian martyrs, twin brothers and physicians, who endured a long martyrdom, remaining miraculously unscathed by water, fire, stones and arrows, before finally being beheaded. Here they kneel on the pyre but the flames have bounced away from them, injuring and creating panic among the torturers. A triumphant Rosa

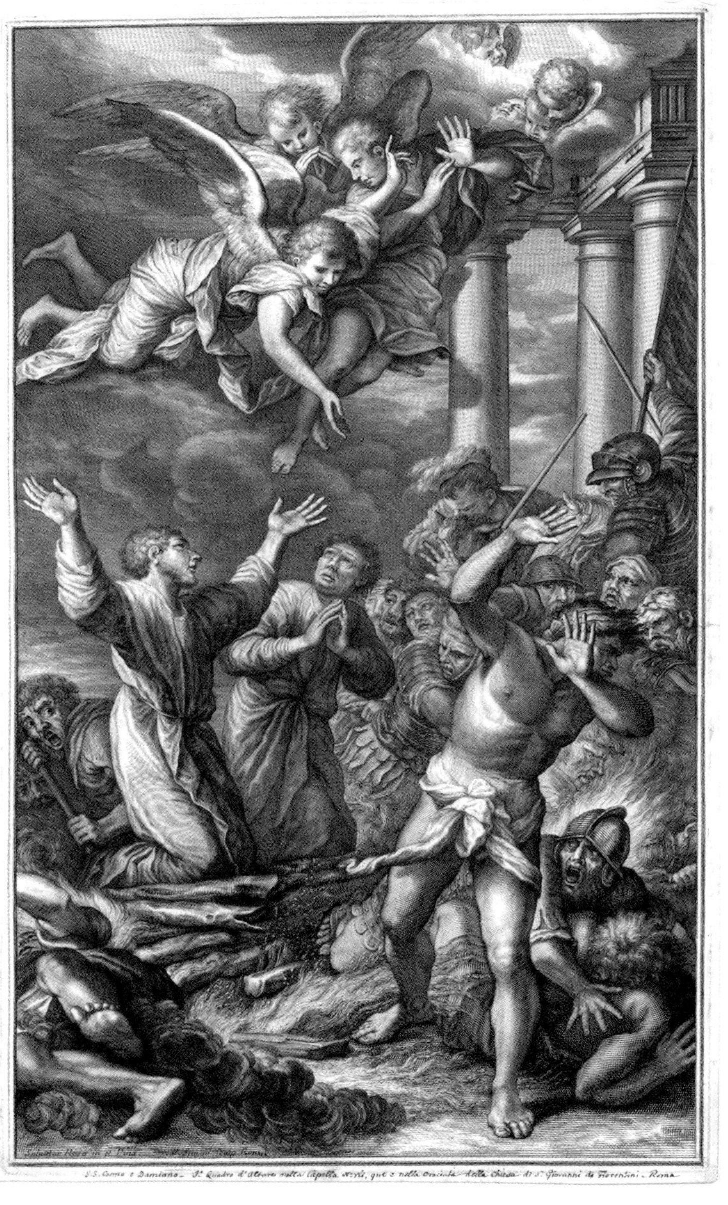

65 Pierre Simon after Salvator Rosa, *Martyrdom of Sts Cosmas and Damian,*
c. 1669–74, engraving.

sought to showcase his undervalued talent as figure painter and the fleeing nude in the foreground, with complex stance and gestures, is a clear reference to Michelangelo's Christ in the Sistine Chapel's *Last Judgement*. For the setting, with its ruined temple, Rosa looked back to the most heroic and Roman of his earlier works, *The Battle of Cimon*, and created an agitated, dramatic group of tumbling, crawling soldiers, their expressions violent and panic-stricken. *The Battle of Cimon* had been praised for the diversity of its actions and perhaps Rosa looked again at the many drawings he had made for it, and which he had kept. He has elided time, and the angels, present before the beheading, are very close to the new martyrs, poised to welcome them to glory. The dramatic chiaroscuro, and the closeness of the heavenly sphere to the earth, suggest memories of Caravaggio's altarpieces, *The Seven Acts of Mercy* and the *Martyrdom of St Matthew*.

Nerli was pleased with the altarpiece and sent Rosa the exorbitant sum of 1,000 scudi in a bag of crimson satin on a silver tray. There ensued a ritual of courtesy. Rosa sent 200 doble back, only to have them returned. In the end Rosa kept the money but sent the Marchese two more paintings. Baldinucci thought that Rosa had achieved his aim and at last impressed connoisseurs with his skill in figure painting.[61] But negative comments swiftly circulated in Rome and Passeri was embarrassed by Rosa's boasting. Rosa, he relates, accosted him on one of his evening walks on the Trinità dei Monti and threw out a hubristic challenge to Michelangelo; 'O come Michelangelo and do a better nude than I have done there, if you know how to; now I have halted the world, and shown them how much I am worth.'[62]

The *Martyrdom of Sts Cosmas and Damian* was Rosa's last moment of triumph and on 18 February 1673 he wrote to Ricciardi, begging for one last visit. It seems that Ricciardi did come, but Rosa died a little over a month later.[63] The priest Francesco Baldovini, who had been a good friend of Rosa's, sent to Baldinucci a touchingly tragi-comic account of Rosa's last days.[64] Passeri added some details, describing how Rosa remained true to himself, angrily and self-pityingly crying out against his fate – 'This is what happens to people who want to paint and write for the sake of eternity'[65] – and impatiently resisting exhortations to Stoicism with the sharp response: 'Make another Salvator, because this one wants to moan.' He endured a series of repulsive remedies and a terrible fear of damnation, somewhat reassured when Baldovini commented that God could not send to Hell a man named Salvatore. The priests of Rome discussed his faith – was he about to die as a schismatic, a Huguenot, a Calvinist or a Lutheran – but Baldovini roundly defended him as a good Catholic. His friends encouraged him to marry Lucrezia, which, slightly chillingly, he did to save his soul. He died, aged 57, on 17 March 1673.

Epilogue

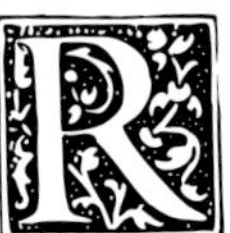

osa's early biographers, who admired and were fascinated by him, nonetheless struggled with the paradox that a painter supreme in landscape, battle and capricci should so provocatively insist that his gifts lay in figure and history painting. Baldinucci praised his landscapes, poetically describing his naturalistic effects of light as it shone on water or rocky cliffs, or gleamed in the shadows of caves and ravines.[1] He enjoyed the poetry and invention of his figure paintings, so redolent of the many 'good books' that Rosa had read. Generous with his praise, for Rosa's rendering of emotion, for his colour and freshness of touch, his bizzarie, Baldinucci nonetheless concluded that the artist could not compete with the great Italian history painters of the past or present. In his rejection of landscape painting, he lamented, Rosa had betrayed his true destiny.[2] Passeri adds to this judgement a long and detailed list of the painful criticisms of Rosa's drawing, colour and drapery that connoisseurs levelled against his figure paintings.[3]

But above all, from these biographers' pages steps forth the artist himself: witty, boastful, and admired for the vivacity and sweetness of his conversation, a charismatic actor whose dark Neapolitan presence fascinated all of those around him.

To this vivid picture the Neapolitan Bernardo De Dominici, in the early eighteenth century, added the extravagant legend that Rosa had taken part in the fisherman Masaniello's revolt in Naples in 1647, describing how Rosa had joined many young Neapolitan painters in Aniello Falcone's glamorous Company of Death.[4] Rosa, satirist and harsh critic of society, now became a fiery freedom fighter. His art, and increasingly his legend, were immensely influential throughout Europe, particularly in England, where his impact was felt not only in painting, but in gardening, art theory, taste and literature.

Rosa's prints were well known in his lifetime, and the *Figurine*, often copied and imitated, played a special part in the growth of his fame. Italian artists Andrea Locatelli, Giovanni Paolo Panini and Giovanni Battista Tiepolo mined them as a source for lively staffage. Throughout Europe there spread a taste for rocky landscapes with small figures, often soldiers, such as those by the German Joachim Franz Beich, and the French Claude-Joseph Vernet. In England landscapes with banditti were fashionable, and, increasingly, Rosa's name was used to invoke a wild alpine scenery; Horace Walpole, when crossing the Alps in 1739, famously exclaimed 'Precipices, mountains, torrents, wolves, rumblings – Salvator Rosa'. The landscapes of Claude Lorrain and Rosa epitomize the contrast between the beautiful and the sublime a contrast immortalized in James Thompson's celebrated lines in *The Castle of Indolence* (1748): 'Whate'er Lorrain light touched with softening hue/ Or savage Rosa dashed, or learned Poussin drew.' After Edmund Burke's publication in 1757 of *A Philosophical Enquiry into the Origins of Our Ideas of the Sublime and the Beautiful*, Rosa's name became synonymous with the sublime, and his savage grandeur was constantly evoked by leading writers on the picturesque, such as William Gilpin and Sir Uvedale Price.

In the 1770s knowledge of Rosa deepened. His satires were often republished in the last thirty years of the eighteenth century, and his figure paintings began to compete in fame with the landscapes. Many celebrated figure paintings were in England, among them the *Marius on the Ruins of Carthage*, and the *Democritus* and *Diogenes*, which were at Foots Cray Place in Kent. Two became the highpoints of the eighteenth-century tour of Norfolk. *Belisarius* was the showpiece of the Belisarius chamber at Raynham Hall, and the most prized possession of Lord Townshend. At nearby Houghton Hall – the property of Lord Townshend's rival, Robert Walpole – hung the *Prodigal Son*. Other works came to be known through engravings, and John Boydell's 1739 catalogue of engravings after important paintings housed in England lists prints after 35 works attributed to Rosa. He would have been thrilled by the praise they won, for to English critics, honing their new skills in artistic debates, these were magnificent history paintings. To Horace Walpole the expression of the *Belisarius* was 'great as Poussins', while the *Prodigal Son* transcended the 'foul and burlesque naturalism of Caravaggio'.[5] In France Diderot echoed this praise, declaring that 'To do Belisarius again after those sublime men [Van Dyck and Rosa] is to write Iphigénie again after Racine, Mahomet after Voltaire.'[6]

John Mortimer, dubbed 'this Salvator of Sussex', idolized Rosa above all other artists; he made a speciality of banditti pictures and monsters, but his *Belisarius* (1772) and his *Caius Marius on the Ruins of Carthage* (1774) are reinterpretations of Rosa's eponymous works. At this date Rosa was often compared to Shakespeare, and his power to convey passionate, often disturbing emotion in part inspired the sensationally macabre works of a small group of history painters, among them Mortimer, James Barry, Henry Fuseli and Joseph Wright. The growing fame of Rosa's history paintings was confirmed by the inclusion of important works in exhibitions at the British Institution, a private society formed in 1805 to display the works of living and dead artists in a gallery in Pall Mall. The exhibition of 1817 included eight works attributed to Rosa, some of which were engraved for the catalogue. The many reviews convey how celebrated Rosa was as a figure painter, the peer of the great Italian classical artists.[7] In Rome in 1819 Shelley exclaimed that only Raphael, Guido Reni and Salvator Rosa could sustain comparison with antiquity. In 1859 the Fortuna was exhibited at the British Institution; it had already been displayed at the Bristol Institution in 1827.

In 1824 Lady Morgan published *The Life and Times of Salvator Rosa* in London and Paris, in both English and French, and a new era of Rosa's fame began. She popularized two legends: that Rosa had fought with Masaniello, and that he had, in his youth, wandered in the mountains of the Abruzzi, where he had been captured and sojourned with picturesque outlaws, or banditti. Rosa, far from the vices and crimes of the city, became the embodiment of a free, untrammelled genius, identified with his own banditti, and the personification of sublime natural scenery. A 'bold and solitary student', this 'Dante of painting' was inspired by 'earthquakes and volcanic flames, in an atmosphere of lightning, and the perpetual crash of falling thunderbolts'.[8] And yet Lady Morgan's defence of Rosa as a history painter is eloquent and impassioned; she writes of the nobility of *Job* and of the *Prodigal Son*, of the 'splendid horrors' of the *Regulus*, and the 'magic eloquence' and powerful emotion of the *Catiline*.[9] In these revolutionary years the *Battle of Cimon* and *Saul and the Witch of Endor*, two great and expressive works by Rosa that were sent to France in the seventeenth century, attracted fresh admiration. Poets, novelists, dramatists and musicians of the Romantic era in England, Germany and France, where Théophile Gautier was his leading admirer, drew vivid material from the myths and legends that surrounded the artist. After the publication of Lady Morgan's biography, painters were inspired by colourful anecdotes from Rosa's life, often showing his stay among the bandits, as in Adrien Guignet's *Salvator Rosa among the Bandits*, well known through prints.

With John Ruskin, however, Rosa's reputation fell. Ruskin condemned the falseness and conventionalism of Rosa's landscapes, which he believed were created by a painter who had never looked closely at the natural world. To him Rosa was a lost spirit, fierce and morose, who saw only that which was gross and terrible. 'The misery of the earth is a marvel to him: he cannot leave off gazing at it. The religion of the earth is a horror to him. He gnashes his teeth at it, mocks and gibes at it.'[10] With that, Rosa grandly exited the stage, to return with the rebirth of scholarly interest in his works in the 1960s.

CHRONOLOGY

1615	Salvator Rosa is born in Arenella on 21 July 1615, the second child of Vitantonio De Rosa and Giulia Greco. His brother, Giuseppe, was born on 14 July 1613, and his sister, Giovanna, on 20 November 1617. Shortly afterwards the family moves to Naples
1621	Vitantonio De Rosa dies; Rosa's mother remarries in 1625
1626	Giuseppe Calasanzio, the founder of the Piarist order, opens his first school in Naples. Rosa, then eleven, and his brother probably attend a second Piarist school near their home
1630	On 1 August Rosa is accepted into the Piarist order as a trainee or novice priest, with the name of Salvator di San Pietro
1631	On 20 March Rosa abandons the Piarist order
1632	Rosa's grandfather, Vito Greco, is named as his legal guardian. His sister, Giovanna, marries Francesco Fracanzano; Rosa, a witness at the wedding, describes himself as a painter with a studio in the Spirito Santo
1634	Rosa signs and dates a *Martyrdom of St Lawrence*. Giovanni Lanfranco, present in Naples at the time, buys Rosa's painting of *Hagar and the Angel*
1635	In the early 1630s Rosa works in the studios of José de Ribera and Aniello Falcone. He goes to Rome for the first time, encouraged by Girolamo Mercuri (1606–1682), then *maestro di casa* of Cardinal Brancaccio. He was probably resident in the cardinal's household
1637	The first mention of Rosa in the Roman parish registers records him in a house in the parish of Sta Maria in Via.

He probably makes a return visit to Naples between 1635
and 1637

1637   By September 1637 Rosa has returned to Naples, and he
         remains there at least until October 1638. He probably
         spent a second period in the studio of Falcone. Niccolò
         Simonelli (c. 1611–1671) commissions a painting,
         probably *Tityus*

1638   In March Rosa's *Tityus* is exhibited at the annual exhibition
         at the Pantheon in Rome, accompanied by a poem by
         Simonelli praising Rosa as the *Demosthenes of Painting*.
         On 13 October Rosa receives payment for a *Martyrdom
         of St Lucy*, already delivered to the Jesuit priest Flaminio
         Magnati. In the autumn Rosa accompanies Cardinal
         Brancaccio to Viterbo, where Brancaccio takes possession
         of his new see. He paints the *Incredulity of St Thomas* for the
         high altar of the Chiesa dell'Orazione e Morte. He forms
         a close friendship with Antonio Abati, who stimulates his
         interest in satire

1639   Rosa is back in Rome, where he takes part in the Carnival,
         making his debut as an actor and introducing to Rome the
         Neapolitan mask of Pascariello

1640   Rosa is recorded in a house in the parish of Santa
         Maria del Popolo, with Girolamo Mercuri and a servant,
         Giuseppe. In the summer he paints three landscapes
         for the Duke of Modena: *Erminia Carving Tancred's Name
         on a Tree*, *View of a Bay* and *Landscape with Lake and Herds*.
         In the autumn, Rosa arrives in Florence. He is court
         painter to Giovan Carlo de' Medici, who pays him a
         monthly stipend of 8 scudi and rents him a house near
         the Croce del Trebbio, where the Academia dei Percossi
         meets. He meets Lucrezia Paolina, who becomes his
         lifelong partner

1641   In August Rosa and Lucrezia's first son, Rosalvo, is born.
         In the spring Rosa is in Livorno, studying the Medici
         galleys in the harbour. He goes to Pisa to attend a theatrical
         performance. On 19 September the Marchese Filippo
         Niccolini (1586–1666), *maestro di casa* of Giovan Carlo, pays

Rosa for two large landscapes and two half-length figures.
The latter may be identified as *Portrait of a Philosopher* and
Poetry. He begins to write poetry and reads a satire to a
literary audience in Siena

1642   On 24 September Rosa is paid for the *Battle between Turks
and Christians*, commissioned by Ferdinando II to celebrate
the birth of his heir, Cosimo

1645   Rosa collaborates with Pietro da Cortona on the
decoration of the mezzanine of the Muletta, Palazzo
Pitti. He frescoes four lunettes with scenes from the life
of Moses. In July Rosa goes to Bologna to look at some
paintings for Giovan Carlo. He makes a pilgrimage to La
Verna and Camaldoli with Belmonte Belmonti. Giovan
Carlo travels to Rome for his investiture as a cardinal,
and Rosa accompanies him

1646   From 1646–8 Rosa spends most of his time in Volterra,
or in the Maffei villas of Monterufoli and Barbaiano. In
1646 he also stays at a villa in the Val d'Arno, belonging
to Raffaele Landini, a dilettante painter and copyist of
Rosa's works. Probably around this date he paints his *Scene
of Witchraft*, which is displayed by Carlo de' Rossi in his
Roman house

1647   In the summer the Neapolitan fisherman Masaniello leads
a revolt against the Spanish rulers of Naples. Rosa writes
his satire *War*, which mentions this event

1648   In January Rosa receives his last payment from Giovan
Carlo de' Medici. He visits Venice with Giovanni Battista
Ricciardi, either in this year or the next

1649   Rosa moves back to Rome in February, and takes a
house in the Strada Felice, near the Trinità dei Monti.
He perhaps makes a grand tour on his return journey,
visiting Parma and Mantua. One account suggests that he
visited Venice with Velasquez, which could have been on
a separate journey after his arrival in Rome. A daughter
is born, and she is sent to an orphanage

1650   Rosa spends much of the summer at the Maffei Villa
Monterufoli with Giovanni Battista Ricciardi. He paints

	the *Democritus in Meditation* and writes a satire, probably *Painting*. He declines an invitation from the Austrian court
1651	Rosa exhibits the *Democritus in Meditation* on the feast of St Joseph, at the Pantheon, where it 'roused Rome to such a degree that you wouldn't believe it'. A son is born and sent to the orphanage
1652	The display of the pendant *Diogenes Throwing Away His Bowl* at the Pantheon follows this success. Cardinal Neri Corsini requests a picture to be sent as a gift to Louis XIV; Rosa paints the *Battle of Cimon*. Cardinal Omodei commissions an *Assumption* for the Milanese church of Santa Maria della Vittoria, and, probably at the same time, a *St Paul the Hermit*, paired with a *St John the Baptist* by Pier Francesco Mola and Gaspard Dughet. In April Rosa declines an invitation to her court from Queen Christina of Sweden. Rosa sells the *Democritus* and the *Diogenes* to Nicolò Sagredo, the Venetian ambassador. In October Lucrezia gives birth to a boy, 'the spitting image of Salvator Rosa', who is immediately dispatched to the orphanage. Between 1652 and 1653 Rosa works on his fifth satire, *Envy*
1653	In May Lucrezia gives birth to a girl, again sent to the orphanage
1654	Rosa reads his satire, *Envy*, at the Umoristi
1655	In October Lucrezia gives birth to a child of unspecified sex, who is then sent to the orphanage. Bartolomeo Corsini pays for a *Scene of Witchcraft*
1656	Rosa paints the *Baptism of Christ* and *St John the Baptist Pointing out Christ* for the Florentine Guadagni family. Fearing attacks on his private life from the Inquisition, he sends Lucrezia and his son Rosalvo to Naples. Rosalvo and Rosa's brother die in the plague that ravaged Naples; Lucrezia returns to Rome. He publishes a series of etchings, the *Figurine*, of warriors and genre figures. In the second half of the 1650s Rosa works on five altarpieces for Carlo de Rossi, intended for the Chapel of the Crucifix in the church of Santa Maria in Montesanto, in the Piazza del Popolo

1657	On 18 May Rosa's son Augusto is born
1659	Sometime before February Rosa goes to Pisa, accompanied by Marcantonio Cesti, to stay with Ricciardi. He rashly exhibits a virulent satirical painting, *Fortune*, at an exhibition at San Giovanni Decollato
1661	In April Rosa reports that he has turned down an invitation, first extended in 1659, to work as court artist in Innsbruck. Two pictures are sent to the king of Denmark. In May 1661 he leaves Rome for Tuscany, and, after a stay in Pisa and Florence, he spends July–November with Ricciardi at his villa at Strozzavolpe, where he works on a series of large etchings. He visits Venice. He is commissioned to paint a *Madonna del Suffragio* for the church of San Giovanno Decollato alle Case Rotte in Milan
1662	Rosa reports on the successful reception of the *Madonna del Suffraggio* in Milan. He travels in the Apennine Mountains, in search of extravagant motifs, and in a famous letter celebrates the wildness of the landscape. The Sacchetti family organize a lavish exhibition at San Giovanni Decollato, mingling Old Masters with contemporary works. Rosa shows five pictures, including *Pythagoras Instructing the Fishermen*, *Pythagoras Emerging from the Underworld* and *Jeremiah Released from the Dungeon*
1663	In search of a new market, Rosa completes a series of large-scale etchings. His *Conspiracy of Catiline* is exhibited at San Giovanni Decollato
1664	A new patron, the Sicilian Don Antonio Ruffo, acquires the two *Pythagoras* paintings
1665	Rosa declines an invitation from Louis XIV of France to the French court
1666	On 1 April Rosa, ill and depressed, writes a now famous letter to Don Antonio Ruffo declaring that will take up his brushes 'only when I feel myself rapt'. He exhibits, at San Giovanni Decollato, *Pan Appearing to Pindar*, *Chiron and Achilles* and *Aethra Showing Theseus the Tokens of His Father*
1668	The exhibition at San Giovanni Decollato is the last in which Rosa takes part, and the papal family, the

Rospigliosi, put on an unusually rich display of Old Master paintings. Rosa shows a *St George* and *Saul and the Witch of Endor*. Rosa is recorded in a new house, on the via Gregoriana

1669   To Rosa's great joy he finally wins a commission from Signore Filippo Nerli for an altarpiece, the *Martyrdom of Sts Cosmas and Damian*, for the Roman church of San Giovanni dei Fiorentini

1670   Rosa is often ill and depressed, his canvases turned against the wall. He perhaps writes his satire *Tirreno*, in which he looks back at his high calling as a poet, and intends to use it as the sad epilogue to a collection of his satires. He paints an altarpiece, *San Torpé*, for the cathedral at Pisa

1673   On 18 February he begs his friend Giovanni Battista Ricciardi for one last visit. Ricciardi comes; Rosa marries Lucrezia; on 17 March he dies

REFERENCES

Introduction

1 Filippo Baldinucci, *Notizie de'professori del disegno da Cimabue in qua*, ed. F. Ranalli (Florence, 1847), vol. v, p. 450.
2 G. B. Passeri, 'Vita di Salvator Rosa, pittore, e poeta', in *Die Künstler-biographien von Giovanni Battista Passeri*, ed. J. Hess (Leipzig and Vienna, 1934), p. 398.
3 Alexandra Hoare, *The Letters of Salvator Rosa: An Italian Transcription, English Translation and Critical Edition* (London, 2018), vol. 1, p. 439, letter dated (?) February 1656.
4 Ibid., p. 657, letter dated 7 February 1665.
5 Baldinucci, *Notizie*, vol. v, pp. 487–8.
6 Hoare, *Letters*, vol. 11, p. 243, letter dated 12 May 1651.

1 Salvatoriello Goes to Rome

1 G. B. Passeri, 'Vita di Salvator Rosa, pittore, e poeta', in *Die Künstler-biographien von Giovanni Battista Passeri*, ed. J. Hess (Leipzig and Vienna, 1934), p. 385.
2 For Rosa's birthdate see Floriana Conte, *Tra Napoli e Milano, Viaggi di artisti nell'Italias del Seicento*, vol. 11: *Salvator Rosa* (Florence, 2014), p. 17.
3 Lucio Festa, 'Uno scolopio mancato e uno vero: Salvator Rosa ed il Fratello', *Napoli nobilissima* (1962), vol. 11, fasc. 11, pp. 69–76.
4 Lorenzo Salazar, 'Salvator Rosa e i Fracanzani (Nuovi documenti), *Napoli nobilissima* (1903), vol. xii, p. 120.
5 Passeri, 'Vita di Salvator Rosa', p. 385; Filippo Baldinucci, *Notizie de'professori del disegno da Cimabue in qua*, ed. F. Ranalli (Florence, 1847), vol. v, p. 438.

6   Bernardo De Dominici, 'Vita di Salvator Rosa', in *Vite de'Pittori,
    Scultori ed Architetti Napoletani*, ed. Fiorella Sricchia Santoro and
    Andrea Zezza (Naples, 2008), p. 410.

7   Ibid. For Rosa's commercial strategy see Loredana Lorizzo,
    'Salvator Rosa e il mercato dell'arte a Roma: dinamiche e strategie
    commerciali', in *Salvator Rosa e il suo tempo*, ed. Sybille Ebert-
    Schifferer, Helen Langdon and Caterina Volpi (Rome, 2010),
    pp. 372–74.

8   Passeri, 'Vita di Salvator Rosa', p. 386; De Dominici, 'Vita di
    Salvator Rosa', p. 414. Viviana Farina, in *Il giovane Salvator Rosa,
    1635–1640 circa* (Naples, 2010), p. 27, suggests that this may be
    the painting now at the Santa Barbara Museum of Art.

9   Baldinucci, *Notizie*, vol. v, p. 438.

10 Rosa's relationship with Ribera has been much-discussed. See
    Michael Mahoney, *The Drawings of Salvator Rosa* (New York and
    London, 1977), vol. I, pp. 40–42; and Conte, *Tra Napoli e Milano*,
    pp. 18–22, both of whom argue against his having formally been
    Ribera's pupil. However, it does seem that Rosa at least studied
    with Ribera, and Baldinucci (*Notizie*, vol. v, p. 437) titles Rosa as
    'discepolo dello spagnoletto' (disciple of Lo Spagnoletto). For a
    survey of the evidence see Farina, *Il giovane Salvator Rosa*, pp. 17–18.

11 De Dominici, 'Vita di Salvator Rosa', p. 412.

12 Miguel Falomir, *Las Furias: Alegoria politica y desafio artistico*, exh. cat.,
    Museo Nacional del Prado, Madrid (Madrid, 2014), pp. 182–3.

13 Giovanni Battista della Porta, *Della Fisionomia dell'Uomo*, ed. Mario
    Cicognani (Parma, 1988), p. 117.

14 Bernardo De Dominici, 'Vita di Aniello Falcone pittore', in *Vite
    de'Pittori, Scultori ed Architetti Napoletani*, ed. Fiorella Sricchia Santoro
    and Andrea Zezza (Naples, 2008), p. 140.

15 De Dominici, 'Vita di Salvator Rosa', p. 416.

16 Fynes Moryson, *An Itinerary* (London, 1617), part III, p. 106.

17 Giambattista Marino, *Lettere di Cavalier Marino* (Venice, 1627), p. 94.

18 Passeri, 'Vita di Salvator Rosa', p. 387.

19 Stefan Albl, 'Salvator Rosa da Napoli a Roma: alcune osservazioni',
    in Viviana Farina, *Il giovane Salvator Rosa*, exh. cat., Museo Correale,
    Sorrento (Monghidoro, 2015), p. 167.

20 Passeri, 'Vita di Salvator Rosa', p. 387.

21 Caterina Volpi, 'Salvator Rosa e il cardinale Francesco Maria
    Brancaccio tra Napoli, Roma e Firenze', *Storia dell'arte*, CXII (2005),
    p. 119.

22 De Dominici, 'Vita di Salvator Rosa', p. 411.

23 Sebastian Schütze and Thomas Willette, *Massimo Stanzione: l'opera
    completa* (Naples, 1992), p. 182, n. 185 and 191.

24 On the closeness of the two academies see Pietro Giulio Riga,
    *Giovanni Manso e la cultura letteraria a Napoli nel primo Seicento: Tasso,
    Marino, gli Oziosi* (Bologna, 2015), pp. 126–30.

25 Girolamo De Miranda, *Una quiete operosa: forme e pratiche dell'Accademia
    napoletani degli Oziosi, 1611–1645* (Naples, 2000), pp. 229–30.

26 Lione Pascoli, *Vite de' pittori, scultori, ed architetti moderni* (Rome, 1730).

27 Farina, *Il giovane Salvator Rosa*, p. 20.

28 De Dominici, 'Vita di Salvator Rosa', p. 418.

29 Christopher Marshall, *Baroque Naples and the Industry of Painting* (New
    Haven, CT, and London, 2016), pp. 239–40.

30 Ovid, *Metamporhoses*, book IV, pp. 447–64.

31 Giambattista Marino, *Adonis*, trans. Thomas E. Mussio (Tempe,
    AZ, 2019), pp. 734–5.

32 Falomir, *Las Furias*, pp. 188–9.

33 Ibid., p. 132.

34 Passeri, 'Vita di Salvator Rosa', p. 388.

35 Longinus, *On the Sublime*, trans. P. Murray and T. S. Dorsch, in
    Classical Literary Criticism, ed. P. Murray (London, 1965), p. 130.

36 Passeri, 'Vita di Salvator Rosa', p. 388.

37 Laura Bartoni, '"Nella Trinità dei Monti che vuol dire nella
    meglior aria di Roma": il quartiere di Salvator Rosa e i suoi
    abitanti; precisazioni e qualche novita', in *Salvator Rosa e il suo
    Tempo, 1615–1673*, ed. Sybille Ebert-Schifferer, Helen Langdon and
    Caterina Volpi (Rome, 2009), p. 410.

38 The date of this painting is controversial: see Caterina Volpi,
    Salvator Rosa (1615–1673), 'pittore famoso' (Rome, 2014), p. 473, cat. no.
    153. In my opinion it must have been painted in Rome.

39 Baldinucci, *Notizie*, vol. V, p. 441.

40 Passeri, 'Vita di Salvator Rosa', p. 388.

41 Isabel Molinari, 'Il Teatro di Salvator Rosa', *Bibiloteca Teatrale*,
    XLIX–LI (1999), p. 214; Alexandra Hoare, *The Letters of Salvator Rosa*,

1615–1673: An Italian Transcription, English Translation and Critical Edition
(London, 2018), vol. I, p. 45.
42 Baldinucci, *Notizie*, vol. V, p. 440.
43 Ibid., as cited in Molinari, 'Il Teatro di Salvator Rosa', p. 222.
44 Molinari, 'Il Teatro di Salvator Rosa', p. 223.
45 As cited in C. D. Dickerson III, 'A Path to Détente? Reflections on
    the Bernini-Rosa Feud of 1639', *Storia dell'arte*, 131 (2012), p. 30.
46 Passeri, 'Vita di Salvator Rosa', pp. 388–90.
47 Caterna Volpi, *Salvator Rosa*, p. 93.
48 Adolfo Venturi, *La R. Galleria Estense in Modena* (Modena, 1882),
    p. 249, docs II–V. These letters pinpoint the date to being
    between July and September 1640.
49 Helen Langdon, 'Salvator Rosa and Claude', *Burlington Magazine*,
    CXV/849 (1973), pp. 779–85.
50 For the text of this letter see Conte, *Tra Napoli e Milano*, pp. 545–51.
51 Leonardo da Vinci, *Notebooks*, ed. Thereza Wells (Oxford, 2008),
    p. 185.
52 Stefan Albl, 'Salvator Rosa da Napoli a Roma', pp. 173 and 242,
    cat. no. 27; Mahoney, *The Drawings of Salvator Rosa*, 25.15.
53 Albl, 'Salvator Rosa da Napoli a Roma', p. 173.
54 Conte, *Tra Napoli e Milano*, pp. 37, 68.

2 Courtier and Painter-poet

1 The early sources disagree on the identity of Rosa's primary
   patron. G. B. Passeri, 'Vita di Salvator Rosa, pittore, e poeta', in
   Die Künstler-biographien von Giovanni Battista Passeri, ed. J. Hess
   (Leipzig and Vienna, 1934), p. 390, says that he was recruited
   in Rome by the Medici agent Fabrizio Piermattei for Prince
   Mattias de' Medici; Filippo Baldinucci, in *Notizie de'professori del
   disegno da Cimabue in qua*, ed. F. Ranalli (Florence, 1847), vol. V,
   p. 448, writes that Rosa met Giovan Carlo de' Medici in Rome
   and accompanied him on his return to Florence.
2 Passeri, 'Vita di Salvator Rosa', p. 391.
3 Elena Fumagalli, ed., *'filosofico umore' e 'maravigliosa speditezza': pittura
   napoletana del Seicento dalle collezioni medicee*, exh. cat., Galleria degli
   Uffizi, Florence (Florence, 2007), pp. 46 and 127.

4 Ibid., p. 46.
5 Plutarch, *Moralia: On the Fortune of Alexander* (Cambridge, MA, and London, 1936), p. 415.
6 Livy, *The History of Rome* (3:26).
7 The date suggested by most scholars is 1642–3, but a later dating seems more likely. Fumagalli (ed., *'filosofico umore'*, p. 49) notes that they are recorded, in January 1647, in the *salone* of the Casino on the via della Scala.
8 Cited in Jonathan Scott, *Salvator Rosa: His Life and Times* (New Haven, CT, and London, 1995), p. 39.
9 Anabel Thomas, *Jacques Courtois at Villa Lapeggi: Seventeenth-century Military exploits and Self-referencing in the Visual Arts* (Siena, 2018), p. 12.
10 Herwarth Röttgen, *Il Cavalier Giuseppe Cesari d'Arpino: un grande pittore nello splendore della fama e nell'inconstanza della fortuna* (Rome, 2002), p. 78.
11 Leonardo da Vinci, *Notebooks*, ed. Thereza Wells (Oxford, 2008), p. 175.
12 Oliver Tostman, 'Cold Anger: Salvator Rosa as a Painter of Battle Pieces', in *Salvator Rosa e il suo tempo*, ed. Sybille Ebert-Schifferer, Helen Langdon and Caterina Volpi (Rome, 2009).
13 Leonardo, *Notebooks*, p. 174.
14 James Hall, *The Self-portrait: A Cultural History* (London, 2014), pp. 14–15; J. J. Pollitt, *The Art of Ancient Greece: Sources and Documents* (Cambridge, 1990), p. 54.
15 Victoria von Flemming, 'Giochi di ruolo: gli autoritratti fiorentini di Salvator Rosa', in *Firenze Milleseicentoquaranta*, ed. Elena Fumagalli, Alessandro Nova and Massimiliano Rossi (Venice, 2010), pp. 289–93.
16 Daniela De Liso, *Salvator Rosa tra pennelli e versi*, ebook (Florence, 2018), p. 3. Rosa is probably referring here to the marines that he painted for Giovan Carlo, though he may be suggesting more generally his power as a landscape painter to create new worlds.
17 Antonio Abati, *Delle Frascherie – fasci tre* (Venice, 1673), p. 88.
18 Passeri, 'Vita di Salvator Rosa', p. 397.
19 Alexandra Hoare, *The Letters of Salvator Rosa, 1615–1673: An Italian Transcription, English Translation and Critical Edition* (London, 2018), vol. 1, p. 57, letter dated 18 (October or November?) 1641.

20 Passeri, 'Vita di Salvator Rosa', p. 393.

21 Baldinucci, *Notizie*, vol. v, pp. 493–4.

22 Carlo Dati, *Lepidezze di spiriti bizzarri e curiosi avvenimenti raccolti, e descritti da Carlo Dati*, ed. Domenico Moreni (Florence, 1829), p. 28.

23 Baldinucci, *Notizie*, vol. v, p. 451.

24 Ibid., p. 454.

25 Ibid., p. 453.

26 Katherine A. McIver, *Cooking and Eating in Renaissance Italy: From Kitchen to Table* (Lanham, MA, 2014), pp. 130–31.

27 Virgil, *Georgics* (2:472). For the text of this discourse see Alexandra Hoare, 'Salvator Rosa as "Amico Vero": The Role of Friendship in the Making of a Free Artist', PhD thesis, University of Toronto, 2010, pp. 550–54.

28 Fumagalli, ed., '*filosofico umore*', p. 176. The paintings are mentioned together, for the first time, in the 1676 inventory of the collection of Leopoldo de' Medici.

29 Baldinucci, *Notizie*, vol. v, p. 454. Baldinucci thought that the painting showed the return of Astrea. But Torricelli thought it showed her departure, as too did Francesco Rovai, and he wrote the poem *A Salvator Rosa che havea dipinto Astrea, che volava al cielo* (To Salvator Rosa, who painted Astrea, flying to Heaven). For the text see Alexandra Hoare, 'Salvator Rosa as "Amico Vero"', p. 540.

30 Baldinucci, *Notizie*, vol. v, p. 452.

31 Nicola Michelassi, 'Il Teatro a Firenze negli anni quaranta del seicento', in Fumagalli, ed., '*filosofico umore*', p. 138.

32 Hoare, 'Salvator Rosa as "Amico Vero"', p. 538.

33 Michelle Rak, *L'Occhio Barocco* (Palermo, 2011), pp. 40 and 148. Rak tells us that Sgruttendio's *La Tiorba a Taccone*, published around the same date as Rosa's painting, makes it clear how close these three roles were.

34 Giulio Cesare Cortese, *Opere Poetiche*, ed. Enrico Malato (Rome, 1967), p. 100.

35 Hoare, *Letters*, vol. II, p. 817, letter c, undated.

36 For the drawing, titled *Two Friends in a Landscape* (held in a private collection in Munich), see Alexandra Hoare, *Salvator Rosa, Friendship and the Free Artist in Seventeenth-century Italy* (London, 2018), p. 122, fig. 78.

37 Eva Struhal, 'Reading with Acutezza: Lorenzo Lippi's Literary Culture', in *The Artist as Reader: On Education and Non-education of Early Modern Artists*, ed. Heiko Damm, Michael Thimann and Claus Zittel (Leiden and Boston, MA, 2013), pp. 105–27.

38 Baldinucci, *Notizie*, vol. VI, p. 44.

39 Lorenzo Lippi, *Il Malmantile Racquistato* (Venice, 1738), canto III, stanzas 68–76, pp. 82–4.

40 Ibid., canto VI.

41 Lucan, *Pharsalia* VI, trans. J. D. Duff (London, 1928), pp. 543–6.

42 Sara Fabbri, '"La Vostra Verrucola, quale io stimavo di qualche horrodezza": Paesaggio reale nella pittura di Salvator Rosa (1615–1673)', *Storia dell'arte*, CXXXIII (2012), pp. 83–106.

43 G. Bonomo, *Caccia alle Streghe: la credenza nelle streghe dal secolo XXIII al XIX con particolare riferimento all'Italia* (Palermo, 1959), pp. 298–9.

44 Aristotle, *Poetics*, trans. Giulio Waldman (Englewood Cliffs, NJ, 1968), p. 7.

45 Giacinto Gigli, *Diario di Roma*, ed. Manlio Barberito (Rome, 1994) p. XXXV.

46 Caterina Volpi, *Salvator Rosa (1615–1673), 'pittore famoso'* (Rome, 2014), p. 474, cat. no. 154. The painting is now framed in a seventeenth-century gilt frame. It is possible, as Volpi suggests, that it is the painting described in Carlo de Rossi's inventory as a small oval scene with a gilt frame.

47 Hoare, *Letters*, vol. II, p. 709, letter dated 15 December 1666.

48 Helen Langdon, 'Salvator Rosa: His Ideas and His Development as an Artist', PhD thesis, Courtauld Institute of Art, London, 1974, p. 199.

49 N. M. Penzer, *The Pentamerone of Giambattista Basile*, trans. Benedetto Croce (New York, 1932), pp. 127–8.

50 Floriana Conte, *Tra Napoli e Milano, Viaggi di artisti nell'Italia del Seicento*, vol. II: *Salvator Rosa* (Florence, 2014), p. 565.

51 Helen Langdon, 'Salvator Rosa. A Variety of Surfaces', in *'Almost Eternal': Painting on Stone and material Innovation in Early Modern Europe*, ed. Piers Baker-Bates and Elena Calvillo (Leiden and Boston, MA, 2018), pp. 328–51.

52 Hoare, *Letters*, vol. II, p. 815, appendix 3, letter A.

53 Sara Fabbri, '"I Quattro Tondi con Incantesimi" di Salvator Rosa nella collezione del Marchese Filippo Niccolini. Il volto oscuro

della Toscana del Seicento', *Notizie da Palazzo Albani*, 38 (2009), pp. 99–102.

54 Paganino Gaudenzio, *La Galleria dell'inclito Marino* (Pisa, 1648), p. 183.

55 Daniello Bartoli, *The Man of Letters*, trans. Gregory Woods (New York, 2018), p. 69.

56 Floriana Conte, *Tra Napoli e Milano*, pp. 552–3.

57 Baldinucci, *Notizie*, vol. V, p. 463.

58 James Patty, *Salvator Rosa in French Literature: From the Bizarre to the Sublime* (Lexington, KY, 2005), ch. 1.

59 Baldinucci, *Notizie*, vol. V, p. 497.

60 De Liso, *Salvator Rosa*, p. 7.

61 Fumagalli, ed., *'filosofico umore'*, pp. 62 and 128, n. 123.

62 Floriana Conte, *Tra Napoli e Milano*, p. 147.

63 Achilles Tatius, *Leucippe and Clitophon*, vol. III, trans. S. Gaselee (London, 1917), p. 8. Ibid. Reinhard Steiner, in *Prometheus: Ikonologische und anthropologische Aspekte der bildenden Kunst von 14.bis zum 17.Jahrhundert* (Munich, 1991), p. 261, argues that Rosa was the first artist to use this description.

64 Andreas Vesalius, *De humani corporis fabrica* (Basel, 1543), p. 465.

65 Paula Findlen, 'Controlling the Experiment: Rhetoric, Court Patronage and the Experimental Method of Francesco Redi', *History of Science*, XXXI (1993), pp. 35–64.

66 Conte, *Tra Napoli e Milano*, p. 30.

67 Aristotle, *Poetics*, p. 7.

68 Caterina Volpi and Franco Paliaga, *'Io vel' aviso perché so che n'haverete gusto': Salvator Rosa e Giovanni Battista Ricciardi document inediti* (Rome, 2012), p. 29.

69 Giovanni Andrea Viscardo, *Precetti Morali e Civili* (Bergamo, 1597), p. 85.

70 Emanuele Tesauro, *La filosofia morale derivata dall'alto fonte del grande Aristotle stagirita* (Venice, 1689), p. 597.

71 Jacopo Salviati, 'Che la Costanza ne'travagli e gloriosa', in Alexandra Hoare, 'Salvator Rosa as "Amico Vero"', p. 555.

72 Baldinucci, *Notizie*, vol. V, p. 456. See also Fumagalli, ed., *'filosofico umore'*.

3 Fortune and Envy

1   Alexandra Hoare, *The Letters of Salvator Rosa: An Italian Transcription, English Translation and Critical Edition* (London, 2018), vol. 1, p. 85, letter dated 21 February 1649.

2   Caterina Volpi and Franco Paliaga, *'Io vel' aviso perché so che n'haverete gusto': Salvator Rosa e Giovanni Battista Ricciardi document inediti* (Rome, 2012), pp. 77 and 81.

3   G. B. Passeri, 'Vita di Salvator Rosa, pittore, e poeta', in *Die Künstler-biographien von Giovanni Battista Passeri*, ed. J. Hess (Leipzig and Vienna, 1934), p. 391.

4   Lione Pascoli, *Vite de pittori, scultori, ed architetti moderni* (Rome, 1730), pp. 70–71.

5   Hoare, *Letters*, vol. 1, p. 137, letter dated January 1650?

6   Caterina Volpi, 'Salvator Rosa e Carlo de Rossi', *Storia dell'arte*, XCIII–XCIV (1998), pp. 356–73; Alexandra Hoare, *Salvator Rosa, Friendship and the Free Artist in Seventeenth-century Italy* (London, 2018), p. 250.

7   Pascoli, *Vite de Pittori*, p. 71.

8   Hoare, *Letters*, vol. 1, p. 221, letter dated 1 April 1651.

9   Juvenal, *Juvenal and Persius*, trans. G. G. Ramsay (London and New York, 1918), satire X.

10 For the obelisk see Pierio Valeriano, *Hieroglyphica* (Basel, 1567), pp. 218v–219r.

11 For the text of this poem see Alexandra Hoare, 'Salvator Rosa as "Amico Vero": The Role of Friendship in the Making of a Free Artist', PhD thesis, University of Toronto, 2010, p. 532. We do not know the date of the poem, which may have been a source of inspiration or was perhaps inspired by the painting but for both artist and poet Democritus derided human corruption.

12 Hoare, *Letters*, vol. 1, p. 225, letter dated 18 April 1651.

13 Volpi and Paliaga, *'Io vel' aviso perché so che n'haverete gusto'*, p. 99, letter dated 25 March 1651.

14 Hoare, *Letters*, vol. 1, p. 248, letter dated 27 May 1651.

15 Ibid., p. 325, letter dated 6 July 1652.

16 Ibid., p. 337, letter dated 17 August 1652. On Rosa's speed of working, see Hoare, *Salvator Rosa*, p. 256.

17 Daniello Bartoli, *The Man of Letters*, trans. Gregory Woods
    (New York, 2018), pp. 15–16.

18 Volpi and Paliaga, *'Io vel' aviso perché so che n'haverete gusto'*, p. 98, letter
    dated 25 March 1651.

19 Filippo Baldinucci, *Notizie de'professori del disegno da Cimabue in qua*,
    ed. F. Ranalli (Florence, 1847), vol. v, p. 501.

20 Volpi and Paliaga, *'Io vel' aviso perché so che n'haverete gusto'*, p. 111, letter
    dated 13 July 1662.

21 Anthony Blunt, *Nicolas Poussin* (London, 1967), p. 171.

22 Passeri, 'Vita di Salvator Rosa', p. 395.

23 Bellori, as cited in Blunt, *Nicolas Poussin*, p. 171.

24 Baldinucci, *Notizie*, p. 463.

25 On Brunetti's letter and encomium see Hoare, *Letters*, vol. I, p. 924,
    n. 3.

26 Floriana Conte, *Tra Napoli e Milano: Viaggi di artisti nell'Italia del Seicento*,
    vol. II: *Salvator Rosa* (Florence, 2015), p. 340, n. 100. The quotation
    is from a letter from Abate Domenico Federici, a correspondent of
    Ciro di Pers.

27 Hoare, *Letters*, vol. I, p. 153, letter dated 2 February 1650.

28 On the dating of the picture and of Bartoli's ekphrasis see Conte,
    Tra Napoli e Milano, vol. II, pp. 348–9, n. 175.

29 The poem is printed in Giovanni Cesareo, ed., *Poesie e Lettere edite e
    inedite di Salvator Rosa*, 2 vols (Naples, 1892), vol. II, pp. 138–48. See
    also Hoare, 'Salvator Rosa as "Amico Vero"', pp. 519–23, Appendix
    II.1, and Hoare, *Salvator Rosa*, pp. 167 and 366, n. 258.

30 Hoare, *Letters*, vol. I, p. 133, letter dated 5 January 1650.

31 Volpi and Paliaga, *'Io vel' aviso perché so che n'haverete gusto'*, p. 105, letter
    dated 7 October 1651.

32 Hoare, *Letters*, vol. I, p. 355, letter dated 2 November 1652.

33 Xavier Salomon, '"Ho fatto spiritar Roma": Salvator Rosa and
    Seventeenth-century Exhibitions', in Helen Langdon, ed., *Salvator
    Rosa*, exh. cat., Dulwich Picture Gallery (London, 2010), p. 85.

34 Conte, *Tra Napoli e Milan*, p. 108.

35 Ibid., pp. 280–81.

36 Ibid., appendix VI, pp. 572–624, prints variants of *Purgatorio*
    and other writings against Rosa. For the text of the satire see
    A. Borzelli, *Una satira contro Salvator Rosa* (Naples, 1910).

37 Hoare, *Letters*, vol. I, p. 403, letter dated 5 May 1654.
38 Passeri, 'Vita di Salvator Rosa', p. 390; Passeri dismissed these
    claims as false.
39 Hoare, *Letters*, vol. I, p. 401, letter dated 27 March 1654.
40 Ibid., p. 403, letter dated 5 May 1654.
41 Ibid., p. 401, letter dated 27 March 1654.
42 Helen Langdon, 'Two Book Illustrations by Salvator Rosa',
    Burlington Magazine, CXVII (1976), pp. 698–9.
43 Cesare Baronio, *Annales Ecclesiastici*, vol. VII (Antwerp, 1603),
    p. 507.
44 Volunnio Bandinelli, *Hor che non piu tra'lamoi delle Spade guerrieri
    risplende il valore in Giostra rappresentata in Fiorenza al Serenissimo Duca
    di Moden* (Florence, 1652), p. 14. An MSS note on the book in the
    British Library attributes this to Bandinelli. See Anne Sophie
    Barrovecchio, *Le complexe de Bélisaire* (Paris, 2009).
45 Procopius VI, *The Wars, Secret History and Buildings*, trans. H. B.
    Dewing (London and New York, 1924), pp. 153–5.
46 Guillaume Du Choul, *Discours de la religion des anciens Romains illustré*
    [1556] (New York, 1976), p. 299.
47 Salvator Rosa, *Satire*, ed. D. Romei (Milan, 1995), p. 49.
48 Caterina Volpi, *Salvator Rosa (1615–1673), 'pittore Famoso'* (Rome,
    2014), p. 490.
49 Richard Wallace, *The Etchings of Salvator Rosa* (Princeton, NJ, 1979),
    p. 16.
50 Cesare Ripa, *Iconologia* (Padua, 1630), pp. 95–6. See also Nancy
    Rash Fabbri, 'Salvator Rosa's Engraving for Carlo de Rossi and His
    Satire, Invidia', *Journal of the Warburg and Courtauld Institutes*, XXXIII
    (1970), pp. 328–30.
51 As cited in Wallace, *Etchings*, p. 18.
52 For this impression see ibid., p. 136, plate 6/1.
53 Ibid., p. 26. Wallace's remains the most interesting discussion of
    the *Figurine*, and I am indebted to it.
54 Hoare, *Letters*, p. 531, vol. II, letter dated 20 November 1660.
55 Ibid., p. 583, letter dated 13 May 1662.
56 Ibid., *Letters*, vol. II, p. 989, n. 3.
57 Ibid., p. 439, letter dated (?) February 1656.
58 Ibid., p. 459, letter dated 9 September 1656.

59 The painting is recorded in an inventory of the collection of Cardinal Flavio Chigi, begun in 1658. It probably dates from 1656 to 1657.

60 Cesareo, *Poesie e Lettere*, pp. 138–48.

61 Ciro di Pers, *Poesie*, ed. Michele Rak (Turin, 1978), p. 111.

62 Ibid., p. 113.

63 Vincenzo Golzio, *Documenti artistici sul Seicento nell'Archivio Chigi* (Rome, 1939), p. 279.

64 For the date of these paintings see Volpi and Paliaga, *'Io vel' aviso perché so che n'haverete gusto'*, p. 58.

65 Hoare, *Letters*, vol. 11, p. 503, letter dated 1 September 1659; and p. 505, letter dated 20 September 1659.

66 Through whom Rosa won this commission is not entirely clear. For a clear summary of the possibilities see ibid., vol. 11, p. 991, n. 1. See also Conte, *Tra Napoli e Milano*, pp. 627–8.

67 Andrea Spiriti, 'Salvator Rosa e Milano: le ragioni di una presenza' in *Salvator Rosa e suo Tempo (1615–1673)*, ed. Sybille Ebert-Schifferer, Helen Langdon and Caterina Volpi (Rome, 2010), p. 93.

68 Hoare, *Letters*, vol. 11, p. 593, letter dated (post-15?) July 1662.

69 Ibid., p. 992, n. 6.

70 Baldinucci, *Notizie*, vol. V, p. 447.

71 Bartoli, *Man of Letters*, p. 8.

72 Dalma Frascarelli, *L'arte del dissenso* (Turin, 2016), p. 95.

4 Magic, Prophecy and Terror

1 Keith Sciberras, *Mattia Preti: The Triumphant Manner* (Malta, 2012), p. 116.

2 Alexandra Hoare, *The Letters of Salvator Rosa, 1615–1673: An Italian Transcription, English Translation and Critical Edition* (London, 2018), vol. 11, p. 613, letter dated 17 March 1663.

3 Ibid., p. 644, letter dated 30 February 1664.

4 G. P. Bellori, 'Nota delle Musei, Librerie, Gallerie et ornamenti di Statue e Pitture nei Palazzi, nelle Case, e ne Guardini di Roma' (Rome, 1664), p. 111.

5   G. B. Passeri, 'Vita di Salvator Rosa, pittore, e poeta', in
    Die Künstler-biographien von Giovanni Battista Passeri, ed. J. Hess
    (Leipzig and Vienna, 1934), p. 396.
6   Hoare, *Letters*, vol. II, p. 635, letter dated 21 October 1663.
7   Ibid., p. 593, letter dated (post-15?) July 1662.
8   Ibid., p. 595, letter dated 29 July 1662.
9   For this anecdote see Plutarch's *Moralia*, trans. Edwin Minar Jr,
    Francis Henry Sandbach and William C. Helmbold (London and
    New York, 1961), vol. IX, p. 729D.
10 Diogenes Laërtius, *Lives and Opinions of the Eminent Philosophers*, trans.
    R. D. Hicks (London and Cambridge, MA, 1970), vol. II, book
    VIII, chapter 40, p. 357
11 A note in the inventory of Don Antonio Ruffo says that the two
    works were done 'ad istanza della regina di Svetia' (at the request
    of the queen). There is no reason to doubt this note. Rosa De
    Gennaro, *Per il collezionismo del Seicento in Sicilia: l'inventario di Antonio
    Ruffo Principe della Scaletta* (Pisa, 2003), pp. 93, 111, 140.
12 Gabriel Naudé, *Apologie pour les grands hommes soupçonnes par magie*
    (Amsterdam, 1712), pp. 160–62. For a discussion of this theme see
    Lorenzo Bianchi, *Rinascimento e Libertinismo* (Naples, 1996),
    pp. 127–36.
13 Giorgio de Sepibus, *Romani Societatis Jesu Musaeum Celeberrimum*
    (Amsterdam, 1678), pp. 2–3.
14 Anthony Grafton, 'Conflict and Harmony in the Collegium
    Gellianum', in *The World of Aulus Gellius*, ed. Leofranc Holford-
    Strevens and Amiel Vardi (Oxford, 2004), p. 339.
15 Athanasius Kircher, *Mundus Subterraneus* (Amsterdam, 1665),
    cited in Joscelyn Godwin, *Athanasius Kircher's Theatre of the World*
    (London, 2009), p. 133.
16 Laërtius, *Lives*, book VIII, chapter 69, pp. 383–4.
17 Tertullian, *De Anima*, chapter XXXII, section i.
18 Paganino Gaudenzio, *Considerazioni Accademiche* (Florence, 1631),
    p. 87.
19 Peter Kingsley, *Ancient Philosophy, Mystery and Magic: Empedocles and
    Pythagorean Tradition* (Oxford, 1995), p. 252.
20 This treatise is anonymous but I have here continued to use the
    traditional name of Longinus. G. Costa, 'Appunti sulla Fortuna del

Pseudo-Longino: Alessandro Tassoni e Paganino Gaudenzio', *Studi Secenteschi*, XXV (1984), pp. 123–43.

21 Longinus, *On the Sublime*, trans. P. Murray and T. S. Dorsch, in *Classical Literary Criticism*, ed. P. Murray (London, 1965), p. 114.

22 Ibid., p. 155.

23 Daniello Bartoli, *Della Geografia trasportata al morale* (Venice, 1664), p. 103.

24 G. Getto, *Barocco in Prosa e in Poesia* (Milan, 1969), p. 99.

25 Dalma Frascarelli, *Paolo Falconieri tra scienza e arcadia* (Rome, 2012), p. 94.

26 Hoare, *Letters*, vol II, pp. 582–3, letter dated 13 May 1662.

27 For a critical discussion of Rosa's letter see Getto, *Barocco*, p. 313.

28 Ingrid D. Rowland, *The Scarith of Scornello: A Tale of Renaissance Forgery* (London, 2004), p. 12.

29 Camilla S. Fiore, 'Athanasius Kircher (1602–1680) and Landscape between Antiquity, Science and Art in the Seventeenth Century', in *Czech and Slovak Journal of Humanities, Historia Artium*, 3 (2016), pp. 79–95; p. 85.

30 Camilla S. Fiore, '"Parmi d'andare peregrinando dolcissamente per quell'Etruria" Scoperte antiquarie e natura nell'Etruria di Curzio Inghirami e Athanasius Kircher', *Storia dell'arte*, 133 (2012), pp. 53–82; p. 65.

31 Athanasius Kircher, *Latium id est* (Amsterdam, 1671), p. 169.

32 Ibid., pp. 141–2.

33 Pliny, *Natural History*, trans. H. Rackham (Cambridge, MA, 1945), vol. IV, Book XVI, pp. 541 and 544.

34 Daniello Bartoli, *De'Simboli trasportati al morale* (Venice, 1830), pp. 348–9.

35 Franco Paliaga, *Pittori, incisori e architetti pisani nel secolo di Galileo* (Ghezzano, 2009), pp. 226–7.

36 Clélia Nau, *Claude Lorrain: Scaenographiae Solis, Graficas Mari Montanana* (2009), p. 114.

37 Longinus, *On the Sublime*, p. 134.

38 Emanuele Tesauro, *Il Cannocchiale Aristotelico*, ed. G. Menardi (Turin, 1970), p. 75.

39 Sallust, *War with Catiline*, trans. J. C. Rolfe (Cambridge, MA, and London, 2013), chapter 4, p. 27.

40 Ibid., chapter 4, p. 27.

41 Ibid., chapter 22, p. 57.

42 Hoare, *Letters*, vol. II, p. 627, letter dated 8 September 1663.

43 Giovanni Battista Della Porta, *Della Fisionomia dell'Uomo*,
    ed. M. Cicognani (Parma, 1988), pp. 399 and 146.

44 B. Gamba, *La Vita di Salvatore Rosa scritta da Filippo Baldinucci fiorentino
    con varie aggiunte* (Venice, 1830), pp. 37–9.

45 Ibid., pp. 37–8, as cited in Xavier Salomon, '"Ho fatto spiritar
    Roma": Salvator Rosa and Seventeenth-century Exhibitions',
    in Helen Langdon, ed., *Salvator Rosa*, exh. cat., Dulwich Picture
    Gallery (London, 2010), p. 89.

46 Hoare, *Letters*, vol. II, p. 749, letter dated 15 September 1668.

47 Charles Zika, 'Images in Service of the Word: The Witch of
    Endor in the Bibles of Early Modern Europe', *Anzeiger des
    Germanischen Nationalsmuseums* (2009), pp. 151–65.

48 Athanasius Kircher, *Ars Magna Lucis et Umbrae in decem libros digesta*
    (Rome, 1646), p. 773.

49 Longinus, *On the Sublime*, p. 134.

50 Paganino Gaudenzio, *Della disunita Accademia accrescimento* (Pisa,
    1644), p. 27.

51 Paolo Lombardi, *Il filosofo e la strega* (Milan, 1997), pp. 59–63.

52 Filippo Baldinucci, *Notizie de'professori del disegno da Cimabue in qua*,
    ed. F. Ranalli (Florence, 1847), vol. V, p. 444.

53 Passeri, 'Vita di Salvator Rosa', p. 392.

54 Hoare, *Letters*, vol. II, p. 769, letter dated 17 August 1669.

55 Ibid., p. 683, letter dated 1 April 1666.

56 As cited in Penelope Murray, *Genius: The History of an Idea*
    (Oxford, 1989), p. 18.

57 Hoare, *Letters*, vol. II, p. 803, letter dated 7 July 1672.

58 Ibid., pp. 777–8, letter dated 26 January 1670.

59 Daniele De Liso, *Salvator Rosa tra pennelli e versi*, ebook (Florence,
    2018), p. 11.

60 Hoare, *Letters*, vol. II, p. 771, letter dated 11 October 1669.

61 Baldinucci, *Notizie*, p. 464.

62 Passeri, 'Vita di Salvator Rosa', p. 396.

63 Hoare, *Letters*, vol. II, p. 809, letter dated 18 February 1673.
    On Ricciardi's visit see p. 1041, n. 2.

64 Baldinucci, *Notizie*, pp. 467–76.
65 Passeri, 'Vita di Salvator Rosa', p. 397.

Epilogue

1 Filippo Baldinucci, *Notizie de'professori del disegno da Cimabue in qua*,
   ed. F. Ranalli (Florence, 1847), vol. v, p. 477.
2 Ibid., pp. 478, 487.
3 G. B. Passeri, 'Vita di Salvator Rosa, pittore, e poeta', in
   Die Künstler-biographien von Giovanni Battista Passeri, ed. J. Hess
   (Leipzig and Vienna, 1934), p. 396.
4 Bernardo De Dominici, 'Vita di Salvator Rosa', in *Vite de'pittori,
   scultori ed architetti napoletani*, ed. Fiorella Sricchia Santoro and
   Andrea Zezza (Naples, 2008), pp. 135–6.
5 Andrew Moore and Larissa Dukelskaya, *A Capital Collection:
   Houghton Hall and the Hermitage, with a Modern Edition of Aedes Walpolianae*
   (New Haven, CT, and London, 2002), p. 364.
6 As given in Michael Fried, *Absorption and Theatricality: Painting and the
   Beholder in the Age of Diderot* (Berkeley, CA, 1980), p. 236.
7 Floriana Conte, *Tra Napoli e Milano, Viaggi di artisti nell'Italia del Seicento*,
   vol. II: *Salvator Rosa* (Florence, 2014), pp. 324–7.
8 Sydney Morgan, *The Life and Times of Salvator Rosa* (London, 1855),
   p. 43.
9 Ibid., p. 142; pp. 225–6.
10 John Ruskin, *Modern Painters* (London, 1869), vol. v, paragraph 14.

SELECT BIBLIOGRAPHY

Articles, Books and Exhibition Catalogues

Conte, Floriana, *Tra Napoli e Milano. Viaggi di artisti nell'Italia del Seicento*,
    vol. II: *Salvator Rosa* (Florence, 2014)
De Liso, Daniela, *Salvator Rosa tra pennelli e versi* (Florence, 2018)
Ebert-Schifferer, Sybille, Helen Langdon and Caterina Volpi,
    eds, *Salvator Rosa e il suo Tempo, 1615–1673* (Rome, 2010)
Farina, Viviana, *Il giovane Salvator Rosa, 1635–1640 circa* (Naples, 2010)
—, ed., *Il giovane Salvator Rosa. Gli inizi di un grande maestro del '600 europeo*,
    exh. cat., Museo Correale, Sorrento (2016)
Fumagalli, Elena, ed., *'Filosofico umore' e 'maravigliosa speditezza'. Pittura
    napoletana del seicento dalle collezioni medicee*, exh. cat., Palazzo Pitti,
    Florence (2007)
Guratzsch, Herwig, ed., *Salvator Rosa: Genie der Zeichnung: Studien und
    Skizzen aus Leipzig und Haarlem*, exh. cat., Museum der Bildenden
    Künste, Leipzig, and Teylers Museum, Haarlem (Cologne, 1999)
Hoare, Alexandra, *Salvator Rosa, Friendship and the Free Artist in Seventeenth-
    Century Italy* (London and Turnhout, 2018)
Kitson, Michael, ed., *Salvator Rosa*, exh. cat., Arts Council and Hayward
    Gallery, London (1973)
Langdon, Helen, 'Salvator Rosa in Florence, 1640–49', *Apollo*, C/151
    (1974), pp. 190–97
—, 'Salvator Rosa: His Ideas and His Development as an Artist',
    PhD dissertation, University of London, 1975
—, 'The Representation of Philosophers in the Art of Salvator Rosa',
    www.kunsttexte.de, 2011
—, 'The Demosthenes of Painting: Salvator Rosa and the Seventeenth-
    Century Sublime', in *Translations of the Sublime: The Early Modern*

Reception and Dissemination of Longinus' 'Peri Hupsous' in Rhetoric, the Visual Arts, Architecture and the Theatre, ed. Caroline van Eck et al. (Leiden, 2012), pp. 163–85
—, ed., *Salvator Rosa*, exh. cat., Dulwich Picture Gallery, London, and Kimbell Art Museum, Fort Worth, Texas (2010)
Limentani, Uberto, *La Satira nel Seicento* (Milan and Naples, 1961)
Mahoney, Michael, *The Drawings of Salvator Rosa*, 2 vols (New York, 1977)
Roworth, Wendy Wassyng, *'Pictor Succensor': A Study of Salvator Rosa as Satirist, Cynic and Painter* (New York and London, 1978)
Salerno, Luigi, *Salvator Rosa* (Milan, 1963)
Scott, Jonathan, *Salvator Rosa: His Life and Times* (New Haven, CT, and London, 1995)
Spinosa, Nicola, et al., eds, *Salvator Rosa tra mito e magia*, exh. cat., Museo e Gallerie Nazionale di Capodimonte, Naples (2008)
Volpi, Caterina, 'Salvator Rosa e Carlo de' Rossi', *Storia dell'arte*, XCIII–XCIV (1998), pp. 356–73
—, 'Salvator Rosa e il cardinale Francesco Maria Brancaccio tra Napoli, Roma e Firenze', *Storia dell'arte*, CXII/12 (2005), pp. 119–48.
—, *Salvator Rosa (1615–1673), 'pittore famoso'* (Rome, 2014)
Wallace, Richard W., *The Etchings of Salvator Rosa* (Princeton, NJ, 1979)

Biographies and Sources

Baldinucci, Filippo, *Notizie de' professori del disegno da Cimabue in qua*, ed. Ferdinando Ranalli, 6 vols (Florence, 1974)
De Dominici, Bernardo, *Le Vite de' pittori, scultori ed architetti napoletani*, ed. Fiorella Sricchia Santoro and Andrea Zezza, 3 vols (Naples, 2003–8)
Hoare, Alexandra, *The Letters of Salvator Rosa: An Italian Transcription, English Translation and Critical Edition*, 2 vols (London and Turnhout, 2019)
Passeri, Giambattista, *Die Künstler-biographien von Giovanni Battista Passeri*, ed. Jacob Hess (Leipzig and Vienna, 1934)
Romei, Danilo, ed., *Salvator Rosa: Satire* (Milan, 1995)
Volpi, Caterina, and Franco Paliaga, *'Io vel aviso perché so che n'haverete gusto', Salvator Rosa e Giovanni Battista Ricciardi attraverso documenti inediti* (Rome, 2012)

ACKNOWLEDGEMENTS

I have been working on aspects of Salvator Rosa for many years, and am grateful to Michael Leaman and Francois Quiviger for inviting me to contribute to the Renaissance Lives series. My greatest debts are to Caterina Volpi, Xavier Salomon and Anthony Langdon, for many exchanges of ideas and information and shared gallery visits in Europe and the United States. I should also like to thank many colleagues and friends, among them Lisa Beaven, Patrizia Cavazzini, Floriana Conte, Simon Ditchfield, Sybille Ebert Schifferer, Viviana Farina, Hilary Gatti, Alexandra Hoare, David Jaffe, Martin Olin, Elizabeth Oy Marra, Ingrid Rowland, Susan Russell, Hannah Segrave, Nicola Spinosa, Eva Struhal, Andreas Stolzenberg, Gudrun Swoboda and Arno Witte, for invitations to test out my ideas at conferences and many other pleasurable conversations over the years.

PHOTO ACKNOWLEDGEMENTS

The author and publishers wish to express their thanks to the below sources of illustrative material and/or permission to reproduce it. Some locations of artworks are also given below, in the interest of brevity:

Art Gallery of South Australia, Adelaide: 54; The British Museum, London: 65; Broughton Hall, Skipton: 31; The Cleveland Museum of Art, OH: 14, 50; The Columbia Museum of Art, SC: 5; Detroit Institute of Arts, MI: 1; photo DeAgostini/Alfredo Dagli Orti via Getty Images: 15; Eastnor Castle Collection: 57; © The Fitzwilliam Museum, University of Cambridge/Bridgeman Images: 45; Gabinetto dei Disegni e delle Stampe delle Gallerie degli Uffizi, Florence/photos Ministero per i Beni e le Attività Culturali e per il Turismo: 4, 7; Galleria Corsini, Rome: 33; Galleria Estense, Modena: 12, 13 (photo Vincenzo Fontana/© Arte & Immagini srl/Corbis via Getty Images); Gallerie degli Uffizi, Florence/ photos Ministero per i Beni e le Attività Culturali e per il Turismo: 24, 64; Gemäldegalerie, Staatliche Museen zu Berlin: 51; The J. Paul Getty Museum, Los Angeles: 47; Kedleston Hall, Quarndon/photo Blantern & Davis, © 2022 NTPL/Scala, Florence: 29; Kimbell Art Museum, Fort Worth, TX: 52; from Athanasius Kircher, *Ars magna lucis et umbr, in X. libros digesta* (Amsterdam, 1671), photo Smithsonian Libraries, Washington, DC: 63; from Athanasius Kircher, *E Soc. Jesu Mundus subterraneus, in xii libros digestus* (Amsterdam, 1664), photo Smithsonian Libraries, Washington, DC: 58; from Athanasius Kircher, *Magnes sive, De arte magnetica tripartium* (Cologne, 1643), photo Boston College Libraries: 56; Knole, Kent/photo Matthew Hollow, © 2022 NTPL/Scala, Florence: 10; Kunsthistorisches Museum, Vienna: 22; courtesy Lord Spencer Collection, Althorp: 18, 19; The Matthiesen Gallery, London/photos courtesy Patrick Matthiesen:

11, 27; The Metropolitan Museum of Art, New York: 26, 32, 44, 49; Musée Condé, Chantilly/photo Michel Urtado, © 2022 RMN-Grand Palais/Dist. photo Scala, Florence: 46; Musée du Louvre, Paris: 38, 62; Musei Capitolini, Rome: 21; Museo di Casa Martelli/photo Ministero per i Beni e le Attività Culturali e per il Turismo: 61; Museo Civico, Viterbo: 8; Museo del Prado, Madrid: 2, 3, 55; National Galleries of Scotland, Edinburgh: 59; The National Gallery, London: 23 (on loan from the Ramsbury Manor Foundation), 28; National Gallery of Victoria (NGV), Melbourne: 42, 43; Nationalmuseum, Stockholm/photo Cecilia Heisser: 60; Palazzo Pitti, Florence: 16 (photo Bridgeman Images), 17 (photo Finsiel/Alinari Archives – reproduced with the permission of Ministero per i Beni e le Attività Culturali e per il Turismo/Bridgeman Images), 20, 30 and 35 (photos Ministero per i Beni e le Attività Culturali e per il Turismo); private collection: 6, 25, 34, 40; Raynham Hall, Norfolk: 41; Rijksmuseum, Amsterdam: 9; from Georgius de Sepibus and Athanasius Kircher, *Romani Collegii Societatis Jesu Musaeum Celeberrimum* (Amsterdam, 1678), photo Getty Research Institute, Los Angeles: 53; Statens Museum for Kunst (SMK), Copenhagen: 36, 37; Victoria and Albert Museum, London: 48; Virginia Museum of Fine Arts, Richmond (Adolph D. and Wilkins C. Williams Fund)/photo Katherine Wetzel, © Virginia Museum of Fine Arts: 39.

INDEX

Illustration numbers are indicated by *italics*